KU-017-239

Contents at a Glance

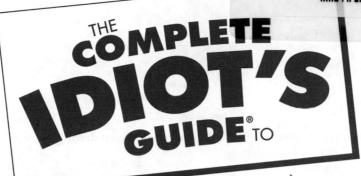

THE
COMPLETE IDIOT'S GUIDE® TO

Adobe®
Photoshop®
Elements 2.0

by Gregory Holden and Joli Ballew

ALPHA

A Pearson Education Company

International Standard Book Number: 0-02-864355-0
Library of Congress Catalog Card Number: 2002111662

04   03   02   8   7   6   5   4   3   2   1

Interpretation of the printing code: The rightmost number of the first series of numbers is the year of the book's printing; the rightmost number of the second series of numbers is the number of the book's printing. For example, a printing code of 02-1 shows that the first printing occurred in 2002.

Printed in the United States of America

Note: This publication contains the opinions and ideas of its authors. It is intended to provide helpful and informative material on the subject matter covered. It is sold with the understanding that the authors and publisher are not engaged in rendering professional services in the book. If the reader requires personal assistance or advice, a competent professional should be consulted.

The authors and publisher specifically disclaim any responsibility for any liability, loss, or risk, personal or otherwise, which is incurred as a consequence, directly or indirectly, of the use and application of any of the contents of this book.

For marketing and publicity, please call: 317-581-3722

The publisher offers discounts on this book when ordered in quantity for bulk purchases and special sales.

For sales within the United States, please contact: Corporate and Government Sales, 1-800-382-3419 or corpsales@pearsontechgroup.com

Outside the United States, please contact: International Sales, 317-581-3793 or international@pearsontechgroup.com

Publisher: *Marie Butler-Knight*
Product Manager: *Phil Kitchel*
Managing Editor: *Jennifer Chisholm*
Acquisitions Editor: *Eric Heagy*
Development Editor: *Michael Koch*
Production Editor: *Katherin Bidwell*
Illustrator: *Chris Eliopoulos*
Cover/Book Designer: *Trina Wurst*
Indexer: *Julie Bess*
Layout/Proofreading: *John Etchison, Rebecca Harmon, Kelly Maish*

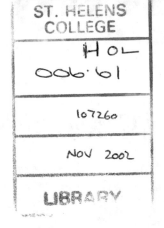

Contents

Introduction

There's a song that goes, "You don't know what you've got until you lose it." Where Adobe Photoshop Elements is concerned, the refrain should go, "You don't know what you've got until you *use* it."

We personally know photographers and very smart computer enthusiasts who use Photoshop Elements with one hand tied behind their backs—they don't take advantage of many (even most) of the professional-quality image-editing tools at their disposal.

Perhaps they're intimidated by the program's name, which conjures up suggestions of the software's big brother, the well-known and highly powerful graphic design application simply called Adobe Photoshop. More often, they don't take the time to try all the things they can do with the program.

A close relative of one of this book's authors uses Photoshop Elements to scan images, boost their contrast and brightness, and paint over obvious blotches and other imperfections. Yet he was amazed when he was shown how much more effective it is to improve brightness and contrast using the Levels command, to erase imperfections with the Clone Stamp tool, or to select only the type in an image using the Magic Wand.

Our goal in this book is to help you feel the same sense of amazement while getting the most out of Photoshop Elements. This program may not be as expensive or complicated as Photoshop, but it enables you to accomplish much of the same sort of image-editing magic. We want you to explore the program's many functions by following along with this book's exercises. This way, you can learn new techniques by editing images we have provided, through trial and error, without having to worry about altering your own personal photos.

Feel free to skip from chapter to chapter to learn exactly what you need to know. Don't feel obligated to read from front to back cover. By all means, take what you've learned and apply it to your own images—with confidence. Photoshop Elements puts the professional design tools in your hands; you only have to try them and use them to perform your own graphic design wizardry.

Who Should Read This Book

This book is for anyone who scans, edits, and prints digital images with a computer. It assumes no knowledge of computer graphics and no experience with graphic design. It explains all the jargon and clarifies the underlying concepts. We're operating on the proven principle that if you want to use Photoshop Elements to work with images, you can and you will. Go through this book with patience, practice, and persistence, and you'll come out with brighter, sharper, and better images on your hard disk, your web page—or even in frames on your walls.

How This Book Is Organized

We've divided this book into the following six parts:

◆ **Part 1, "Introducing Photoshop Elements,"** welcomes you to Photoshop Elements, gives you some tips on how to obtain good images to work with, and provides some hands-on experience with basic everyday functions.

◆ **Part 2, "Building an Elementary Skill Set,"** instructs you in basic digital image theory, and then gets you started with selecting images and working with layers.

◆ **Part 3, "Working with Photographs,"** shows you how to bring your digital photos to life, improve their color, and smooth out flaws.

◆ **Part 4, "Getting Creative with Text and Graphics,"** provides exercises and techniques for adding text and doing your own painting and drawing.

◆ **Part 5, "Advanced Techniques and Special Effects,"** throws back the curtain on some of the flashiest techniques, including filters, special effects, and transformations.

◆ **Part 6, "Presenting Your Pictures,"** takes your image-editing projects to completion, showing you how to print, publish your work online, or send your digital image files to a digital photo-processing service.

If you need some help along the way, check the glossary at the back of this book to find clear explanations of technical jargon related to digital images.

Throughout this book we emphasize learning by doing. From the first chapter on, we don't just show you how to perform tasks—we encourage you to roll up your sleeves and follow along with us. So crack open that CD-ROM envelope in the back of the book and put the disc in your computer's CD-ROM drive right now, so you can use the sample images contained there and get hands-on experience with Photoshop Elements.

Hardware and Software Requirements

To use Photoshop Elements, your computer needs to meet the following minimum requirements:

- Intel Pentium processor (Windows) or PowerPC processor (Macintosh).

- Windows 98, ME, 2000, or XP; or Mac OS 9.1, 9.2.*x*, or 10.1.3–10.1.5.

- 128MB of RAM (Windows or Macintosh), and virtual memory turned on (Macintosh).

- 200MB (Windows) or 400MB (Macintosh) of free hard disk space.

- A color monitor capable of displaying thousands of colors at a resolution of 800×600 or greater.

In addition, you need a web browser such as Internet Explorer 5.0 or later to view the program's built-in Help files, and a CD-ROM drive.

Extras

Along the way, we throw in extra bits and miscellaneous tasty morsels in the form of four different sidebars:

In Focus

Here we offer shortcuts, workarounds, tips, tricks, and practical advice.

Shop Talk

Here we define the key terms and ideas you'll need to know.

Swatch Out!

We warn you of potential pitfalls to avoid when editing images.

It's Element-ary

We give you some extra information that will help you work smarter.

Acknowledgments

Just as it takes many palettes and toolbars to work together to create a program such as Photoshop Elements, this book was the result of a team of professionals working together.

First, our agent and adviser Neil Salkind brought together this book's two co-authors for the first time (hopefully not the last) and connected them to Alpha Books, with the assistance of Jessica Richards, Kevin Borders, Stacey Barone, and Sherry and David Rogelberg.

Eric Heagy of Alpha Books proved himself the soul of patience and spirit of helpfulness as he went far beyond the call of duty to see this book to fruition. Development editor Michael Koch and technical editor Don Passenger worked long hours to make this the best-quality book it could be; it turned out better both graphically and textually thanks to their efforts. Copy editor Michael Welch made sure everything read the way it should. And Katherin Bidwell did countless "photo merges" to get the book through the production process.

Special thanks go to Thayer Lindner, who contributed many of the photographs, and Scott Wills, who contributed some key images to the color insert.

Special Thanks to the Technical Reviewer

The Complete Idiot's Guide to Adobe Photoshop Elements 2.0 was reviewed by an expert who double-checked the accuracy of what you'll learn here, to help us ensure that this book gives you everything you need to know about Photoshop Elements. We extend our special thanks to Don Passenger.

Trademarks

All terms mentioned in this book that are known to be or are suspected of being trademarks or service marks have been appropriately capitalized. Alpha Books and Pearson Education, Inc., cannot attest to the accuracy of this information. Use of a term in this book should not be regarded as affecting the validity of any trademark or service mark.

Part 1

Introducing Photoshop Elements

It's elementary, dear Photoshopper. Before you can start brightening and brushing up your images using the many cool Photoshop Elements tools, you've got to start at the beginning and learn the basics.

This first part of the book takes you on a tour of Photoshop Elements so you can learn something fundamental that many users skip over—where to find everything you need, and what all those buttons, boxes, and menu options actually *do*. You'll also learn how to capture images so you can have good material to work with before you begin editing. Finally, you'll learn how to find files, open new image files, and get help from Photoshop Elements itself when you're in a jam and this book isn't close at hand.

An Element-ary Approach to Elements

In This Chapter

- ◆ Explore the Photoshop Elements window
- ◆ Open tools for selecting, painting, and drawing
- ◆ Learn to use and arrange palettes
- ◆ Discover the shortcuts and options bars
- ◆ Find and use the built-in Photoshop Elements Help system

Digital imaging is bringing photography, retouching, and printing within everyone's reach. Functions such as retouching and painting, which could once be done only by technicians, can now be done by hobbyists and casual consumers. Adobe Photoshop Elements offers an excellent midrange product that enables you to enter the world of digital photo editing.

Adobe developed Photoshop Elements for those of us who own digital cameras, scanners, or who regularly send and receive pictures through e-mail. Photoshop Elements enables us to change, edit, correct, and otherwise work on these pictures in a user-friendly environment that gives you access to some high-powered tools.

Photoshop Elements has a lot to offer, which may make it seem complicated at first glance. But it also has many shortcuts and wizards that, when properly used, make it easy to do extraordinary tasks with images and photos. The more you use the program, the more you should like the results you can accomplish. By the end of this chapter, you'll be ready to start editing your own digital images like a pro.

Starting Up Photoshop Elements

It's easy to get started with Photoshop Elements. Just do one of the following:

- If you're a Windows user, double-click the Adobe Photoshop Elements 2.0 icon on your desktop, or, if a dozen or more open windows are obscuring your desktop, choose Start → Programs → Adobe → Photoshop Elements → Adobe Photoshop Elements 2.0.

- If you're a Mac user, find the Adobe Photoshop Elements folder, double-click it to open it, and then double-click the Adobe Photoshop Elements icon. (It's a good idea to choose File → Make Alias to create an alias for this icon and place it on your desktop so you can find it more easily in the future.)

In any case, the Welcome window soon appears to greet you with some ways to get a quick start with the program.

Using the Welcome Window

The Welcome window (shown in Figure 1.1) isn't just there to greet you and make you feel at home. It does that, all right, but it also gives you a chance to click some buttons that let you get started with particular tasks if you're in a hurry to start editing.

Figure 1.1

The Welcome screen greets you when you launch Adobe Photoshop Elements.

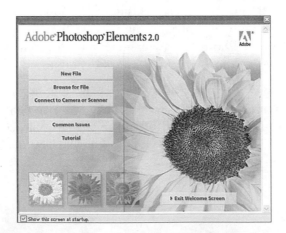

Hover your mouse pointer over each of the buttons on the Welcome screen. As you do so, notice that each one lights up in turn. Here are brief descriptions of what you can do with each button:

- **New File.** Click here to open a new image window within the Photoshop Elements window. You can either paint or draw directly on the image window, or open an existing image file within the main Photoshop Elements window.

- **Browse for File.** Click here, and a visual navigation tool called the File Browser opens so you can find an image file on your computer. Chapter 3 describes this feature.

- **Connect to Scanner or Camera.** If you have a scanner or camera connected to your computer and you want to bring an image from the camera into Photoshop Elements, click this button. To use this feature successfully, you need to install the software that came with your scanner or camera. See Chapter 3 for more information about importing images from scanners or cameras.

- **Common Issues.** Click this button, and a miniature window called a palette opens within the Photoshop Elements window. Photoshop Elements comes with a number of such palettes. This particular one, How To, includes "Recipes"—step-by-step instructions for performing various common tasks with the program.

- **Tutorial.** Click here, and Photoshop Elements launches your Web browser. The browser window displays links that lead to a group of interactive tutorials for fixing images, creating animations, and other topics. The tutorials are installed on your hard disk during installation; you don't need to be connected to the Internet to view them.

In Focus

If you are already working in the main Photoshop Elements window, you can make the Welcome screen reappear by choosing Window → Welcome.

- **Exit Welcome Screen.** Click here or on the Close box at the top of the Welcome screen if you simply want to close this window and move to the main Photoshop Elements window so you can start working with the program.

Also make note of the check box in the bottom left-hand corner of the Welcome screen. Uncheck it if you don't want to view the Welcome window when you start up Photoshop Elements in future.

Right now, click New File to start using Photoshop Elements right away. The Welcome screen closes and the New dialog box appears. For now, don't worry about the settings in this dialog box (you'll find out more about how to create new files in Chapter 3). Click OK to close this New File dialog box and open a new untitled image within the Photoshop Elements window.

Touring the Interface

Once you've opened a new image window, make sure you have the other main parts of the program interface available to you. Although the PC and Mac versions of Photoshop Elements offer slight visual differences, the interface is pretty much the same in terms of functionality. Some of the keyboard shortcuts vary, however—the PC version uses the Ctrl and Alt keys, and the Macintosh version uses the Cmd and Opt keys.

Choose Window → Tools to display the toolbox if it isn't visible. (If a Windows menu option is checked, that means it is visible; if it is not checked, it's not visible.) Also choose Window → Shortcuts and Window → Options, if needed, to display two other primary features of the Photoshop Elements environment: the shortcuts bar and options bar (see Figure 1.2).

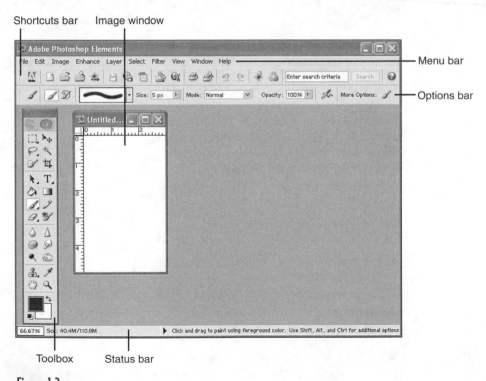

Figure 1.2

A new image window opens within the main Photoshop Elements window.

In Focus

If you are more experienced at working with computer graphics programs or other software programs that use multiple palettes, you will be at ease with the Photoshop Elements interface. You have a good deal of control over the components you have visible in order to perform various tasks. Most of the components are accessible from the Windows menu. You select a Windows menu option to display the component, such as the shortcuts bar, the toolbox, or a palette. If you select an already-checked menu option, it is unchecked and becomes hidden.

Other parts of the Photoshop Elements working environment are customizable. For instance, if you choose View → Rulers, you display rulers within image windows. Because the program has so many options, the screen images you see in this book may not look exactly the same as what you see on your own screen.

Each image you create or edit in Photoshop Elements is contained in its own image window. Although you've got only one image window open right now, you can have as many open at the same time as you want and as your memory and screen space allow. However, only the one whose title bar (that's the bar at the top of the window) is dark blue is "active." You can only edit the active window.

Ordering Up from the Menu Bar

The Photoshop Elements menu bar appears at the top of your program window (Windows) or the top of your computer screen (Mac). Click each menu in turn to see the options unroll beneath them:

- The **File menu** provides all the options needed to open, save, print, and create new images. In addition, you'll find a number of slick new options. Create Photomerge, for example, enables you to create a panorama out of a series of related images.

- The **Edit menu** offers easy access to your basic edit (cut, copy, paste), history (undo, redo), and preference functions.

- The **Image menu** enables you to rotate, crop, or transform all or part of your pictures.

- The **Enhance menu** offers tools that provide quick image fixes (you'll find out more about quick fixes in Chapter 9).

- The **Layer menu** enables you to control and adjust sections of an image called layers, as you'll discover in Chapters 7 and 8.

◆ The **Select menu** offers many ways to control what parts of an image to select, so you can change the appearance of just those parts while leaving the rest of the image alone.

◆ The **Filters menu**, one of Photoshop Elements most powerful and expandable features, offers instant access to artistic and corrective functions that change the way your image looks.

◆ The **View menu** lets you zoom in and out, show rulers, and control how you look at an image window. Try it out—click one of the open image windows and choose View → Grid to make a grid appear that can help you position objects.

◆ The **Window menu** enables you to display or hide the Photoshop Elements *palettes*, tools, and other features.

◆ The **Help menu** includes general help, system information, tutorials, and more (see Chapter 3 for more).

Shop Talk

A **palette** is a window that floats within the main Photoshop Elements window and that contains buttons, popup menus, and other interactive tools that help you edit and learn about images. Palettes look different from windows—they can float above other windows, but you can't cover a palette with an image window. Palettes have a very thin top bar and tiny square close button in the upper-left corner. You can resize palettes by dragging their edges or corners. All of the Photoshop Elements palettes reside in the Palette Well when they're not in use.

Exploring the Toolbox

To get acquainted with the toolbox, hover your mouse pointer over each of the tools in turn. Little labels called *tool tips* appear when you linger over each tool for a moment. Click the Brush tool on the left to select it. Then choose Window → Hints to open the Hints palette within the Photoshop Elements window. Click and drag the blue bar at the top of the palette to move it into the main work area within the Photoshop Elements window (that's the area with the gray background).

In Focus

Tool tips don't appear unless the Show Tool Tips option is checked in the Photoshop Elements general preferences. Choose Edit → Preferences → General to display general preferences.

As you can see, the Hints palette is context-based. It displays information about the currently selected tool or other item. It's a great way to get details about what a tool does and how to use it while you're working with the program.

Click the Brush tool in the toolbox, then click and hold down anywhere within the blank image window to start brushing. Try to draw yourself a friendly greeting like the word "Hi!" shown in Figure 1.3.

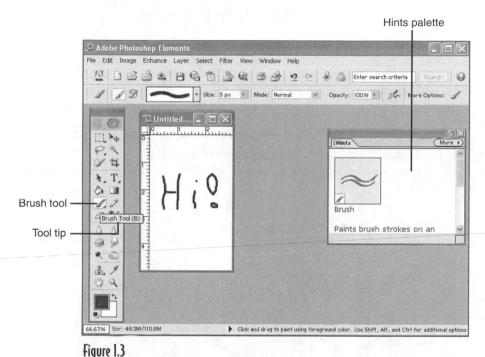

Figure 1.3

The Hints palette provides interactive information about the Photoshop Elements tools.

The toolbox is divided into six basic sections divided by horizontal rules:

- ◆ At the top of the toolbox is a button (the flower picture) that links you directly to the Adobe Online updates site, where you can download available program updates for Photoshop Elements if you are connected to the Internet.

- ◆ The next six buttons offer text and selection tools. Below, you'll find eight shape and drawing tools. Next are six image adjustment tools.

In Focus

Each of the tools in the toolbox has a corresponding shortcut key. The key appears in the tool tip next to the tool's name. For example, the tool tip Lasso tool (L) indicates that L is the shortcut key—press L and the Lasso tool is automatically selected.

- ◆ The last group includes an eclectic set of four "everything else" tools.

- ◆ At the bottom of the toolbox are buttons that display and select your foreground and background colors. The small double arrow lets you swap your foreground and background colors; the tiny double box enables you to restore the default (black on white) colors.

Uncovering Hidden Tools

Do you like to uncover secrets or hidden things? If so, the toolbox is for you. Next to seven of your tools, you'll find tiny downward-pointing triangles. Each of these triangles leads to hidden related tools. Click the Shape Selection tool, for instance, and hold down your mouse button. In a second or so, the hidden tool menu appears, as seen in Figure 1.4.

Figure 1.4

Press and hold on any tool marked with the small downward arrow to reveal the associated hidden tools.

To select one of the hidden tools, drag your mouse to the tool of choice and release the mouse button. Photoshop Elements updates the toolbox to display your choice.

The Shortcuts Bar and Options Bar

The two bars that appear directly beneath the menu bar are among the most important parts of the Photoshop Elements interface. The shortcuts bar appears on top by default and contains icons for creating new files, opening and saving files, dragging palettes out of the Palette Well, and so on. Pass your mouse pointer over the icons to view the tool tips for each tool.

The options bar, which appears beneath the shortcuts bar by default, contains options that are specific to the tool you've chosen. To get some quick experience using both of these bars, select the Brush tool; as a result, the options in the options bar become specific to the Brush tool. The current brush shape appears in the big box that has the Show Selected Brush Presets tool tip and the drop-down list arrow next to it.

Click the New icon at the far left of the short-cuts bar to open a new image window. Click OK when the New dialog box appears. Then click the Brush Size drop-down list arrow to choose a new brush shape from the dizzying array of options. Write a second message to yourself in the new image window (see Figure 1.5). If you still have your original image (your drawing of the word "Hi!") open, compare it to this one drawn with a different size and pattern of brush. Click and drag each window's title bar to reposition it so you can see both windows, the toolbox, and the Hints palette at once.

> ### It's Element-ary
>
> The Adobe.com icon next to the New icon at the far left of the shortcuts bar launches your browser and takes you to the Adobe.com website where you can find out more about Photo shop Elements and other Adobe products. (You have to be connected to the Internet for this to work.)

Adobe.com
icon

New   Show selected
icon   brush presets

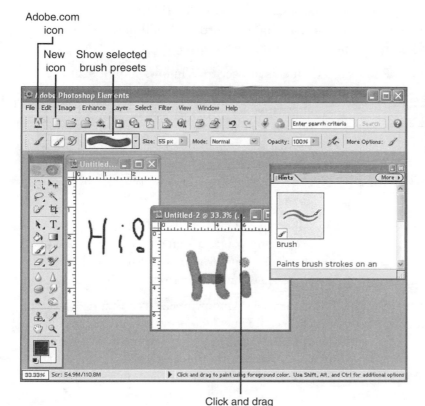

Click and drag
to move window

Figure 1.5

The shortcuts and options bars let you quickly perform many image-editing tasks.

Exploring the Shortcuts Bar

The shortcuts bar buttons (shown in Figure 1.6) perform many different functions. Some of them are described in forthcoming chapters (the QuickFix button is described in Chapter 9, for instance). The following sections show you a few tasks that can help with virtually all functions.

Figure 1.6

The shortcuts bar provides quick access to the most popular program features.

Open   Save   Undo/Step backward   Search

Browse   Redo/Step forward   Help

Enter search criteria   Search   Navigator

Follow these steps to explore the shortcuts bar options and get some experience with them:

1. Click Open. The Open dialog box appears. You can use this dialog box to locate a file on your computer so you can work with it. You'll find out more about opening files in Chapter 3; for now, click Cancel.

2. Click Browse. The Photoshop Elements answer to Windows Explorer or the Mac Finder appears: the File Browser. The File Browser gives you a visual alternative to the Open dialog box. You can browse for files on your computer, but you get a visual representation of what each file looks like before you open it. Click the Close box to close the File Browser; you'll work with it in Chapter 3.

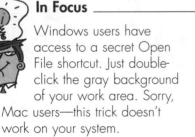

In Focus

Windows users have access to a secret Open File shortcut. Just double-click the gray background of your work area. Sorry, Mac users—this trick doesn't work on your system.

3. Click Save. The Save As dialog box appears, prompting you to assign a file name to one of the open image windows and to save them somewhere on your hard disk. Click Cancel.

4. Click Online Services. The Online Services window opens (see Figure 1.7) with a set of links that let you add new "Recipes" (step-by-step instructions on how to perform tasks), additional features, and (if you are connected to the Internet) a link to a photo-finishing service called Shutterfly that prints your digital photos and mails them to you. (You'll find out more about Shutterfly in Chapter 22.)

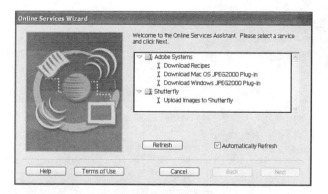

Figure 1.7

The Online Services button connects you to photo-printing services and updated software.

5. Click Cancel to close the Online Services window and return to the Photoshop Elements window for more exploration.

6. Click one of the image windows to make it active, and draw something on it with the Brush tool. Then click the Step Backward button in the shortcuts bar—your work disappears. Click Step Forward to make it reappear again.

Search Field

Photoshop Elements offers terrific onscreen access to its user manual. To search this manual, enter a phrase into the box that normally has the default words Enter Search Criteria and click the Search button (on the Mac, you click a magnifying glass icon). Photoshop Elements launches your default web browser and displays the matching entries from the online Help files (See Chapter 3 for more about using the Photoshop Elements built-in Help system.)

Detaching the Options Bar

Like the shortcuts bar, the options bar can function as a floating bar that you can close or move around the screen. It doesn't have to stay in a single location beneath the shortcuts bar. Click

In Focus

One of the nice things about the Step Backward and Step Forward buttons is that, if you click one of them repeatedly, you can move through a series of steps. Click Step Backward three times, for instance, and you undo your three previous actions. You can also undo one single action out of a sequence of actions with the History palette, as explained in the section "Palettes and the Palette Well" later in this chapter.

Swatch Out!

Each time you press F1 or choose Help → Adobe Photoshop Elements Help, you launch a new browser window, which can be confusing. Make sure you don't already have a Help window open before you launch a new one.

the dotted vertical line near the left edge of the options bar, hold down your mouse button, drag the options bar into the main work area, and release the mouse button. Figure 1.8 shows the detached bar.

Figure 1.8

The options and shortcuts bar can be detached for more flexibility.

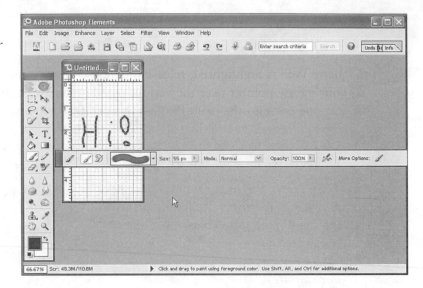

Detaching a bar gives you a lot of flexibility when your workspace gets crowded. You can move the options bar to the bottom of your screen, out of the way, in order to view image files better. You can dock the options bar back in its original space. Click and hold down the blue bar and drag the bar back to its location beneath the shortcuts bar. Release the mouse button, and the bar is docked. When the bar is undocked, try double-clicking the bar at the far left edge to collapse it into a compact space; double-click the bar again to restore it to its previous expanded size.

Palettes and the Palette Well

You've already seen that Photoshop Elements has a wide variety of palettes for different purposes, and that you'll find out more about them in the chapters that follow. But there's another way to access palettes—the Palette Well. The Palette Well appears at the far right of the shortcuts bar; if the shortcuts bar isn't visible, the Palette Well isn't available either. What's more, you may have to enlarge the Photoshop Elements window by clicking and dragging either the left or right edges or double-clicking the bar to display the Palette Well in its entirety (see Figure 1.9).

Figure 1.9

The Palette Well gives you a convenient place to store palettes.

Practice storing a palette right now by clicking the Hints palette's blue bar, holding down the mouse button, and dragging the palette right into the Palette Well. When the Palette Well is highlighted, release the mouse button, and the palette is stored. Pass your mouse pointer over the various palette tabs stored in the Palette Well; click and drag one out into the main Photoshop Elements window to start working on it. It can be tricky to find exactly the palette you want in the Palette Well; for everyday use, you'll probably find the Windows menu easier to use.

Each one of the Photoshop Elements palettes offers a unique function and appearance. Too many such palettes exist to discuss every one in detail here; many will be discussed in chapters that pertain to the functions they let you perform. You should, though, open a few palettes to get a look at them and learn how to work with them.

To begin, choose Window → Navigator to display the Navigator palette (see Figure 1.10).

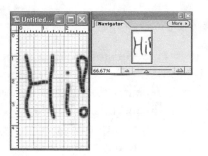

Figure 1.10

The Navigator palette lets you zoom in or out interactively.

Click and hold down the slider and slide it to the right to zoom in on the active window. Move the slider to the left, and you zoom out. You can also zoom in by using the Zoom tool in the toolbox, or by pressing Ctrl++ (Windows) or Cmd++ (Mac). Zoom out by pressing Ctrl+– (Windows) or Cmd+– (Mac).

Choose Window → Color Swatches to display the Color Swatches palette, which lets you choose colors. As Figure 1.11 shows, Color Swatches has some general features that are common to all palettes, including Minimize and Close boxes, a title bar, and draggable corners and edges that let you resize the palette.

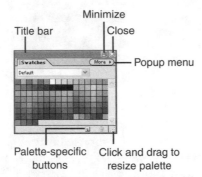

Minimize

Title bar   Close

Popup menu

Palette-specific   Click and drag to
buttons   resize palette

Figure 1.11

Palettes contain standard tools that let you control their appearance.

When you click the More button, a popup menu appears with a new set of options that are specific to this palette (see Figure 1.12). But be aware that, if you click a palette's tab in the Palette Well, the More button does not appear.

Figure 1.12

Many palettes have their own popup menus.

Next, choose Window → Undo History to display the Undo History palette (see Figure 1.13), which is one of the Photoshop Elements most unique features. This palette recounts your most recent set of Photoshop Elements commands and enables you to move backward (undo) and forward (redo) through that history. If you even want to undo a single step that you think you did several actions ago but can't quite remember what it was, this is the palette for you.

Figure 1.13

Move back and forth in your undo history with the Undo History palette.

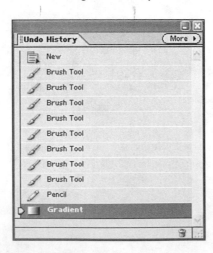

Combining Palettes

A cool Photoshop Elements trick enables you to combine palettes together into a single presentation. Click the little tab that displays the name Color Swatches, hold down the mouse, and drag the palette so that it's over the Undo History palette. You'll notice that when one palette is directly atop the other, the one on the bottom becomes highlighted. Release your mouse button; the two palettes are combined into one merged floating palette, as seen in Figure 1.14. Just click any of the tabs at the top of the palette window to bring that particular palette to the front.

In this chapter, you've explored the main features of the Photoshop Elements interface. In the next chapter, you'll learn how to browse through files on your computer and open them up in Photoshop Elements.

> ### It's Element-ary
>
> If you have trouble moving palettes or they don't want to go in the locations you want, choose Window → Reset Palette Locations to close open palettes and open the How To and Hints palettes. When you open new palettes, you'll be able to control them more easily.

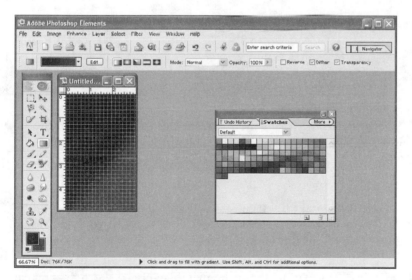

Figure 1.14

Drag one palette atop another to create a merged presentation.

Finding Help

This book does its best to give you the basics of using Photoshop Elements. But it doesn't cover every last detail about the program. If you're looking for an obscure keyboard shortcut or further explanation on a process not covered here, turn to the Photoshop Elements online help system. (It's called an "online" help system because it uses a web browser, but you don't have to actually be online to access and use Help.)

Using Online Help

It's easy to start up online help and explore the different ways to use it. If you're working in Windows, press F1. Otherwise, choose Help → Photoshop Elements Help. Your default web browser opens and displays the Photoshop Elements Help welcome screen, shown in Figure 1.15.

Figure 1.15

The Photoshop Elements Help window uses a web browser to help you find answers.

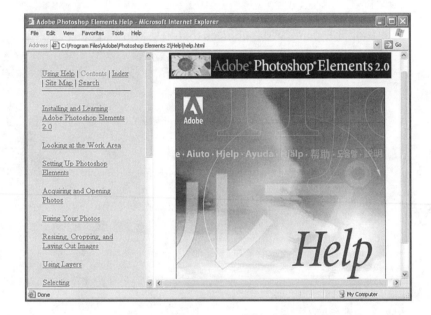

Click a topic in the Navigation frame (that's the frame on the left-hand side of the Help window) to view a detailed explanation of that topic in the right-hand frame. By default, Help opens with a table of contents in the Navigation frame. Here are your options:

- ◆ Click Search: A text box labeled Find pages containing appears. Enter the topic **Windows Shortcuts** (in Windows) or **Macintosh Shortcuts** (if you're a Mac user) in the box, and press Search. In a few seconds, a list of links appears in the Navigation frame. Click the Windows or Macintosh Shortcuts link to go to a Help page that contains information about the many keyboard shortcuts you can use with Photoshop Elements.

- ◆ Click Index to display an alphabetical index. The Index is your best option if you know the name of a topic you want to research but you don't know what Contents category contains it.

◆ Click Site Map at the top of the Navigation Pane if you're not sure at all what you're looking for and you don't mind looking through a long list of all topics in the Help system until you find what you're looking for.

Hints, Recipes, and Tutorials

Photoshop Elements offers so many options under the Window menu that it's easy to look for some of the choices that help you learn how to use specific tools or perform functions. Suppose, for example, you've created a new image window as described in this chapter and you want to add text to it. You click the tool that looks like the letter T in the toolbox because you think it has something to do with creating text, but you're not sure. Choose Window → Hints to display the Hints palette. When you click the Text tool, the Hints palette displays its name (the Horizontal Text tool) and gives you some quick hints about how to use it.

To get step-by-step instructions on how to enhance text, draw shapes, or perform other tasks with Photoshop Elements, choose Window → How To to open the palette by that name (see Figure 1.16). Click the drop-down list at the top of the How To palette and choose a specific task from the list.

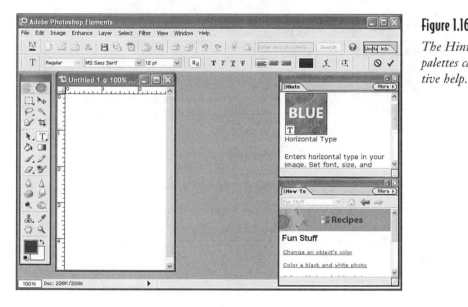

Figure 1.16

The Hints and How To palettes can give you interactive help.

In Focus

If you've got some time on your hands and are looking for alternate step-by-step instructions on particular topics, choose Help → Photoshop Elements Tutorials. The Photoshop Elements Online Help page appears in your browser window, with links to a group of tutorials. Virtually all the tutorials are covered in this book, however. You can also click the Adobe.com icon in the shortcuts bar to go to Adobe's website, where you can access a larger number of tutorials than the built-in Help system can provide.

The Least You Need to Know

- The Welcome screen and the main program window both provide ways to let you start using Photoshop Elements.

- The toolbox contains tools for selecting, drawing, and editing.

- The menu bar contains options for opening, editing, saving, and viewing images.

- The shortcuts and options bars give you quick access to many functions.

- You can access palettes from the Window menu or the Palette Well.

- You can create merged palettes by dragging one atop another.

- Pressing Help gives you access to the Help system.

Getting Started

In This Chapter

- Learning how to open and display images
- Locating and previewing images with the File Browser
- Viewing a "contact sheet" displaying multiple image files
- Opening images from a scanner or digital camera

Once you've gotten to know your way around the Photoshop Elements interface and have captured some digital images, it's time to roll up your sleeves and start editing them. Aside from installing and starting up the software, you're also likely to open an existing image so you can view it and polish it up visually.

In this chapter, you'll first learn the simple way to open files (big hint: It's as easy as File → Open). You'll also learn how to say "Open Sesame" and have a Photoshop Elements genie called the File Browser locate and open files for you. You'll get some practice opening files directly from a digital camera, too.

But simply opening an image isn't the only way to get started working with Photoshop Elements. You'll learn how to create a new image window where you can either paste an existing image or start drawing your own creation from scratch. Finally, you'll learn how to make the best use of the software's extensive built-in Help files in case you need a jump-start.

In Focus

You can also open files by choosing Window → File Browser. You then use Photoshop Elements' own File Browser to locate and display your image files visually, as described in "Browsing for Files" later in this chapter.

The Open File Policy

Before you can start exploring the different ways Photoshop Elements gives you for opening files, you need to capture your image (as described in Chapter 3) and store it on disk. This section assumes that you've either stored the image on your computer's hard disk or that, if you don't have your own scanned images available, you can open any of the images on this book's CD-ROM. The section "Importing Files" in Chapter 3 explains how to open an image that's stored in your digital camera.

Launching Your Grand Opening

Photoshop Elements can do a lot of things, but it can't do its work unless you've loaded one or more pictures into image windows. Once they're open, you can use the available tools and menu items to process your images. The simplest approach to opening a picture is both straightforward and probably familiar to anyone with any Windows or Macintosh experience. Follow these steps:

1. Do one of the following:

   ◆ Select File → Open.

   ◆ Type Ctrl+O (Windows) or Cmd+O (Mac).

   ◆ Double-click the gray background of the Photoshop Elements workspace (Windows only).

2. The Open File dialog box appears, as shown in Figure 2.1. (Figure 2.1 shows the Open dialog box as it appears in Windows XP using Thumbnails view. Your Open dialog box might not look exactly the same. Choose Thumbnails from the View menu icon in the Open dialog box's toolbar if you want to view thumbnail images.)

3. Navigate to the *house.tif* image in the Chapter 2 folder on this book's CD-ROM, and open the file by doing one of two things:

   ◆ Click the file name to highlight it, and then click Open.

   ◆ Double-click the file name.

   The Open dialog box closes and the image you selected is displayed in a new window.

Figure 2.1

The Open dialog box displays a preview of a selected image.

In Focus

If you know what type of file you're looking for, choosing the image type from the Files of Type drop-down list in the Open dialog box helps you locate it quickly. If you're looking for a particular kind of file, choose that type of image file from the Files Of Type drop-down list in the Open File dialog box. If you're looking for a Photoshop Data image, for instance, choose Photoshop (*.psd) from the Files of Type list. Only the Photoshop Data images are displayed. Choose All Formats if you want to view all files. (See Chapter 4 for more about file types.)

The Open dialog box is the simplest way to open your images; choose it when you're in a hurry or when you know exactly what you want to open and exactly where it is located. If you're not sure what you want to open or if you want to look around to choose the best image, choose the File Browser to visually explore the directories and folders on your hard drive. The "Browsing for Files" section later in this chapter describes the File Browser.

Touring the Image Window

Now that you've opened up an image, take a few minutes to explore some features that are unique to that window.

Title Bar

In addition to listing the name of your file, the image window's title bar (see Figure 2.2) shows you the current magnification of your image (for example, 100%, 50%, 33.3%) and the *color mode*. It also shows the layer you are on in a multilayered image (see Chapter 7 for more about layers). Choose View → Zoom In or Zoom Out to change the magnification.

Figure 2.2

An image window has its own title bar.

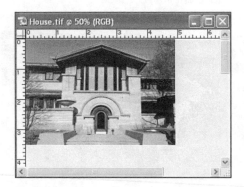

Shop Talk

The term **color mode** refers to the way Photoshop Elements stores color information about an image. The program supports three color modes: RGB, grayscale (gray), or bitmap. RGB, which stands for red-green-blue, offers full color definition for every part of your image. Grayscale discards color information, storing only brightness values, from darkest (black) to lightest (white), with a range of gray tones that fall between. Bitmap images use only two values, either black or white, with no intermediate tones. See Chapter 4 for more about color modes.

You can do more with an image window than you'd probably guess at first glance. Try a few tasks with the image you have open. Click and drag the title bar to move the image elsewhere within the Photoshop Elements window; if you're using Windows, click the *Minimize* button to reduce the image to a title bar tucked away at the bottom of the Photoshop Elements window. Then click the Adobe Photoshop Elements button in the Windows taskbar to restore the image to its previous size and position. Finally, drag an edge to enlarge or resize the window without resizing the image itself.

If you're on a Macintosh, clicking Minimize causes the "window blind" effect, in which the window collapses to its title bar, and clicking it again restores the window to its original size.

Shop Talk

The **Maximize** and **Minimize** window functions operate in much the same manner under both Windows and Macintosh.

The Maximize button, one of three buttons in the upper right-hand corner of an image window, toggles between full-screen and intermediate presentation. When pressed the first time, your computer attempts to display your image window at its biggest possible size within the Photoshop Elements window. Clicked again, it returns to the intermediate image window presentation.

The Minimize button toggles between open and closed presentations. In Windows, the window zips down to the Start bar and is hidden from the main desktop. On the Macintosh, the window collapses into its title bar. Clicked again, the Minimize button restores your window to its previous configuration.

Gather Information About Your Image

Once you open an image, what you decide to do with it partly depends on its characteristics. You can learn about an image's characteristics in the status bar, which appears at the bottom of the Photoshop Elements window (Windows) or at the bottom of your image (Macintosh).

Use the status bar (see Figure 2.3) to get up-to-date information about the currently active image. Take a tour around the status bar by clicking its three components: the zoom text box, the selectable information display, and the task context area. These three areas work together to tell you about the active image and the currently selected tool.

First, click inside the zoom text box and select the current number to highlight it. Enter a different number and then press Enter. The image's magnification changes accordingly. As you can see, the zoom text box lets you zoom in or zoom out interactively. The higher the number, the more your image magnifies (the maximum magnification is 1600 percent). The lower the number, the lower the magnification (you can reduce magnification until only one *pixel* is visible in the image).

Shop Talk

A **pixel** is a "picture element," the smallest piece of a digital image. Your images are made up of rows and columns of pixels, forming a rectangle. Each pixel has a distinct color associated with it.

When you're preparing images for the web, file size and physical dimensions become critical. You want the smallest file size you can get without sacrificing image quality, and you want a height and width that will fit comfortably on a web page. Click the triangle in the status bar to display the file information popup menu; choose one of the menu options to find out more details about *house.tif*; The status bar displays the details next to the zoom text box. The first three menu options are pretty straightforward:

- ◆ **Document Sizes** shows the image's file size.

- ◆ **Document Profile** displays the image's color mode.

- ◆ **Document Dimensions** reveals the image's size (usually in pixels).

Figure 2.3

The Photoshop Elements status bar provides current image information.

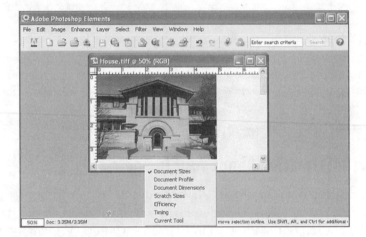

The next few file information popup menu options aren't so straightforward. They come in handy when your computer memory is running low and you have to work on memory-intensive images. They let you know if Photoshop Elements needs more RAM (Random Access Memory, the memory your computer uses to operate applications) to operate efficiently:

- ◆ **Scratch Sizes** reports important information about how much of your system's memory Photoshop Elements currently uses. The number on the left reports the amount of RAM used to display all currently open images. The number on the right reports the total amount of RAM available to Photoshop Elements for processing images. (A *scratch disk* refers to a portion of RAM (memory) or disk set aside to store intermediate results of your image-processing tasks.)

- ◆ **Efficiency** displays the percent of time spent performing image-processing tasks versus handling overhead tasks (such as working with the scratch disk). Whenever the value falls below 100 percent, the indicator reflects that Photoshop Elements is operating below peak efficiency.

- **Timing** indicates the amount of time it took to complete the last image-processing operation you performed.

- **Current Tool** shows the name of the selected and active tool, which may be handy if you don't keep the toolbox visible sometimes.

In this section, you've opened a picture in Photoshop Elements and have identified the various components of the image window. Next, you'll learn about using the File Browser to locate, identify, and open your image.

In Focus

When you left-click the information display, you access a secret display that shows even more information about your image! You'll see the current image width, height, resolution, and "channels." Channels refer to the number of colors associated with each pixel. RGB images have three channels; grayscale and bitmap have just one.

Browsing for Files

Suppose you've got a folder just chock full of photos from that field trip you took with your son's third-grade class to the science museum. You've got more than two dozen images, in fact, and you need to find that single picture of your son's friend Nigel standing next to Mr. Neutron. The problem is, all the photos came back from the photo lab on a CD-ROM with generic numbers—nothing that says "Nigel" or "Mr. Neutron." File Browser to the rescue!

In Photoshop Elements, the File Browser tool enables you to visually inspect and organize all the image files on your computer. The browser helps you to scan through all of the files on your computer with power and flexibility. Try it yourself, and you'll discover that the File Browser doesn't just display file names, and is not limited to one directory. The File Browser gives a visual representation of *all* the files on your computer. What's more, with Photoshop Elements version 2.0, Adobe gave the File Browser a complete overhaul.

To launch your File Browser, do one of the following:

- Choose File → Browse.

- Choose Window → File Browser.

- Press Ctrl+Shift+O (Windows) or Cmd+Shift+O (Mac).

It's Element-ary

In previous versions of Photoshop Elements, the File Browser resided in the Palette Well by default. In version 2.0, you can dock it there manually yourself by choosing Dock to Palette Well from the More popup menu.

◆ In the Welcome window that appears when you first start Photoshop Elements, click the Browse for File button.

Each method opens the File Browser. As Figure 2.4 shows, when you select an image file in a folder, information about that file appears in the lower and middle panes on the right.

Figure 2.4

The File Browser enables you to navigate visually through files.

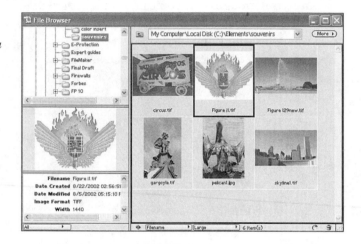

Navigating with the File Browser

Once you get used to the File Browser, you'll find it incredibly useful. While Photoshop Elements is open, you might just be tempted to use it in place of Windows Explorer or the Macintosh Finder. Here are some tips to help you better navigate with the File Browser:

◆ **See it at once**   See the contents of an entire disk at once by clicking your main disk drive in the file navigation area. All folders appear with small folder icons. Double-click a folder that contains image files; the pictures appear as small thumbnail images in the large display area in the right half of the File Browser.

◆ **Preview a picture**   Get a larger preview of an image by clicking its thumbnail icon to select it. A larger version appears in the File Browser's preview area. The facts and figures about the selected image are displayed in the file information area just beneath the preview area.

◆ **Know where you are**   Determine where you are in your file system by clicking the file navigation drop-down list at the top of the File Browser. The series of folder navigation messages that drop down instantly show you which directory you are in.

- ◆ **Manage and open your files**   To open a file just double-click its thumbnail. Photoshop Elements opens it as a new image window. To move a file, click and drag it atop the folder that you want to contain it. To delete a file, select it and click the trashcan icon at the lower-right corner of the File Browser. (When a dialog box appears asking you to confirm that you want to delete the file, click No unless you actually want to delete it.)

- ◆ **Rotate your images**   If you can, find a horizontal thumbnail that's displayed in the File Browser in a vertical orientation (or vice versa). Click the thumbnail, and then click the Rotate button next to the trashcan button to rotate the image by 90 degrees. Click Rotate three more times to restore the image's thumbnail to its original position. Rotation is only applied to the thumbnail, not the actual image.

In Focus

To reverse the direction of rotation, hold down the Alt key (Windows) or Opt key (Macintosh) when clicking the Rotate button.

When you turn an image using the Rotate button in the File Browser palette controls, you don't actually change the image on your hard drive. Instead, you change a small information file associated with your current directory. Whenever you open a picture file, Photoshop Elements consults this directory "meta-file." When it discovers that you've requested a rotation, it rotates the image as it's opened. To permanently rotate an image, click the rotate button as needed, open the file in Photoshop Elements, and then save the rotated image back to disk.

More File Browser Tricks

By now, you probably think you've explored everything you can do with the File Browser. Don't forget that little button labeled More in the top-right corner. Click it. You'll see a long list of further options unroll from a popup menu, as Figure 2.5 shows.

Many of the More popup menu items are easy to figure out—Rotate 180 degrees lets you flip an image horizontally or vertically, for instance. However, some of the more obscure menu options are the most powerful and interesting. Try them out yourself.

Figure 2.5

The More popup menu contains many additional navigation options.

Rename a Batch of Files

Use the File Browser to rename all the files in your directory. Here's how.

1. Open a directory in the File Browser.

2. Choose More → Select All.

3. Choose More → Batch Rename. The Batch Rename dialog appears (see Figure 2.6).

Figure 2.6

Batch Rename lets you rename all files in a folder at once.

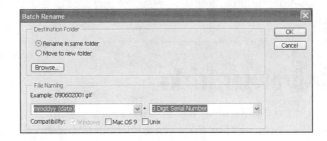

Swatch Out!

Take care when you rename. You cannot "batch undo" a batch renaming operation. Also, save the renamed files to a new folder so you can quickly check whether you renamed all the files you wanted, and to make sure you got the names right.

4. Select a new file name format or "rule" from the drop-down list on the left (in the figure, the format "mmddyy" has been chosen).

5. Select a serial number type from the drop-down list on the right (in the figure, "3-Digit Serial Number" has been chosen).

6. Click OK. Photoshop Elements renames all the files you selected.

View a File "Contact Sheet"

Another File Browser trick improves your ability to get a visual overview of a large number of image files at the same time. By default, the File Browser is broken into multiple sections, which makes it difficult for you to see more than six images at once—unless you switch to thumbnail view, in which case you can see dozens. To view multiple images in the form of a digital *contact sheet*, follow these steps:

1. Click the More button and, if necessary, uncheck the Expanded View option to remove the preview area, file navigation area, and file information area from the File Browser.

2. Click the More button and, if necessary, uncheck the Large Thumbnail option. Photoshop Elements hides most of the file details and leaves you with a scrollable list of image thumbnails.

3. If you need to, click the More button and, if necessary, uncheck the Show Folders option to hide any directories. This leaves you with a display of image files only, as shown in Figure 2.7.

Shop Talk

The term **contact sheet** comes from the realm of traditional darkroom photography. The photographer places an entire roll of film (cut into manageable pieces) on a sheet of photographic paper and exposes it. Once developed, the print displays thumbnail-sized images of the entire roll.

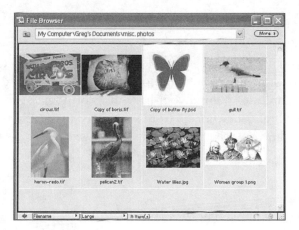

Figure 2.7

You can transform the File Browser into a "contact sheet" display.

Reveal a File's Location

The File Browser is so useful, you may *only* want to use it to locate a file. Once you find what you want, you can then open and work with the file in another program, such as a web page editor. Discover how easy it is to use for yourself:

1. Choose Window → File Browser to display the File Browser.

2. Click through folders in the file navigation section of the File Browser to locate the image you want to work with.

3. Click the file's thumbnail to select it.

4. Choose More → Reveal Location in Explorer (Windows) or More → Reveal Location in Finder (Macintosh). The image is displayed in either Windows Explorer (as shown in Figure 2.8) or in the Macintosh Finder.

Figure 2.8

The File Browser can open a file in Windows Explorer.

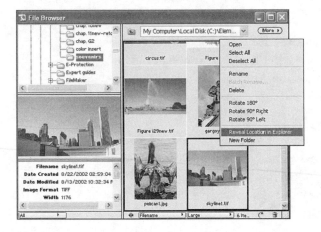

Creating New Files

Much of the time, you'll probably be using Photoshop Elements to view, edit, and touch up digital images such as photos. But if that's all you do with the program, you'll be using it with one hand tied behind your back. It's worth taking some time to discover how to create a brand-new image from scratch using the Photoshop Elements drawing tools. To begin, you need to create a new image window, as follows:

1. Do one of the following:

   ◆ Select File → New.

   ◆ On the Welcome screen, click New File.

   ◆ Click the New File icon on the shortcuts bar.

2. The New File dialog box appears. Enter the new name **test-drawing** in the Name field.

3. Set the size of your new image. In Figure 2.9, a new window is being created that is 5 inches tall and 3 inches wide, with a resolution of 150 pixels per inch, and using RGB color mode.

Figure 2.9

The New File dialog box lets you specify the name and dimensions of a new image window.

4. Choose RGB from the Mode drop-down list. It's a good idea to stick with RGB color for most of your Photoshop Elements image work, because it gives you the best quality either for onscreen display or if you intend to publish the image on the web. Indexed mode has the capacity to display only a limited number of colors, while CYMK mode is relevant only if you are preparing an image for a printer who will produce a printed booklet.

5. In the Contents area, choose Transparent to leave your image completely blank. (If, on the other hand, you want to fill your image with a color, choose either White or Background Color.)

6. Click OK.

In Focus _____

If you prefer to use pixels rather than inches, select pixels from the pull-down menu to the right of the width and height measurements. Approximately 72 pixels equal one inch.

After you follow these steps, Photoshop Elements creates your new image window and opens it for you. You're now ready to work in your new, blank image window. You can paste all or part of an image in the new window from another image window. You can add text (see Chapter 13), use the painting tools (see Chapter 14), use the brushing tools (see Chapter 15), or draw your own shapes (see Chapter 16), like the one shown in Figure 2.10.

Figure 2.10

A new image window can contain text or your own original art.

The Least You Need to Know

- ◆ The File Browser gives you a visual way to locate and organize images.

- ◆ The number at the left of the status bar enables you to change image magnification.

- ◆ The information display area in the status bar provides detailed information about an image.

- ◆ The Files of Type drop-down list in the Open File dialog box enables you to view only one type of image file in a folder or on a disk.

- ◆ The New File dialog box enables you to specify the name and dimensions of a new image window.

Chapter 3

Capturing Images

In This Chapter

◆ Choosing a good image to scan

◆ Calibrating your scanner for reliable previews

◆ Optimizing the file size of scanned images

◆ Framing and zooming to improve digital photos

◆ Saving your digital photos in the right format

Photoshop Elements gives you lots of powerful tools for editing photos. But even the best tools in the world can't save really bad images. Your first job as a digital photo editor, then, is to obtain good images to work with.

When you take an image with a digital camera or scan a printed photo or drawing, you *capture* that image. Capturing an image means that you convert it from its original form—a real three-dimensional object, or tones on a piece of paper—into bits of digital information called *pixels*. You save the image in a computer format to a file on your computer. You can then open the image in Photoshop Elements.

This is why this chapter comes so early in the book: Before you can open and edit computer image files, you've got to create them. This chapter's goal is to give you some tips on scanning and working with digital cameras and scanners to create great images you can make even better with Photoshop Elements.

Importing Files

Chances are your scanner or digital camera comes with its own software for opening images. It might seem at first like a challenge to determine how to move those images from the camera to Photoshop Elements so you can edit them. But if you already have Photoshop Elements open, you don't have to open up the other application. You can save time by using Photoshop Elements to initiate the process of importing images from your digital device, provided your scanner or camera supports either the *TWAIN* or *WIA* (Windows Image Acquisition).

Shop Talk

TWAIN is a standard set of instructions that enables your computer to connect with graphics hardware, including many scanners and digital cameras. TWAIN, surprisingly enough, is not an acronym. Instead, the standard derives its name from a well-known phrase in *The Jungle Book* by Rudyard Kipling: "never the twain shall meet." The TWAIN Working Group's website (www.twain.org) contains plenty of information about the TWAIN standard and quickly dispels the myth that TWAIN stands for "Technology Without An Interesting Name."

WIA (Windows Image Acquisition) is an application programming interface (API) that enables Windows-based software applications such as Photoshop Elements to acquire digital images from hardware devices such as scanners and digital cameras. You can find out more about WIA by going to the Microsoft Developers Network Library (http://msdn.microsoft.com/library/default.asp) and searching for Windows Image Acquisition.

Here's how to import images from a digital device such as a scanner or digital camera into Photoshop Elements:

1. Make sure your camera or scanner software is installed correctly and you have rebooted your computer after installation.

2. Connect the device to your computer as instructed by the manufacturer. Most current hardware uses a USB connection, but this may vary.

3. Make sure your device has power and is turned on.

4. Launch Photoshop Elements.

5. Choose one of the following options:

   ◆ Click Connect to Camera or Scanner on the Welcome screen.

   ◆ Click the Import icon in the shortcuts bar.

   ◆ Choose File → Import.

6. The Select Import Source dialog box appears. Select your device from the Import drop-down list. The Import list options vary depending on the actual hardware you have installed on your computer.

7. Wait for your scanner or camera software to launch. Follow the manufacturer instructions to choose your image (if you're using a digital camera) or scan your image (if you're using a scanner) and return the results to Photoshop Elements.

After you finish selecting or scanning, you return to Photoshop Elements. Your image appears in a new image window, ready for you to use.

Scan 'Em and Capture 'Em

Ever want to be a magician? When you start to use a scanner, you're performing a sort of magic trick—and you don't even need to have anything up your sleeves. When you scan a photo, poster, or anything on a piece of paper, you change it from one form of visual information to another. Presto! The camera lens inside the scanner moves across the image and turns it into little squares called *pixels*. Each pixel contains bits of data that a computer can read and display on your screen.

In Focus

What really happens when you scan a photo? Photographic professionals call a photo a continuous-tone image—the tones in the image change continually from one shade to another. When you scan a continuous-tone image, you turn it into a digital image that a computer can interpret and display. By scanning the photo, you turn the information within it into a bitmap—a map of the image that consists of those little pixels of digital information.

One of your primary goals in scanning an image is (or should be) to capture a good range of tonal information. For a grayscale image, this means a wide range of tones between white and black—the tones should blend smoothly from one to another without harsh jumps from a light shade of gray to a much darker one. For a color image, this means you should capture all of the colors that were in the image originally without damaging any information or losing any colors along the way.

Picking Good Images

The quality of the image as it appears on a computer monitor depends, in part, on how you configure and run the scanner. But it also depends on the quality of the image itself. Whenever possible, pick an image that displays well on a computer screen. The phrase "garbage in, garbage out" is as relevant to digital images as it is to other matters.

Computer monitors aren't the best medium for viewing pictures. Monitors vary widely in quality. Some have high resolution, some low; some are old and faint, while others are new and crisp in their display. If you're scanning images and editing them in Photoshop Elements with an eye toward publishing them on the World Wide Web, you need to realize that you have absolutely no control over the quality or size of the monitor on which they will appear. For that reason, you need to pick images that have qualities such as the following:

- ◆ **Good lighting**   To be easily viewable on a computer screen, images need to be relatively bright. Images with subtle, foggy tones might look fine on glossy photo paper, but will leave people squinting when they view them on a computer screen.

- ◆ **Good contrast**   Contrast is the difference between the light and dark areas in an image. Images that have a substantial amount of contrast, such as photos taken outdoors on bright sunny days, will scan better than images taken in a dimly lit basement.

Shop Talk

The *resolution* of a digital image is the amount of information contained within it. Digital information in bitmap images is contained in the little squares called *pixels*. Therefore, resolution is usually expressed in terms of pixels per inch (ppi) or dots per inch (dpi).

- ◆ **Manageable size**   You can make a scanned image any size you want. Most computer users, though, have 15-inch, 17-inch, or 19-inch monitors. If you plan to display your images online, keep them small so they'll fit in a web browser window.

The image shown on the left in Figure 3.1 is an example of one with good contrast and lighting; the one on the right would be difficult to scan and display on a computer monitor.

Whenever possible, start with an image that has good contrast and that is sharply focused. But if you have an image that isn't up to ideal standards and you still want to work with it, chances are that image can still be made presentable with the tools described throughout this book. You're likely, at the very least, to make the image better than it was, and you just might end up with a masterpiece, too.

Figure 3.1

Use images that have good contrast and lighting.

Considering the Final Output

As mentioned in the previous section, images intended for presentation on the web should have special considerations. Specifically, the image's physical dimensions need to be manageable, and its resolution should be relatively low. Before you start scanning (or taking digital photos, for that matter), it's important to take into account what you want to do with an image after you capture it.

The final form that a digital image takes has everything to do with how you scan and edit it. Where images that are intended to be published on the web are concerned, file size is of paramount importance. The smaller the file size, the faster the image will appear in someone's browser window, even over a relatively slow dialup modem connection. You need to crop such images tightly and set the resolution low before you do the scan.

On the other hand, if you plan to print out an image on expensive photo paper and frame it on your wall, file size isn't the primary consideration. In this case, you should set the resolution as high as your printer will allow. If you have a 600-dpi printer, it doesn't make much sense to set the resolution at 1,200 dpi. But it does make sense to crop the image to fit the final output size (which, hopefully, will fit inside your frame) and set the resolution to 600 dpi to get the highest level of quality you can. The more planning you can do in advance, the better your results will be.

Selecting Color Mode

Resolution and physical dimensions are only two of the settings you can specify before you start scanning. You can also set the *color mode* you want to use.

Chapter 4 describes color modes in more detail, but here's a quick overview: Most scanners let you specify *RGB, CMYK*, or indexed color for the images you scan. In most cases RGB is fine for the images you want to open and edit in Photoshop Elements. If you want to keep file size small for the web, however, choose *indexed color*. If you plan to print your images in a brochure or other publication that is processed by a printer, use CMYK.

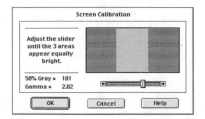

Shop Talk

A **color mode** is a way of accurately reproducing color in an image by combining a handful of colors in different ways to produce a wide range of colors. **RGB** color mode, for instance, combines three "additive" colors: red, green, and blue. **CMYK** color mode uses a "subtractive" set of colors that correspond to printers' inks: cyan, magenta, yellow, and black, the last of which is represented by the letter K. **Indexed color** uses a palette with a limited number of colors, such as a total of 216 or 256 different colors.

Calibrating Your Scanner

Wait! Don't skip ahead to the next section. Calibrating your scanner is really exciting—even sexy. All right, that's a bit of an overstatement. Calibrating your scanner can be exciting, though, if you've had a lot of trouble getting good images. A scanner that's calibrated can make a dramatic difference in the quality of your photos.

What does it mean to "calibrate" your scanner, exactly? It means that you configure the scanner with your monitor so that, when you view an image preview, your monitor accurately reflects the way it appears.

First, you make a test scan of your image. Then you open the software that came with the scanner and open the calibration controls. The exact menu options vary depending on the software you use. In DeskScan II, for example, you choose Help → Calibrate Screen, and follow the instructions in the Screen Calibration dialog box (see Figure 3.2).

Figure 3.2

Calibrate your monitor so it provides an accurate preview.

In Focus _____

Suppose you don't even have a scanner, or the device you had isn't working right? You have plenty of places to get images scanned. Copy shops such as Kinko's will let you use their scanners, as will many photo labs. Even chain drugstores have digital "picture makers" that scan images so you can print them out or save them to disk.

If you're an America Online customer, you can mail your printed photos to a photo service, and they'll scan the images and return them to you on disk (along with your original prints). On AOL, enter the keyword **PicturePlace** and then press Go.

Photoshop Elements has an arrangement with an online photo service called Shutterfly (www.shutterfly.com). You can send Shutterfly your photos and they'll return them to you in digitized format, too.

Previewing

Once you've calibrated your scanner, the next step is to launch the software that came with it so you can do the actual scanning. Sometimes, scanners come with applications that act as *plug-ins*; in other words, they work within another graphics application such as the high-powered professional graphics application on which Photoshop Elements is based: Adobe Photoshop.

After you install the software following the instructions that come with your scanner, start up the program, turn on the scanner, and make a preview scan of your first image. A preview scan gives you an idea of what an image looks like before you do the actual scan.

Previewing also gives you the chance to tell the scanner exactly how much of the scanning bed you want to use. In most cases, you're not going to need to use the entire space available, but only a relatively small area that is taken up by the actual photo or other item you are scanning. By using the Crop tool that comes with your scanning software, you can select the part of the scanning bed you want to use, which saves time and reduces the file size of the resulting image as well. You can also use the preview process to crop the image and make the adjustments described in the following sections.

In Focus _____

Most scanners give you the option of specifying a standard preview size. If most of your images are 4 by 6 inches, for instance, you can set the preview size slightly larger (such as at $4^1/_4$ by $6^1/_4$ inches). This can save a considerable amount of scanning time.

To do the preview, position the image in the scanner, and then look for the button that says Preview, such as the one in the lower left-hand corner of the DeskScan II window shown in Figure 3.3.

Figure 3.3

A preview scan lets you make adjustments before you do the final scan.

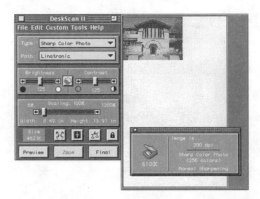

When you press the Preview button you'll hear a whirring sound as the optical device in the scanner does its business. A preview image appears onscreen with a marquee box (a rectangle made up of dashes) around the image. This box lets you crop the image. Cropping an image means that you select the part of the image that you want to appear in the final version, and leave out parts of the image that aren't essential.

It's always a good idea to do a preview scan before the actual scan. For one thing, the preview scan lets you know whether or not the image is positioned in the scanner correctly or whether it is skewed in some way. A preview scan also lets you make relatively simple adjustments to contrast and brightness—but keep in mind that you can make these adjustments in Photoshop Elements, too.

Shop Talk

The term **cropping** refers to the practice of identifying a contiguous part of an image you want to preserve and parts you want to cut out. Computer graphics programs let you crop an image by drawing a container around the part you want to preserve; when you choose the program's Crop command, the rest of the image is deleted.

Cropping the Image

Cropping an image is important and you should do it whenever possible because it makes an image smaller—not only in terms of its physical size but its file size as well. When you crop an image, you reduce the number of individual pixels in it. The fewer the pixels, the less space the image consumes on disk. The smaller an image file is, the quicker it appears online. If you've just done a preview scan, drag the lines of the box to resize it so that the box's outline closely matches what you want as the subject of your photo.

In Figure 3.4, to illustrate cropping, the box has been placed around the girl; the nonessential areas around the figure are being "cropped out."

The resulting cropped image will be much more compact than if you simply scanned the entire photo and put it on your web page. (The image will look better, too, if your cropping improves the image's composition and impact.)

Figure 3.4

Cropping a scanned image makes the file size smaller.

It's Element-ary

You don't have to crop your image exactly in your scanning software. In fact, you don't have to crop it at all. You can crop the image more precisely in Photoshop Elements because you can magnify it—and you can also change the contrast and brightness. However, some scanners provide an additional reason to crop before you scan: They adjust contrast and color saturation to better capture the part of the image you want.

Optimizing File Size

The size of the digital file you scan is partly a function of cropping. But it's also a function of the resolution and color mode.

When you scan an image you have different sorts of resolution to take into account. *Scan resolution* is an expression of the amount of image information (pixels) stored in a file and is controlled by the settings in your scanning software. But you should also keep *output resolution* in mind. This is an expression of the capability of a printer or other output device to produce detail. High-resolution imagesetters used in offset printing can produce an output of 2,540 dots per inch (dpi) or more, compared to the 300-dpi or 600-dpi resolution of a midrange inkjet or laser printer.

The higher the resolution, the larger the file size. If you set your scanning software to an output resolution of 1,200 dpi or more, you can quickly end up with an image that takes up 5MB, 8MB, or even more disk space. Choose an output resolution that matches the resolution of your own output device so you don't use up hard disk space so quickly.

If you scan a black-and-white drawing in color mode, you'll just end up with an image that's far larger than it needs to be. It'll take up more space on your hard disk, take longer to upload to your website, take longer to appear onscreen, and so on.

Setting the Resolution

Remember how you learned that scanned images are made up of little dots called pixels? Those dots are small, but they aren't always the same size. When you scan an image, you have the option of making the dots *really* small so the image appears extra smooth. This is called setting the *resolution* of an image.

The smaller the dots are, the better an image might appear in a printed booklet, brochure, or flyer. The size of the dots is expressed in dots per inch (dpi). The higher the number of dots per inch, the smaller the dots are, and the finer the image will be. The image on the left in Figure 3.5 has a resolution of 72 dpi; the one on the right has a 300 dpi resolution.

Figure 3.5

The higher the resolution, the sharper the image—and the bigger the file size.

In an image with 1,250 dots per inch, the dots are so small that you can't see them at all; this level of resolution is used in printing. Many laser printers print at a resolution of 300 or 600 dots per inch. A resolution of 300 dpi is finer than 72 dpi. Because an image scanned at 300 dpi has much more information in it, however, it takes up much more computer memory than the 72 dpi version. Also, computer monitors can display no more than approximately 72 dpi.

If, on the other hand, you are scanning images that you expect to output on a laser printer as well as publish them on a web page, it's advisable to scan at 150 or 300 dpi. You can use the high-resolution (300 dpi, that is) version for your paper publication.

Then you can open the scanned image in Photoshop Elements (as explained later in this chapter) and save it in a lower-resolution, 72-dpi version. You can then put the 72 dpi image on your web page.

Scanning

Press the Scan button. Listen to your scanner whir away as those colors are turned into pixels. Because you're only scanning at 72 dpi, it shouldn't take too long to scan your image. When you're done, the image should appear in your scanning software's window.

In Focus

If you plan to publish your images on the web, scan them at 72 dpi—or perhaps at 100 or 150 dpi to begin with, so you can reduce the resolution later on to 72 dpi. This might seem like a coarse resolution, but no one can see anything finer than 72 dpi on a computer screen, so don't waste disk space scanning at 300 dpi if you're only going to end up publishing the image online.

Saving Files

Before you make any more changes, save your image to disk by choosing File → Save. In the dialog box that appears, enter a name for your file and navigate to a folder or directory where you want to save it. In most cases, you'll see a drop-down menu at the bottom of this box. This menu presents options for what file format you want your image to be saved in.

Because you are scanning an image so you can open and edit it in Photoshop Elements, it's best to save the file in Photoshop Data format (PSD). You can then use Photoshop Elements to save the image in another format, as described in Chapter 12.

In Focus

When you assign a name to your image, be sure to include the correct file name extension. You can type the extension by hand, but Photoshop Elements will also add it automatically when you select the appropriate file format from the Format drop-down list in the Save As dialog box. This is important because computers only recognize image files with extensions such as *.gif, .tif,* or *.psd.*

If you name your image *me* and you save it in PSD format, name it *me.psd.* If you save it in JPEG format and you work on a Mac, call it *me.jpg.* On a PC, call it *me.jpg.* There's no difference in the final result or in the quality.

Digital Cameras

Digital cameras bring a new level of convenience to capturing images that can be viewed and edited on a computer. While scanners are pretty much office-bound, digital cameras can be carried around easily and used to capture candid scenes outdoors or in.

So many digital cameras flood the market that we aren't going to attempt recommendations at which model is best for you to buy. Rather, we'll assume that you already have a digital camera and you're looking for some tips on how to use it to capture images that will be relatively easy to view and edit in Photoshop Elements.

Framing Your Image

Many digital cameras make taking a photo a simple matter of pointing and shooting. It's the pointing—the framing of the image—that makes a big difference in the final product.

CAUTION

Swatch Out!

The LCD has a couple of downsides. It uses up more battery power than simply looking through the viewfinder. It can also be hard to see if the sun is shining directly on the LCD. Try to find a camera with an LCD that tilts so you can move it out of the sunlight—or, better yet, a backlit LCD.

Most digital cameras give you the option of either looking through the viewfinder (the little window on the back of the camera) or the Liquid Crystal Display (LCD), the miniature screen that lets you preview images. Use the LCD whenever possible because it's more precise. But remember that the little framing square that's supposed to indicate what's going to be in the final image isn't perfect. Rather than framing everything so it's right up to the edge of the frame, leave some extra room around the edges (see Figure 3.6).

If you leave enough room around your subject, you give yourself the option of cropping more closely when you edit the image in Photoshop Elements.

Figure 3.6

The image on the left is framed too tightly; the other is just right.

Previewing

One of the great advantages of using digital cameras over conventional, film-based cameras is the ability to preview images and simply throw them out and redo them if they aren't quite right. By all means, take advantage of this feature.

One reason to do a preview is to check whether you've zoomed in on your subject adequately. Virtually all digital cameras enable you to zoom in and out to some degree, even if it's only by a factor of two or three times. Keep in mind that your images are digitized and made up of those little squares called pixels; while you can resize an image in Photoshop Elements to make it seem like the subject is closer, the image quality will suffer when those pixels are resized. As a general rule, you should try to zoom in as close as possible to your subject before taking the photo (see Figure 3.7).

Figure 3.7

Zoom in when you take the photo; don't depend on Photoshop Elements to resize it.

Deleting and Retaking

Don't be afraid to retake an image if you're uncertain if it's right. Keep in mind, for one thing, that most of the less expensive digital cameras don't let you focus manually. Rather, they use a focal area in the middle of the image that controls the focus. If you don't have your image centered quite right, it might not be in focus. Reposition it and reshoot if you're in doubt.

Saving Files

As you'll see in Chapter 3, Photoshop Elements gives you the ability to import an image from your digital camera. However, at times you may need to save images to disk using the software that came with your camera.

When you save images to disk, you need to choose a file format—a set of instructions that processes the digital information in the image and arranges the pixels in a particular way. Many image formats compress files to make them consume less disk space. Because you're planning to edit the image in Photoshop Elements, you should avoid compressing it now—let Photoshop Elements do that for you later. Save the file in Photoshop's own image format, Photoshop Data (PSD), or in Tagged Image File Format (TIFF), which preserves the image's original quality so you can then edit as needed.

> **It's Element-ary**
>
> Photoshop Elements has the ability to sharpen images. (This is one of the "Quick Fixes" described in Chapter 9.) But you can't depend on the application to sharpen the fine details in someone's fuzzy, out-of-focus face, though. Try scanning in at high resolution to begin with, and then reduce the resolution when you edit in Photoshop Elements.

Video Frame Capture

Almost all of the instructions that apply to capturing images using a digital camera apply to capturing still images from a digital video camera.

We've found that, when you take a digital video image, you need better lighting and higher contrast than with digital camera images. Scenes taken indoors in dim light don't always appear sharp, even when edited in Photoshop Elements. Take extra care when framing and focusing video images so you give Photoshop Elements something good to work with.

> **In Focus**
>
> Scanning slides requires some special considerations. When you're scanning a slide, you not only have to capture the information within an image, but depending on how the slide was created, you might also need to convert the image from negative to positive format. You may want to invest in hardware specially designed to scan slides rather than a flatbed scanner. However, some flatbed scanners are equipped with Transparent Media Adapters (TMAs) that are intended to process slides.
>
> If you don't have a slide scanner available, see if your flatbed scanner can handle slides—and if it has a high enough resolution to work with slides. Dedicated slide scanners have a high resolution—typically, 2,400 dpi or higher. A high resolution helps you to get an adequate amount of detail out of your slides.

Copying Images from the Web

You aren't limited to your own cameras or scanners when looking for sources of digital images. You only have to look around the web for sites that offer drawings, icons, and other images you can use that are free for personal use—known, in other words, as royalty-free clip art.

Where do you find clip art, exactly? You can do a search for a specific type of image by entering a word or phrase in the search box of a search service such as Google (www.google.com) or AltaVista (www.altavista.com). You can also go to a site that lets you search for specific types of clip art, such as Clipartguide.com's Animal Pictures & Clip Art page. If you use Microsoft Word or another Microsoft Office program, you get access to the Microsoft Clip Gallery Live, an extensive library of images you can use.

Try it now. Assume you're looking for an image of a dog, for example. Connect to the Internet, start up your web browser, and go to www.clipartguide.com/clipart_animals.html. Enter "dog clip art" in the box next to the Clipart Search button, and then click the Clipart Search button. You go to one of many clip art sites whose contents Clipartguide.com has indexed.

Swatch Out!

The words "royalty-free" are ones to pay attention to when it comes to clip art. Most artists attach conditions as to how and where their images can be used. Sometimes they ask for a usage fee—especially if their images are to be used in an advertisement or on a commercial website. Read the fine print before you copy, because clip art doesn't always mean "free."

In Focus

You can also purchase stock images (a group of generic images that you can use for various purposes) individually or a set on CD-ROM. Go to Yahoo! (www.yahoo.com), search for the term "stock photo" or "stock art," and press Enter. A web page will appear with links to dozens of companies that will be happy to sell you all kinds of stock images.

Be nice to the artists who let you use their work. Give them a credit line, if they ask for one, and if they request a fee (usually nominal), send it along.

The Least You Need to Know

- When possible, scan images with good lighting and contrast.

- Calibrate your scanner so your scans are accurate.

- Preview before you scan to choose exactly what you want to capture.

- Don't frame images too tightly; leave space so you can crop them in Photoshop Elements.

- Reduce resolution to reduce the file size of scanned images.

Part 2

Building an Elementary Skill Set

Even the flashiest, most avant-garde house needs to be built on a firm foundation. This part gets you acquainted with the solid, basic skills you need to learn in order to work with images using Photoshop Elements.

First, you'll learn about the two kinds of images you can work with: rasters and vectors. You'll also delve into the different color theories used to create digital images. Then you'll learn about the many ways you can select areas of an image, including the Rectangular and Elliptical Marquees, the Lasso, the Magic Wand, and the new Selection Brush. Finally, you'll explore the ways in which you can divide images into multiple layers.

Understanding Images and Graphics

In This Chapter

- ◆ Understanding rasters and pixels
- ◆ Drawing your own vector graphics
- ◆ Changing an image's resolution
- ◆ Converting rasters to vectors
- ◆ Choosing a compression format

Before you start working with Photoshop Elements in detail, it's a good idea to take a few minutes to get some basic information about digital image types and color modes so you know what you're doing when you use the program's tools and menus.

Photoshop Elements lets you work with two kinds of images: raster images (also known as bitmaps) and vector graphics. For the most part, this book focuses on rasters because that's what digital photos are, and our assumption is that you are using the program primarily to edit digital photos.

However, you can also use Photoshop Elements as a drawing program as well, so you can create simple artwork that stands on its own (such as logos), or add interest to your photos by adding vector objects such as textual captions, or circles or other balloon-like containers that hold captions. In this chapter, you'll learn about the differences between vectors and rasters by working with both. You'll also get some experience with another fundamental aspect of image editing with Photoshop Elements: the colors you can choose to give your images added life and interest.

Taking a Closer Look at Rasters

Rasters are made up of little squares called *pixels* that make them appear jagged when viewed up close. Each pixel contains one or more bits of digital information that a computer uses to display colors—hence, the term *bitmap*, which is synonymous with raster.

Counting Pixels

Despite their small size (or perhaps *because* of their small size), pixels can convey an amazing amount of digital information. A digital photo can also contain an amazing number of pixels.

> **CAUTION**
>
> **Swatch Out!**
>
> If you change the physical dimensions (the width or height, that is) of your image, make sure the Constrain Proportions check box is checked when you do so. Constrain Proportions means that as one dimension is changed, the other changes accordingly so the original shape of the image is maintained. Otherwise the image will become distorted.

You can see this for yourself. Choose File → Open and, in the Open dialog box, open this book's CD-ROM. Open the Chapter 4 folder and double-click the *lake.tif* file to open it in Photoshop Elements. Once the image is open, choose Image → Resize → Image Size to display the Image Size dialog box.

If pixels aren't displayed in the Width or Height boxes near the top of the Image Size dialog box (see Figure 4.1), click the arrows next to the right-hand box next to Width and Height and choose Pixels from the drop-down list. As you can see, this image measures 871 pixels in width. This means there are 871 pixels from left to right. It also has 584 pixels from top to bottom. This means the image contains a total of 508,664 pixels or more than half a million pixels.

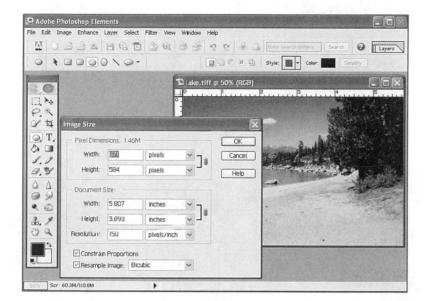

Figure 4.1

More than half a million pixels create the colors in this image.

Understanding Resolution

In the preceding section, you learned that the physical dimensions of an image (its height and width) can be expressed as numbers of pixels. The *lake.tif* file is 871 pixels in width and 584 pixels in height, which equals 5.8 inches wide by 3.9 inches in height. Make a note of the file size as well, which is displayed near the top of the image window after Pixel dimensions: 1.46MB (for 1.46 megabytes).

Note that the number of pixels in an image doesn't have to be fixed. The resolution of a raster image determines how many pixels it actually contains: the more pixels, the more information there is in the image, and the finer the detail and range of colors. In the image you just opened in the preceding section, *lake.tif*, you have more than half a million pixels. The resolution of this image is 150 pixels per inch (ppi), as you can see from the Resolution box of the Image Size dialog box.

Go to the Image Size dialog box now, and change the resolution by clicking in the box next to Resolution. Move the cursor across the number 150, press Backspace to delete it, and type **300.** What happens? The number of pixels in the image grows dramatically, but the size in terms of inches does not. You've squished twice as many pixels into the same space. The file size has also grown dramatically, to a whopping 5.5MB.

In Focus _____

Resolution is one of the most important things you can adjust when you want to change image quality or file size. Increasing the resolution from a common resolution of 150 to 180 ppi to 300 ppi can make the image seem finer and sharper. A resolution of 200 to 300 ppi should work well for printing on a color inkjet printer.

On the other hand, if you're preparing images for the web, you should keep the resolution at a relatively low 72 ppi: It keeps the file size low, and it matches the resolution most monitors are able to display. But be careful—throwing away pixels can detract from the quality of your image and can cause you to lose information about multiple layers if the image contains them. You may want to save the image with the original resolution so you can return to it if needed.

Dealing with Image Compression

As you learned in the previous section, a raster image with a high resolution can easily contain millions of pixels, and can take up several megabytes of disk space. To make digital images easier to store and transport over networks, a number of file formats have been developed. A file format is a way of saving the information on a disk so that a computer program like Photoshop Elements can interpret and display it.

Shop Talk _____

Image **compression** is a feature available to image formats such as TIFF or JPEG. Compression enables you to save the information in an image in such a way that the file size is reduced, with varying impact on image quality. The idea is to take the bits of information in the image and eliminate parts that are unnecessary or of relatively low importance to the image as a whole, so you can still view the image, but it takes up less space on disk.

The *lake.tif* file that you worked with in the preceding section uses the Tagged Image File Format (TIFF) to store information within it. (That's what the file extension *.tif* stands for.) TIFF comes in two varieties: standard and LZW compression. With *lake.tif* open in the Photoshop Elements window, choose File → Save As. When the Save As dialog box appears, change the file name as it appears in the File Name box to *lake2.tif*. Click Save. A TIFF Options dialog box appears (see Figure 4.2).

The options at the top of the TIFF Options dialog box let you choose whether or not the image should be compressed when it is saved. If you click None, no compression will be performed; the file size will be as big as it can be. If you click LZW, the image will be compressed in such a way that no data will be lost; it's known as a *lossless* compression method. ZIP compression is also lossless; it's commonly used in the Windows world. JPEG compression does result in some loss of data: it's known as a *lossy* compression scheme.

If you do want to compress the image and compare the resulting file size, click the button next to LZW. Otherwise, click Cancel.

Vector Graphics: They're Just Lines and Shapes

The moment you see the word "vector," do your eyes start to glaze over? Do you conjure up images of science-fiction space battles? Relax. Vector graphics *can* be complex, but all you really need to know to work with such images in Photoshop Elements is that they consist of lines and other shapes.

In Photoshop Elements, vector graphics include shapes you draw and text you add to images. Vectors make high-quality illustrations. But drawings comprised of vectors take up far more disk space than rasters. Rasters are smaller and more portable, which is why they are used on the World Wide Web as well as many other media and programs that display images.

You may not use vectors all the time. Photoshop Elements, after all, *is* primarily intended for editing photos and other images that consist of pixels. But knowing what vectors are and how to use them will help you get the most out of the software and help you whip up a simple poster or greeting card in a snap.

Paths: A Fancy Name for "Shapes"

Another techy-sounding term, *path*, is used to describe a shape that makes up all or part of a vector image. A path isn't necessarily a line; rather, it can be a curve, a circle, or the shape of a letter.

A path is an instruction to a computer to draw a shape in a particular way. When you draw a path, Photoshop Elements gives your computer instructions like, "Begin to draw a line at point 10.4. Proceed to point 10.20." The computer draws a solid line rather than stringing a bunch of pixels together, as it does with a raster image. A combination of paths, taken together, make up a text label or a complete drawing, as in the drawings shown in Figure 4.3.

Figure 4.3

Unlike many painting programs, Photoshop Elements lets you draw vectors.

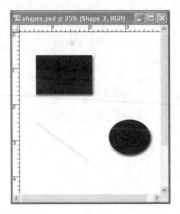

Being Clear About Resolution

What, you may ask, is the difference between the shapes you just drew and shapes you might draw in a built-in painting program? The big difference is that vector images are resolution-independent. You can scale them to any size or print them at any resolution and they will not lose clarity—in contrast to rasters (images that consist of pixels), which can appear jagged when viewed or printed at high resolution.

Try it yourself: Choose File → New to open a new image window in the Photoshop Elements window. Click and hold down on the Shape selection tool and choose the Polygon tool. Draw a polygon in the blank image window. Right-click the polygon and choose Free Transform Shape from the popup menu. Click and hold down on one of the selection handles that appear around the polygon, and then drag to move the image. Click the Zoom tool and zoom in on the image—notice that it doesn't lose clarity. If you were to resize the image and print it out, you'd see that it appears just as clear as it did originally.

You can get an idea of this yourself by opening your operating system's built-in paint program. (Leave Photoshop Elements open as well.) In Windows, choose Start → Programs → Accessories → Paint. On the Macintosh, search for MacPaint and then double-click the MacPaint program icon. Draw some lines and shapes. Then click the magnifying glass icon and click the image to zoom in on it; notice that it appears jagged (see Figure 4.4).

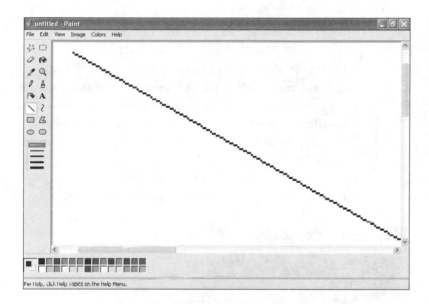

Figure 4.4

Built-in painting programs create jagged raster images.

Now switch to Photoshop Elements. Click this program's magnifying glass tool near the bottom of the toolbox (the formal name is the Zoom tool). Click the images you draw and zoom in on the line; notice that it doesn't grow less sharp or jagged until you view it very close up. It does appear jagged when viewed at high resolution, but that's because your computer monitor is made up of dots—the smoothness of lines depends on the resolution (the number of dots per inch) of your monitor.

Computer monitors can display both vectors and rasters. But raster images can easily grow to many megabytes in size, while vector graphics aren't always as big. Why? The file size of a raster image is determined by the number of pixels it contains. A single image might require a computer to compress and resolve millions of separate pixels. In contrast, the file size of a vector graphic depends on how many paths it contains and what shape they are. A path is just a set of

In Focus

In Windows, the sample image files are typically installed in a default location C:\Program Files\ Adobe\Photoshop Elements 2\Samples.

drawing instructions, and computers are flexible in how they draw shapes. It can display paths clearly and sharply, either onscreen or on paper.

Converting Vectors to Rasters

You can copy a vector image from another application such as Adobe Illustrator and paste it into Photoshop Elements. When you copy the contents of your computer clipboard, Photoshop Elements asks whether you want to convert the image to a raster or leave it as a vector image.

> **It's Element-ary**
>
> When you paste an image and convert it from a vector to a raster, it is pasted at the resolution of the image into which you paste it. For instance, if the image is 150 dpi, the vector that you're pasting into it will be pasted as a 150-dpi image.

An image in Photoshop Elements can consist of both raster and vector information. You can see this for yourself by opening one of the sample images that come with Photoshop Elements. It's called *working.psd*. Choose File → Open and, in the Open dialog box, locate the Photoshop Elements 2 folder. Within this folder, there's a folder called Samples, and within this folder is *working. psd* (shown in Figure 4.5) and other sample images.

Figure 4.5

The textual contents of this image are vectors, but the rest are rasters.

The Least You Need to Know

- Raster compression formats enable you to save image information while conserving file size.

- Raster images consist of individual squares called pixels.

- Vector graphics are created with the Photoshop Elements drawing tools.

- Vector graphics consist of paths, which describe shapes.

- Photoshop Elements enables you to import vector images in either vector or raster format.

Selecting Bitmaps

In This Chapter

- ◆ Understanding how selections work
- ◆ Selecting rectangular and elliptical areas
- ◆ Deselecting and reselecting an area in an image
- ◆ Moving selected areas
- ◆ Changing marquee preferences

Life would be easy if every image you captured turned out just right the first time. But life wouldn't be as much fun, either: You wouldn't have any need for Photoshop Elements, and you wouldn't get to try any of the program's cool tools for selecting parts of an image so you can move, cut, edit, or otherwise transform images into your original creations.

This chapter introduces you to the options that Photoshop Elements provides for making elliptical and rectangular (and, for that matter, circular and square) selections. You'll understand how to make selections and adjust them so you grab exactly the pixels you want to change. You'll also get some hands-on experience with some of the more elementary selection tools you're likely to use.

So What's a Selection, Anyway?

Selections are easy to understand. Just think about what the Fairy Godmother does in the Disney movie *Cinderella*—she selects an object, and then transforms it. She waves her own selection tool, her magic wand. Poof! She grabs a pumpkin and she turns it into a coach. Zing! She herds a group of mice, brings them over to the coach, and transforms them into horses.

Change those mice into little pixels that are grouped into bitmaps, and you begin to grasp how selections work. (If you need a refresher course on what pixels are, see Chapter 4.) When you select part of an image, you graphically identify a group of pixels within it. You draw a border called a *marquee* around the pixels you want to edit. Figure 5.1 shows a rectangular marquee drawn around the head of the gargoyle so it can be moved, drawn on, or copied and pasted somewhere else.

Shop Talk

If you've been to an old-time movie theater (as opposed to one of those new-fangled multiplex or googleplex facilities), you know what a **marquee** is. It's a bunch of flashing lights that are supposed to highlight a feature film and that seem to move around. The marquee in Photoshop Elements is a series of dashes that you draw yourself right on top of the image you want to edit. You aren't drawing on the image itself; you're only drawing a selection area. The size and shape of the marquee depends on the selection tool you're using, and on how you move your mouse around. The dashes seem to move; in fact, they're sometimes called "marching ants."

Drawing a selection area on an image is very much like the first step in *cropping* an image: you draw a box around part of an image. The difference is that your only purpose, in cropping, is to identify which parts of the image you want to save and which areas you want to delete. One big difference is that when you crop something you only end up with a rectangular area; in selecting, you can draw ellipses and circles as well as rectangles and squares. But the principle is the same: You draw a marquee around the area you want to act upon.

Shop Talk

When you **crop** an image, you draw a container around the part you want to preserve. Everything outside the container is deleted. The container described in the following section is the Rectangular Marquee tool, but you can also use the Elliptical Marquee tool as described later in this chapter and the Lasso tool as described in the following chapter. When you choose Image → Crop from the Photoshop Elements menu bar, the deleted area disappears—in other words, is "cropped out."

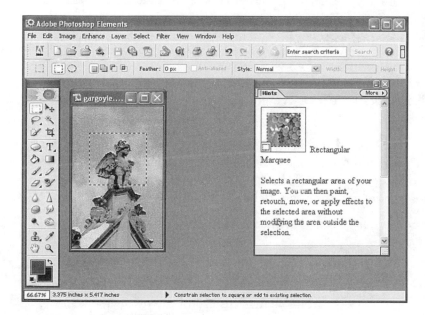

Figure 5.1

Select part of an image by drawing a marquee around it.

Exploring the Basic Selection Tools

Most of the tools you're going to want to use are in the toolbox. The others are scattered around the program. The main resources are explained in the following sections.

Thinking Inside the Selection Box: Rectangular Selections

The two selection tools you are most likely to use are the Rectangular Marquee tool, shown in Figure 5.2, and the Elliptical Marquee tool. (See Chapter 1 if you need a refresher course on how to use the toolbox.) You'll find these tools in the toolbox. The Rectangular Marquee tool's options bar appears directly beneath the shortcuts bar by default.

Figure 5.2

You'll find the Rectangular and Elliptical Marquee tools at the top of the toolbox.

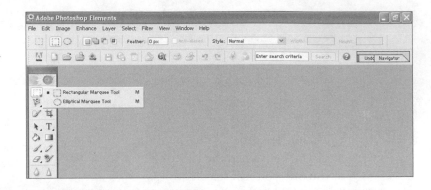

The best way to get acquainted with the Rectangular Marquee tool is to start using it. Follow these steps:

1. Choose File → Open from the Photoshop Elements menu bar, click Open in the shortcuts bar, or press Ctrl+O (Windows) or Cmd+O (Mac). The Open dialog box appears.

2. Click the arrow next to the Look in drop-down list (Windows) or the unnamed drop-down list (Mac) and double-click the folder in your Photoshop Elements program that contains sample files. In a standard Windows installation, this is C:\Program Files\Adobe\Photoshop Elements 2\Samples\.

3. Double-click the file *Car Show.psd* to open it (or single-click the file and click Open).

> ### It's Element-ary
>
> If you have configured Windows Explorer or My Computer so that file name extensions aren't displayed, you won't see the three-letter extension *.psd*. If you want to display file name extensions, Open Windows Explorer and then choose Tools → Options from the Windows Explorer menu bar to display the Folder Options dialog box. Uncheck Hide File Extensions For Known File Types, and then click OK.

4. Click the Rectangular Marquee tool in the toolbox and pass the mouse pointer over the image. Notice that, instead of the usual arrow, the pointer looks like a plus sign (+). This enables you to draw a selection area. Click just above and to the left of the fourth car from the left (the red one).

5. Hold down the left mouse button and drag down and to the right, across the car (you can actually drag from one point to any other point in any direction—we just picked from upper left to lower right as an example). Gasp in wonder as a rectangle of "marching ants" unfolds and eventually frames the car.

6. Release the mouse button. Voilà! You've selected the car.

Now that you've selected the red car, you might as well *do* something with it.

1. Choose Edit → Copy to copy the selection to your computer's clipboard.

2. Position the pointer anywhere within the selection marquee you just drew. (Notice that the plus sign turns into an arrow when it's inside the marquee.) Click and drag the box to the right, until you've framed the car to the right of the one you just selected.

In Focus

If you click and then press and hold down the Shift key while dragging with the rectangular marquee, you'll draw a perfect square rather than a rectangle.

3. Release the mouse button.

4. Choose Edit → Paste to paste the red car over the tan one. For some extra fun, repeat choose Edit → Paste to paste the red car over each of the cars in the drawing.

5. When you're done rearranging cars, choose File → Save As. When the Save As dialog box appears, save your file with a different name so you can still work with the original sample file *Car Show.psd* if you need to.

The preceding steps show how to cut and paste something you've selected from one part of an image to another. You can also cut and paste from one image file to another. Select part of an image, copy it to the clipboard, open the new image, and paste it. When you paste the image it is highlighted with the selection marquee. Click anywhere within the marquee to move the selection to the desired location. To make another image active, click on the solid bar at the top of the image window.

Thinking Outside the Box: Elliptical Selections

It's hip to be square, but when it comes to selections, ellipses and circles are just as cool. Where, you ask, is the Elliptical Marquee tool? By default, this tool is hidden behind the Rectangular Marquee tool, but you can uncover it by doing one of the following:

In Focus

If the Rectangular Marquee tool isn't the one currently displayed, click the tool at the far left of the options bar and choose Reset Tool or Reset All Tools to restore the toolbox tools to their default settings.

◆ Click and hold down on the Rectangular Marquee tool in the toolbox. When the hidden tool menu appears, slide your mouse pointer down and to the right to select the Elliptical Marquee tool.

In Focus

As you might expect, clicking and then pressing and holding down the Shift key while you draw an elliptical selection enables you to draw a circle. Ellipses can be hard to draw over a sharply defined area; if you'd rather draw from an ellipse (or a rectangle) from the center outwards, press and hold down the Alt key (Windows) or Opt key (Mac) and then click while you draw the shape.

♦ Alt+click or right-click (Windows) or Ctrl+click (Mac) on the Rectangular Marquee tool in the toolbox to immediately switch to the Elliptical Marquee tool (this trick works with all hidden tools).

♦ Press Shift+M to select the hidden tool (in this case, the Elliptical Marquee tool).

♦ Click the Elliptical Marquee tool button in the options bar.

Elliptical tools work especially well when the item you want to select is already elliptical in shape, such as the head of one of this book's authors (see Figure 5.3).

Figure 5.3

Not surprisingly, the Elliptical Marquee tool is perfect for selecting elliptical objects.

New selection
Add to selection
Subtract from selection
Intersect with selection
Options bar

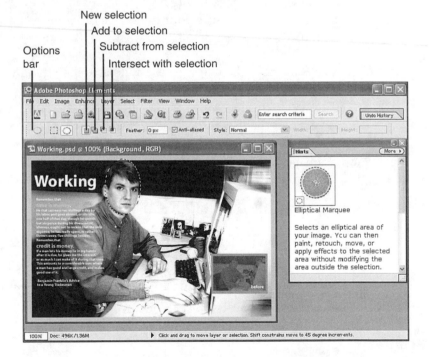

Adjusting Selections

Sometimes, it's hard to get selections right the first time. Try it out for yourself: Choose File → Open. Click the drop-down list at the top of the Open dialog box (it's labeled Look in the Windows version, but is unnamed in the Mac version) to locate the folder that contains the Photoshop Elements sample files. (In a standard Windows installation, this is C:\Program Files\Adobe\Photoshop Elements 2\ Samples\. Double-click the folder to open it. Double-click the file *Working.psd*. Select the Elliptical Marquee tool, and click just above and to one side of the head of the young man in the photo. Drag down across the face, drawing the ellipse.

Chances are you didn't get your elliptical selection exactly right. It's a common problem—you don't quite get the top of someone's hairdo, or you're in danger of cutting off someone's size-15 shoes. Not to worry—Photoshop Elements provides you with a number of ways to tweak selections. In the options bar, for example, the New Selection button is selected by default so you can make a new selection every time you click an image. The other options bar buttons (Add To Selection, Subtract From Selection, and Intersect With Selection) enable you to change what you've selected, as described in the following sections.

CAUTION

Swatch Out!

It's a good idea to uncheck the box next to Anti-Aliased in the Elliptical Marquee tool's options bar. Anti-aliasing refers to the practice of softening the edges of pixels to create a less jagged-looking outline. If Anti-Aliasing is checked it can be very difficult to make a precise selection of a well-defined shape, however.

Deselecting and Reselecting

Suppose you've tried to make an elliptical selection and you want to try again. First, you need to deselect what you selected. You can deselect part of an image in several ways:

- Click anywhere in the image outside the marquee if New Selection is high-lighted in the options bar.
- Choose Select → Deselect.
- Press Ctrl+D.
- Right-click and choose Deselect.

In any case, the selection marquee disappears so you can make a new selection.

Adding to a Selection

Suppose you make a selection and you're so satisfied with it that you just can't restrain yourself—you want to select more, more, more! You can leave your original selection highlighted and then—calmly, now—make a new selection by clicking the Add To Selection button in the options bar.

Try it yourself by following these steps:

1. If it's not already open from the previous exercise, open the *Working.psd* file and draw an elliptical marquee around the man's head.

2. Click Add To Selection in the options bar.

3. Press and hold down Shift, and draw a circle around the baseball that's next to the keyboard. (Notice that the original marquee remains selected.)

4. Leave the head and the baseball selected and, just for fun, select the Rectangular Marquee tool.

5. Draw a rectangle around the word "Working." As you can see, Add To Selection and the other options bar buttons work the same with both rectangular and elliptical tools.

The image should resemble the one shown in Figure 5.4.

Figure 5.4

Add To Selection enables you to select separate areas within an image.

Subtracting from a Selection

Suppose you've done a perfect job of selecting one area, you click Add To Selection, and then you decide to remove the original selection. Do you deselect everything and start over?

In Focus

If you really want to create polygonal marquees, you get more control by using the polygonal lasso, as described in Chapter 6.

Certainly not. Click Subtract From Selection in the options bar. Then draw a selection marquee over the area of a selection that you want to subtract. When you release the mouse button, what you selected will no longer be selected. If you drew a rectangle or ellipse over a previous rectangle or ellipse, the whole marquee disappears.

Things get really interesting when you subtract only part of a selection. Try it with the test image *Working.tif*. Use Add To Selection to select the head, the baseball, and the title "Working" in this image. Click Subtract From Selection, and then draw over part of one of the three selection marquees. The part you drew over disappears. Draw over the other two selection areas. You are left with some interesting polygonal marquee shapes (see Figure 5.5).

Figure 5.5

The Subtract From Selection button enables you to "erase" part of a marquee.

Intersecting with a Selection

Suppose you want to select the point at which two marquees intersect—in other words, the area that the two selections have in common where they overlap. You can do this with the Intersect With Selection button in the options bar. The best way to learn how this tool works is to try it yourself with a new image. Follow these steps:

1. Click File → Open, and open the *rectangles.psd* file located in the Chapter 5 folder on this book's CD-ROM.

2. Make sure you have deselected Subtract From Selection in the options bar by clicking New Selection. Select the Rectangular Marquee tool, and draw a marquee around the uppermost of the two rectangles.

3. Click Intersect With Selection in the options bar. Now draw a selection rectangle around the second rectangle.

4. Release the mouse button. The area of overlap between the two selection rectangles is highlighted (see Figure 5.6).

> **It's Element-ary**
>
> Intersect With Selection, Add To Selection, Subtract With Selection, and New Selection all work pretty much the same with all selection tools—not only the Rectangular and Elliptical Marquee tools covered in this chapter, but also the Lasso and Magic Wand, which Chapter 6 describes.

Figure 5.6

Intersect With Selection enables you to select the area overlapped by two selections.

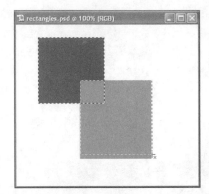 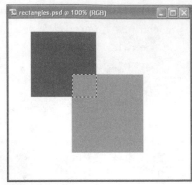

Feathering Selections

By default, marquees enable you to select a sharply defined area. You can achieve a smoother, more elegant effect by selecting a region and feathering the edges, which means to create a softer, fading edge. Try it by following these steps (which also give you practice in cutting and pasting selections between files):

Shop Talk

Feathering softens the edges of selections—for example, the corners of a selection rectangle become rounded. However, you might not see the effects when you make a selection, only when you edit it. The greater the number of pixels, the fuzzier the image appears when you cut and paste it. If you want to soften more along the outer edge of a selection so you don't lose the inner edge, specify a Feathering setting, make the selection, choose Select → Modify → Expand, and expand by a few pixels. Then choose Edit → Copy and Edit → Paste to paste the feathered-and-expanded selection.

1. Open the *Working.psd* file one more time.

2. Click the Elliptical Marquee tool in the toolbox.

3. Select the young man's head in the image.

4. Choose Edit → Copy to copy the image to the clipboard.

5. Click New in the Elements menu bar (in the upper left corner of Photoshop Elements). In the New dialog box, specify 600 pixels in the Width box and 200 pixels in the Height box.

6. Click OK to open a new image within Photoshop Elements (this will be a second open image because you have not closed *Working.psd*). Because you just opened this image, it is currently the active one.

7. Choose Edit → Paste to paste the image into the new window.

8. Switch back to the *Working.psd* file by clicking on the solid bar at the top of the image. In the Feather box in the options bar, backspace over the default value 0 and type **10**.

9. Repeat the preceding Steps 3 and 4 to select and copy the same head you selected earlier. Then switch focus back to your new image and again paste the selection.

The result should look similar to Figure 5.7.

Figure 5.7

Feathering enables you to soften the edges of a selection.

Changing the Marquee Shape

You already know that if you press and hold down Shift while drawing a rectangular or elliptical marquee, you draw either a perfect square or perfect circle. You can get a higher degree of control by choosing an option from the Style drop-down list in the options bar or by changing the appearance of the marquee itself.

Constraining the Shape

Two options in the Style drop-down list in the options bar enable you to control the shape of rectangular or elliptical selection marquees:

◆ Fixed Aspect Ratio is similar to holding down the Shift key while making a selection in that it forces a proportioned marquee selection. However, instead of drawing only circles and squares, you can draw rectangles and ellipses with specified height-to-width ratios (of course, specifying a one-to-one ratio results in a circle or square).

◆ Fixed Size enables you to specify the exact height and width of the selection marquee you want to draw.

When you select Fixed Size, the Width and Height boxes become active, so you can enter the height and width in pixels. When a height and width are specified, you only have to click in an image to have the selection marquee appear instantly with the specified dimensions.

Changing the Marquee's Appearance

Some options under the Select menu enable you to change a marquee in a number of different ways. You can see the effects yourself clearly if you make a selection on a plain white background. Then choose Select → Modify and make a selection from the submenu that appears to try out each option yourself:

- Choose Border to open the Border Selection dialog box. Enter a value in pixels in the Width box, and then choose OK. Watch the marquee grow thicker or thinner depending on what you specify.

- Select Smooth to open the Smooth Selection dialog box. Enter a value in the Sample Radius box, and then choose OK. The edges of the selection marquee are smoothed. (This works best with rectangular marquees.)

- Select either Expand or Contract to change the size of the existing selection on a pixel-by-pixel basis. If you draw a marquee and choose Select → Modify → Contract and enter **10**, you'll contract the marquee by 10 pixels in both height and width.

In this chapter, you have seen how to make basic elliptical and rectangular selections using the Marquee Selection tools from the toolbox and how to adjust selections using the options bar and Select menu. In the next chapter, you'll try out some tools for selecting freeform shapes, and you'll explore some even more sophisticated techniques for transforming selections.

The Least You Need to Know

- Marquees enable you to highlight selected parts of an image.

- The toolbox buttons enable you to toggle between the Rectangular and Elliptical Marquee selection tools.

- The commands on the options bar enable you to add to and subtract from selections.

- You can soften the edges of a selection by feathering its borders.

- The Copy and Paste buttons in the shortcuts bar enable you to cut and paste selections from one image to another image.

Chapter 6

Selecting Freeform and Vector Objects

In This Chapter

- ◆ Going freestyle with the Lasso tool
- ◆ Painting selection areas with the Selection Brush
- ◆ Picking colors with the Magic Wand
- ◆ Rotating, expanding, and contracting selections
- ◆ Saving and loading selections

Most of the objects you need to select in Photoshop Elements aren't bounded by straight lines or smooth curves. They're among the myriad of things in the world that have irregular shapes, from trees to clouds, from castles to cookies. Some of these are bitmap images, while others are made up of the drawn paths called vectors that you learned about in Chapter 4. To get an accurate handle on both bitmaps and vectors, Photoshop Elements provides you with the three tools you'll explore in this chapter: the Lasso, Selection Brush, and Magic Wand.

Freeform Lassoing

The Lasso you'll find in the Photoshop Elements toolbox resembles the one that cowboys use in rodeos and out on the proverbial range. It's intended to round up things (whether cattle or pixels) that won't fit in a nice neat rectangle. With a little practice, you'll learn how to rope in practically any group of pixels you encounter.

Rounding 'Em Up with the Regular Lasso

To select something that's irregular in shape and outlined with curved rather than straight lines, just draw a container around it with the regular lasso.

Try it yourself by selecting the outline of the black sculpture in the foreground of Figure 6.1 by following these steps:

1. Place this book's CD-ROM in your CD-ROM drive.

2. Choose File → Open from the Photoshop Elements menu bar.

3. In the Open dialog box, click the arrow next to Look in.

4. Open your CD-ROM drive.

5. Open the *sculpture.tif* image file, which is located in the Chapter 6 folder of this book's CD-ROM.

6. Click the Lasso tool in the toolbox.

7. Pass the mouse pointer over the image. Notice that the lasso conveniently remains in the shape of a lasso; the knot in the lasso is where you actually draw your selection marquee. It's a bit like throwing a lasso around the head of an animal. With practice, you'll get the hang of it.

8. Click and hold down anywhere around the edge of the sculpture, and draw an outline around it.

The shape should look similar to Figure 6.1.

In Focus

With the **normal lasso,** don't stop drawing until you reach the point at which you began dragging. You need to overlap with the starting point. If you don't, Photoshop Elements completes the selection for you by drawing from your stopping point in a straight line to the starting point, which may not actually result in the shape you want.

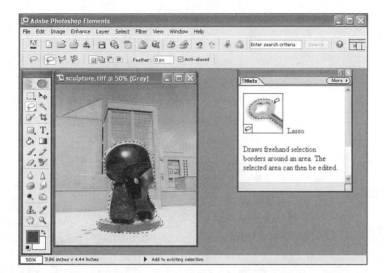

Figure 6.1

The Lasso tool is perfect for making freeform selections.

The Polygonal Lasso

The regular (or freehand) Lasso tool appears in the toolbox by default but, as you can tell from the little arrow in the corner of the Lasso button on the toolbox, some other tools are hidden beneath it. You can uncover them by doing one of the following:

◆ Click and hold down on the Lasso tool. When the hidden tool menu appears, slide your mouse pointer down and to the right to select either the Polygonal Lasso or Magnetic Lasso tool.

◆ Right-click the Lasso tool and select from the drop-down menu.

◆ Alt+click (Windows) or Ctrl+click (Mac) the Lasso tool to immediately switch to the Polygonal Lasso tool. Press Alt+click or Ctrl+click again to switch to the Magnetic Lasso tool.

◆ Press Shift+L to select the hidden Lasso tool.

◆ Click either the Polygonal Lasso or Magnetic Lasso tool button in the options bar.

The Polygonal Lasso tool is your best choice when what you want to select is bounded by straight lines that don't fit together in right angles (in other words, a polygon). Try it with the sample *sculpture.tif* image file:

1. Reopen *sculpture.tif* if necessary or deselect the sculpture you selected earlier, if it's still selected, by clicking Ctrl+D (Windows) or Cmd+D (Mac).

2. Select the Polygonal Lasso tool by doing one of the actions in the previous list.

3. Start to select the outline of the buildings behind the sculpture by clicking once anywhere on the outline of the building. A moving line of "marching ants" appears: Notice that, when you move the pointer around, the line moves with you. Every time you click, the line "follows" you around.

4. Click the nearest corner of the outer edge of the buildings.

5. Click the next corner, the next, and so on, following the line of the buildings until you have returned to the starting point.

The resulting selection should look similar to Figure 6.2. Take your time and practice with the Polygonal Lasso tool. It's easy to click in the wrong place and end up with a spider web design rather than the polygon you're trying to create.

In Focus

If Photoshop Elements creates some anchor points that obviously aren't on the line you want, you can immediately press Backspace or Delete while holding down the mouse button to delete the most recent anchor points, one at a time. If the Magnetic Lasso or Polygonal Lasso tool goes off in the wrong direction, back up and then click your mouse over the path you want to follow.

Figure 6.2

With the Polygonal Lasso tool, you trace the outline of a polygon.

Magnetic Lasso

As you can see, if you're trying to make a very exact selection of an irregularly shaped object, you're likely to have a tough time if you use either the Lasso tool or Polygonal Lasso tool. Choosing View → Zoom In can help you get a closer look. But for really complex selections, the Magnetic Lasso is the tool of choice.

The Magnetic Lasso helps you draw a selection marquee around an irregularly shaped object by detecting the contrast in color within the image. It works most

effectively when you're trying to select something that contrasts sharply with its surroundings. However, you can adjust the sensitivity of the Magnetic Lasso so it works
with a low-contrast image, too. (See the fol-
lowing section, "Changing Lasso Preferences,"
for more.)

Now that you've tried to select both the foreground and the background of the *sculpture.tif*
image, you'll appreciate how the magnetic
lasso can make selecting easier—with some
patience and practice. Deselect the previous
selection, choose the Magnetic Lasso tool, and
position the cursor at a point where the edge of
what you want to select contrasts from its surroundings. In *sculpture.tif*, the obvious thing to
select is the edge of the black sculpture.

In Focus

You can immediately erase
an entire selection and start
a new one by double-
clicking anywhere in the
image with any of the lasso
tools. However, a new selection
point is inserted at the point where
you double-clicked. Be sure to
double-click at a point where
you want to start making a new
selection.

Click the edge, and then slowly guide your mouse pointer around the edge. You don't
have to click anywhere; Photoshop Elements creates a line around the image and adds
anchor points on its own. Keep moving around the edge until you return to the starting point (see Figure 6.3).

Figure 6.3

*Photoshop Elements creates
its own selection outline
using the Magnetic Lasso
tool.*

Changing Lasso Preferences

Each of the lasso tools contains a corresponding set of controls in the options bar.
Actually, the options for the regular and polygonal lassos are the same:

- Four buttons grouped close together—New Selection, Add To Selection, Subtract From Selection, and Intersect With Selection—enable you to change what you've selected in case you didn't get it right the first time.

- Feather enables you to soften the edges of the lasso you draw (see "Feathering Selections" in Chapter 5 for more details about feathering).

- Anti-aliasing is checked by default. It gives a lasso softened (that is, anti-aliased) edges. If you uncheck it, the lasso marquee will have more jagged edges than usual.

The Magnetic Lasso options (see Figure 6.4) enable you to perform some unique functions that control how sensitive the lasso is, how many anchor points are created, and how wide of an area it searches for color contrast.

- Width specifies, in pixels, the width of the marquee drawn by the Magnetic Lasso. The value can be from 1 to 40 pixels.

- Edge Contrast tells Photoshop Elements how sensitive to changes in color contrast the Magnetic Lasso should be. Values can vary from 1 to 100 percent. If the image you are working on has high contrast, use a higher value so you get a clean outline when you draw it. If the image is low in contrast, keep the setting low so Photoshop Elements will be sensitive to more subtle changes in color.

- Frequency is a number from 0 to 100 that tells Photoshop Elements how frequently it should insert anchor points. The higher the number, the more points the tool inserts. The number you enter depends on the image's shape. For an image with jagged edges, enter a low value (fewer anchor points). For an image with smooth curves around the edge, use a higher frequency to get more anchor points and a smoother outline.

- Pen Pressure controls sensitivity to a stylus if you're drawing on a tablet. If you don't use a stylus, don't worry about this. If you do, select the option if you want the edge width to decrease as you push the stylus with more pressure.

Figure 6.4

Control how well the Magnetic Lasso tool draws an outline by setting these preferences on the options bar.

Working with the Selection Brush

Marquee tools work fine when you want to make a selection that's a well-defined shape. But what if you want to paint or draw your own selection in a design of your own invention? You'll get a lot more control over the shape by turning to a tool that's new to Photoshop Elements 2.0: the Selection Brush.

Brushing Up on Hand-Drawn Selections

Anyone who's proficient at drawing or painting, especially in a computer graphics program, should enjoy using the Selection Brush tool. The Selection Brush enables you to draw a border around a selection. You'll find it in the toolbox, too (see Figure 6.5).

Figure 6.5

The Selection Brush tool enables you to brush your own selection area.

To get some practice using the Selection Brush tool, open the photo of Boris the Cat (*boris.tif*) in the Chapter 6 folder on this book's CD-ROM, and then follow these steps:

1. Click the Selection Brush in the toolbox.

2. Click the Brush Presets pop-up palette (see Figure 6.6) and select a style from the dizzying array of brush styles provided.

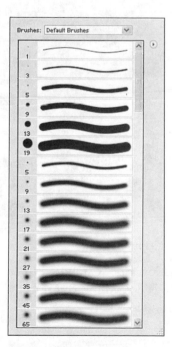

Figure 6.6

Choose a selection brush style to draw just the shape you want.

3. Click the Size arrow (see Figure 6.7) and specify the brush's width (for this example, 8 pixels); move the slider to the right to increase the width and to the left to decrease it (a preview of the new size appears in the Brush Presets palette when you select a size).

Figure 6.7

Move the Size slider to adjust the width of the brush.

4. From the Mode menu, select Selection, which creates a selection marquee as you draw; Mask creates a colored line. (By default, the Mask color is red; you can click the Overlay Color box and select a new color if you want.) For this example, choose Selection.

5. Once you have all these specifications straight, draw an outline of Boris the cat. For example, use an 8-pixel brush (as shown in Figure 6.8) and use the Selection option. You can stop drawing one line and move to another without losing the previous selection. You don't need to return to the starting point, either; all of your separate selection lines remain highlighted.

Figure 6.8

The Selection Brush enables you to brush your own selection area.

6. Choose Edit → Copy.

7. Choose File → New from Clipboard to create a new canvas from what's in the clipboard, which is everything you selected when you drew with the Selection Brush (see Figure 6.9).

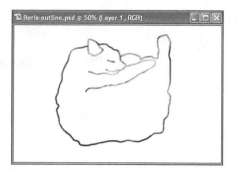

Figure 6.9

The Selection Brush lets you create selections that can become works of art in themselves.

So many sizes and styles of brushes are available to you in the Brushes palette that we can't possibly list them all here. We invite you to open a blank new document and click around in the palette to see all that's available. When you click the palette, another drop-down list, Brushes, appears at the top. Select an option from the list to change the brushes displayed. You can also click the arrow to the right of the displayed brushes to refine the display—choose Small Thumbnail to view many options in a small space, for instance.

Making a Mask Selection

In the previous section, you used the Selection Brush to identify the area you want to select. You did this by choosing Selection from the Mode drop-down list in the Selection Brush's options bar. If you choose Mask from the Mode drop-down menu, you can make a *mask* selection.

When you draw a mask, you highlight the area *not* to be selected with a colored overlay. For example, when you draw the mask and then choose Edit → Copy, everything in the image except the mask is copied to the clipboard.

When you choose Mask, two new options appear in the options bar. Opacity refers to the ability of the mask to conceal the parts of the image that are not selected. The higher the opacity, the more the contents beneath the mask are concealed. Click the Overlay Color box to choose a color for the mask: By default, the mask is a dark red intended to resemble rubalith tape, which is used in printing to create masks. But you can make the mask any color you want.

Waving the Magic Wand

If you thought the Magnetic Lasso tool streamlined selecting complex shapes, you'll be amazed at how the Magic Wand can automate selections even further. The Wand works by selecting all pixels in the area of the pixel on which you click that are similar in color to that pixel. For instance, if you click one spot of blue sky in an image with the Magic Wand, you select the entire blue sky. You'll understand the idea better if you try it yourself. Follow these steps:

1. Open the file *big-gargoyle.tif* in the Chapter 6 folder on this book's CD-ROM.

2. Choose File → Save As.

3. Click the arrow next to Save In to locate a directory on your own hard disk where you can save the image so you can work with it.

4. Select the Magic Wand tool in the toolbox.

5. Click anywhere in the blue sky surrounding the gargoyle. The goal is to select only the blue sky. If you only selected a single spot in the image with that mouse click, check the options bar. If Contiguous is checked, this tells the program to only select the pixels that are immediately next to the one on which you actually clicked. Uncheck Contiguous, and then click in the blue sky again.

6. Now the blue sky is selected. Click the Paint Bucket tool. The Paint Bucket enables you to fill a selection area or a shape with the foreground color in a single mouse click.

7. Make sure White is selected as the foreground color, and that Foreground is specified in the Fill box in the options bar.

8. Click anywhere in the selected area to make the formerly blue sky look instantly cloudy by filling it with white. Figure 6.10 shows the Before and After versions.

Figure 6.10

Choose a Selection Brush style to draw just the shape you want.

9. Choose Edit → Undo Paint Bucket or press Ctrl+Z (Windows) or Cmd+Z (Mac) to undo the change. Keep the image open so you can get some more experience with the Magic Wand in the following section.

Adjusting Tolerance

By adjusting the Tolerance setting in the options bar, you can tell Photoshop Elements to be either more or less sensitive (in Photoshop Elements-speak, tolerant) when selecting colors. In theory, setting the tolerance to a lower number tells Photoshop Elements to select fewer colors; a higher number specifies more colors). In reality, it's a matter of trial and error. You have to keep adjusting the tolerance several times before you select the areas you want (and even then, the Magic Wand might not get it exactly right).

You can experiment with the *big-gargoyle.tif* image:

1. If necessary, choose Select → Deselect to deselect the blue sky you selected earlier.

2. Select the Magic Wand.

3. Enter a relatively low number, such as 32, in the Tolerance box.

4. Click one of the little patches of snow. All of the patches of snow should be selected.

5. Enter a relatively high number, such as 82, in the Tolerance box.

6. Click a patch of snow. Much more of the image than just the white patches are selected; Photoshop Elements now selects the gray areas that are especially light (in other words, close to white).

7. Choose Select → Deselect to undo your selection. Leave the gargoyle image open for the next series of exercises.

Figure 6.11 shows the difference between a low and high tolerance setting.

This exercise gives you more experience with the Magic Wand. Set the tolerance to 32, and select the snow in the *big-gargoyle.tif* image. Click the Eyedropper tool in the toolbox. The Eyedropper tool is an amazing and powerful tool. It enables you to select a color not from the Color Picker, but from the image you're working on. By default, the Eyedropper lets you select the foreground color, but you can select the background color by pressing Alt+click (Windows) or Opt+click (Mac) with the Eyedropper.

Try it now: Select the Eyedropper by either clicking its toolbox icon or pressing the I shortcut key. Then click a gray area of the gargoyle. Click the Paint Bucket, and fill each of the white areas with the color. Choose Select → Deselect, and you've made the gargoyle snow-free!

Figure 6.11

Different Tolerance settings cause the Magic Wand to select a higher or lower range of colors.

Changing and Transforming Selections

Some of the options in Photoshop Elements for adjusting selections apply to virtually any selection tool you decide to use. They're (mostly) found in the Select menu, and it's good to get acquainted with them.

In Focus

Choose Select → Modify → Contract to display the Contract Selection dialog box, where you can specify the number of pixels by which you want the selection to shrink. Choose Select → Similar to select pixels that are similar in color and adjacent to the pixels you've currently selected.

Growing, Expanding, and Contracting Selections

If you make a selection and then choose Select → Grow, the selection area expands slightly to include adjacent pixels that are similar in color. You can use this to make the snow seem to grow on the image you used in the previous section. Open *big-gargoyle.tif*, click the Magic Wand, and select the white snow. Then choose Select → Grow. Choose Select → Grow again or press Ctrl+Y (Windows) or Cmd+Y (Mac). Watch the selection area grow.

Here's another, different way to expand selections: Choose Select → Modify → Expand. In the Expand Selection dialog box, enter the number of pixels by which you want the selection area(s) to expand. Click OK. The selected area grows symmetrically in height and width by the number of pixels specified.

Filling Selections

Once you've made a selection, you can fill the highlighted area with the Paint Bucket. Here's a more elegant approach: Make the selection, and then choose Edit → Fill or press Shift+Backspace (Windows) or Shift+Delete (Mac) to display the Fill dialog box. Select the color with which you want to fill the selection by choosing an option from the Use drop-down list. Click OK to fill the selection.

To fill the selection with the background color, press Ctrl+Backspace (Windows) or Cmd+Delete (Mac). To fill a selection with the foreground color, press Alt+Backspace (Windows) or Opt+Delete (Mac). To instantly open the Fill dialog box, press Shift+ Backspace (Windows) or Shift+Delete (Mac).

Inverting Selections

You've already seen how to select the blue sky in the *big-gargoyle.tif* image using the Magic Wand tool. It's just as likely that you'll want to select the gargoyle in the image. A quick way to do this is to select the solid blue background of the image, then choose Select → Inverse to switch to selecting everything in the image other than what is currently highlighted.

In Focus

Another Select menu option, All, enables you to select the entire image file all at once.

Rotating Selections

If you want to rotate a selection, choose Image → Rotate. Then choose one of the options (90 degrees Left, 90 degrees right, 180 degrees, Flip Horizontal, or Flip Vertical) from the submenu shown in Figure 6.12.

The options in the upper section of the Rotate submenu enable you to rotate an image whether it's selected or not. The options in the middle section apply to selections. They're pretty self-explanatory, except perhaps for Free Rotate Selection. When you choose this option, a bounding box appears around what you've selected. Click and drag on one of the corners of the bounding box to rotate the selection around its center.

Figure 6.12

The Rotate submenu enables you to adjust selection marquees or the pixels they contain.

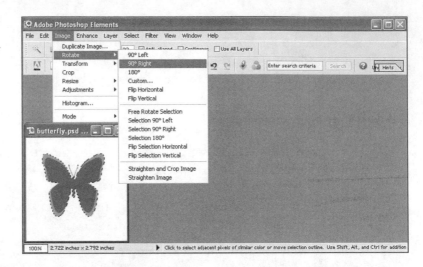

Using the Shape Selection Tool

Something is different about Figure 6.11 compared to the previous images in this chapter: It's a vector, an image made up of line segments that you can draw with the Shape tools. (We cover these tools and how to use them in Chapter 16.)

When you're working with vectors as opposed to bitmaps, you should make use of a special selector: the Shape Selection tool. It's the fourth one down from the left in the toolbox. Click and hold down the Selection tool that's visible, and then choose the Shape Selection tool from the list of hidden tools (see Figure 6.13).

Figure 6.13

The Shape Selection tool is specially designed to select drawn vector shapes.

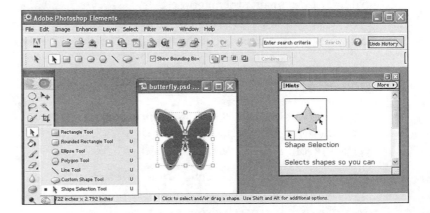

Saving and Loading Selections

Sometimes you need to make exactly the same selection over and over in different images. Suppose, for instance, you want to create a design that consists of a group of repeated circles, each containing a different pattern. One needs to have stripes in it, one polka dots, one diagonal lines. You have several drawings available that contain the patterns you want to use, but each drawing is in a separate file. You can make exactly the same selection in each file by making a selection, saving it, and then loading it in the next image.

First, make the circular selection you want using the Elliptical Marquee tool while holding down the Shift key. Then choose Select → Save Selection. Give the selection a name in the Save Selection dialog box and click OK. Then, when you open a new image, you only need to choose Select → Load Selection. Choose the selection in the Load Selection dialog box, and click OK. The circular selection you previously saved appears in the new image.

The Least You Need to Know

- The Lasso tool makes it easy for you to select irregular shapes.
- The Polygonal Lasso tool enables you to select a polygon.
- The Selection Brush enables you to draw your own selection.
- The Magic Wand tool enables you to select a color or group of similar colors.
- The Shape Selection tool is great for selecting the vector shapes you've drawn.

Chapter 7

Introducing Layers

In This Chapter

- Understanding multilayered images
- Controlling layout with the Layers palette
- Creating a layered image
- Editing and deleting layers
- Linking and flattening layers

Suppose you take a family photo and then scan and edit it in Photoshop Elements. That photo contains only a single layer of information. But when you look at it, you start to wish you could break it into different sections so you can edit them independently. Wouldn't it be nice, for example, if you could make the sky bluer, and adjust the grass in the foreground of the image, while leaving the people in the middle of the image unchanged? Wouldn't it be nice to go a step further and spruce up the background with some snow-covered mountains to make it look like you took an alpine vacation?

You can do all of these things in Photoshop Elements by working with layers. If you divide an image into layers, you can work with each part separately—and without having to make intricate selections. You can combine layers from one image with layers from another to come up with a truly original creation. This chapter gives you an overview of layers as well as some hands-on experience in preparing the Photoshop Elements version of a "layer cake."

Getting the Layer of the Land

As a kid, you probably did your share of cutting and pasting paper to build a scene. Chances are you started with a big sheet of colored paper—the background. On top of the background, you pasted some paper you had cut into the shapes of buildings—the second layer. On top of the buildings, you pasted other shapes such as windows, doors, and the like—the third layer.

Now, you can go beyond scissors and paste to use Photoshop Elements as a sort of digital layering tool. You can cut and paste pieces of images to create your own layers, merge layers, and rearrange them any way you want. It might sound a bit abstract right now, but layers will be uncovered when you try the hands-on exercises in the sections that follow.

Getting to Know the Layers Palette

You can find the controls that enable you to work with layers in the Layers palette. The best way to get to know the Layers palette is to begin working with it. Follow these steps:

1. Start up Photoshop Elements.

2. Choose File → Open to launch the Open dialog box.

3. Select the *lake-layers.psd* file in the Chapter 7 folder on this book's CD-ROM and choose Open.

4. Open the Layers palette by dragging it out of the Palette Well or by choosing Window → Layers. Figure 7.1 shows the image and Layers palette.

As you can see, the Layers palette displays five layers in this image—the white background layer and the four separate layers above it. Click each of the layers in turn and see what happens: Each of the layers within the image is highlighted with a bounding box to show that it's been selected.

The Layers palette provides a wide range of controls over how layers appear in an image, as Figure 7.2 shows.

Figure 7.1

The Layers palette displays the layers within an image.

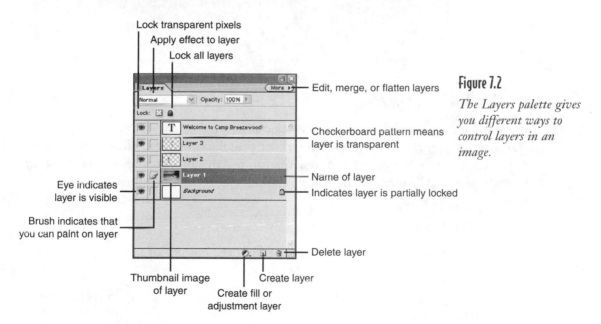

Figure 7.2

The Layers palette gives you different ways to control layers in an image.

Customizing Palette Icon Size

By default, the Layers palette contains a thumbnail image of a layer next to its name. You can save some space by choosing a smaller icon or no icon at all. On the other hand, you can choose a bigger icon to get a better glimpse of a layer's contents. You make the changes by changing the palette options. Follow these steps:

1. Choose More in the upper right-hand corner of the Layers palette.

2. Choose Palette Options from the popup menu that appears.

3. In the Layers Palette Options dialog box (shown in Figure 7.3), choose the icon size you want.

4. Choose OK.

Figure 7.3

You can change icon size to fit your needs.

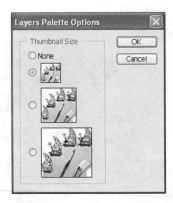

Changing the Order of Layers

The sample image this chapter uses isn't especially complicated. But in an image that contains seven, eight, or even more layers, changing the order of layers can make a big difference in how the image appears. You can test this by opening the *lake-layers.tif* file, located in the Chapter 7 folder on this book's CD-ROM, and then following these steps:

1. Select the Move tool in the toolbox.

2. Click and hold down the mouse on the text at the bottom of the image. A selection box should appear around the text.

3. Drag the text up so it's just atop the feet of my daughters, and then release the mouse button.

In Focus

Deselecting the text after you rearrange its layer makes it easier to see the effect of the change.

4. In the Layers palette, select the layer that contains the text you just selected (it's marked with a big T, which stands for … well, you can probably guess).

5. Drag the layer down by placing the mouse over the icon for this layer, and then left-clicking and hold while dragging the layer until it's just above Layer 1, and then release the mouse button.

Once you've moved the text from Layer 5 to Layer 2, the result is that it looks like the girls in the image are walking atop the text. Figure 7.4 shows the "before" (on the left) and "after" versions.

 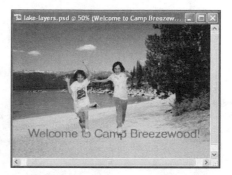

Figure 7.4

You can rearrange layers using the Layers palette.

Creating a Layered Image

Working with layers gives you the ability to combine or edit images in ways you may never have imagined. You can add a photo of Uncle Joe to that photo from the family reunion he couldn't attend. You can place a dog atop a surfboard, a fish in space … the list of possibilities is as big as your imagination. To get you started, I'll show you how I created the simple layered image shown earlier.

Assembling Images

First, assemble the images that have the components you want to combine. For this example, we scanned two photos, one of the girls running through a sprinkler, the other of the mountain scene.

Next, we selected the outlines of the two girls. This was a laborious process, even though we were using the Magnetic Lasso tool described in Chapter 6 (see Figure 7.5).

We copied each outline and saved it in a new image (see Figure 7.6).

Figure 7.5

After you capture an image, select the object you want to copy.

Figure 7.6

Isolate images so you can copy them to new layers.

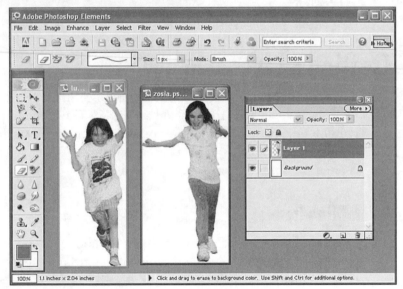

Adding and Naming Layers

Photoshop Elements gives you several different ways to create a layer:

- ◆ Choose Layer → New → Layer.

- ◆ Press Ctrl+N (Windows) or Cmd+N (Mac).

- ◆ Click the More button at the top of the Layers palette and choose New Layer from the shortcut menu.

- ◆ Click the New Layer icon at the bottom right-hand corner of the Layers palette.

Now, for a more elegant method of copying a selection from one image and pasting it to a new layer in another, multilayered image, follow these steps:

1. Make sure the *lake-layers.psd* file is open in Photoshop Elements.

2. Open the image *zosia.psd* on the CD-ROM.

3. Make sure Layer 1, the layer that contains Zosia's image, is selected in the Layers palette. Then click More and choose Duplicate Layer from the shortcut menu.

4. In the Duplicate Layer dialog box (see Figure 7.7), choose *lake-layers.psd* from the Destination drop-down list.

Figure 7.7

Duplicating a layer in one image to another image.

5. Click OK. The image is added as a layer to *lake-layers.psd*.

6. Right-click the layer you just added and choose Rename from the shortcut menu.

7. Type a new name for the layer in the Name box of the Layer Properties dialog box.

8. Choose OK.

Editing a Layer

Once you have layers arranged the way you want, you can fine-tune their appearance. You can do the following:

◆ Move the layer with the Move tool.

◆ Change the *opacity* of a layer by clicking the arrow next to Opacity and moving the slider to the right or left.

◆ Paint on the layer using the Paint Brush, Bucket, or other drawing tool.

Shop Talk

Opacity is a way of describing how effectively something blocks the transmission of light through it. If something is 100-percent opaque, you can't see anything beneath it. Moving the opacity slider to the left gives the layer less opacity and more of a "ghosted" effect; moving it to the right gives the layer more opacity and more effectively hides the layers beneath it.

If you Ctrl+click (Windows) or Cmd+click (Mac) on the thumbnail of a layer in the Layers palette, you immediately select the opaque area in the layer—in other words, everything that's not the transparent layer behind it.

It's Element-ary

You can also delete a layer by clicking and dragging it atop the trashcan icon in the bottom right-hand corner of the Layers palette.

Linking Layers

You have two layers in an image that were just made for each other; they are positioned just the way you want, they look great together, and heck, they're practically

In Focus

Linking layers gives you a way to temporarily edit them as one. However, Photoshop Elements gives you more permanent ways to join layers. You can group them together or merge them into a single layer. Chapter 8 covers the grouping and merging of layers.

◆ You can also select a layer and apply a filter from the Filter menu. (You'll learn more about working with filters further in Chapter 17.)

When you first create a layer, it is transparent. But when you edit the layer, your edits are made on the active layer that contains the visible content, not the transparent background.

Deleting Layers

Deleting a layer is easy as easy as right-clicking the layer you want to remove and choosing Delete from the shortcut menu. That's all there is to it. However, before you permanently delete a layer, consider the next best thing: Click the eye icon next to the layer in the Layers palette. When the eye icon is not visible, that means the layer isn't visible, either. By hiding a layer, you can test the effect of deleting it without actually eliminating it for good.

inseparable. You might as well link the layers to merge them into one. This way you can edit and move them all at once if you want to. To link Layers 2 and 3 in *lake-layers.tif* (the layers depicting the two girls), select Layer 2 in the Layers palette, and then click the second column in Layer 3—the column just next to the eye icon and to the left of the thumbnail. The link icon appears in the column to show that Layer 3 is linked to Layer 2 (see Figure 7.8).

If you ever need to unlink a layer, just click the Link icon to remove the link.

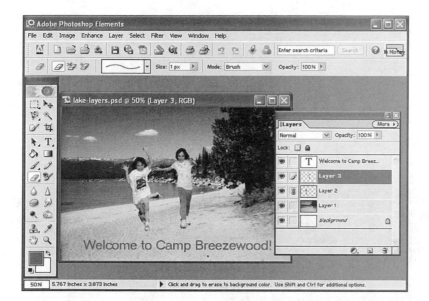

Figure 7.8

Linking layers enables you to edit and move them all together.

Flattening Layers

Sometimes, layers get in the way of what you want to do. Layered images take up a lot of disk space. You might want to open and use the image in a program that doesn't use PSD, PDF, and TIF files. You may want to add the image to a web page, for instance.

In such cases you need to flatten the layers into a single background layer. The quick way is to choose Layer → Flatten Image. Photoshop blends all layers into one. The other way is to save the file with a different name. You can do it yourself by following these steps:

1. Open *lake-layers.psd* if it's not open already.

2. Choose File → Save As to display the Save As dialog box.

3. Enter a new file name—*lake-unlayered.tif*—for the unlayered image in the file. In the Format box, make sure Photoshop (*.psd, *.pdd) is selected. Click As A Copy.

4. Uncheck the box next to Layers to save the image without layers (see Figure 7.9).

5. Choose Save.

The image is saved without layers. Notice that the Save As dialog box gives you the option to save the image with layers, as long as it's in Photoshop, PDF, or TIF format.

Figure 7.9

The Save As dialog box enables you to save an image without layers.

In Focus

Flattening layers is a drastic change. Be sure you've finished all your arranging and editing of layers before you flatten them into one. You can choose Edit → Undo or Edit → Step Backward to "unflatten" the image, as long as you're in the same Photoshop Elements session. Consider saving the flattened image with a different name so you can preserve the original layered arrangement if you need it. But save it with a .psd, .pdf, or .tif extension, or the layer information won't be saved.

As you saw when you worked with the Save As dialog box in the previous exercise, and toyed around with the check boxes, Photoshop Elements gives you the option to save the layers within a multilayered image, provided the image is in PSD, PDF, or TIF format.

You may want to save a PSD image in TIF format so you can open and edit it in an image-editing program such as Paint Shop Pro for Windows or GraphicConverter for the Macintosh. If so, just choose File → Save As, choose TIFF (*.tif, *.tiff) from the Format drop-down list, and make sure Save Layers is selected.

Now that you've had an introduction to layers and how to use them, in the next chapter you'll delve into some more advanced ways to manipulate and control layers and create some striking graphic effects.

The Least You Need to Know

- Dividing an image into layers enables you to work with image areas separately.

- The Layers palette enables you to view, rearrange, delete, and add layers.

- Layers enable you to combine and edit portions of multiple images.

- Layers can be rendered invisible and have variable opacity settings.

- Linking layers enables you to edit and move them together.

- Flattening an image combines all layers into one.

Chapter 8

Getting Into Layers

In This Chapter

- ◆ Merging layers
- ◆ Changing a layer's appearance
- ◆ Rearranging layers
- ◆ Blending layers
- ◆ Adding adjustment layers

In the previous chapter, you learned about the basic approaches to working with a layered image. This chapter dives into some more interesting and involved techniques of working with layers, such as merging layers, changing the appearance of layers, and working with adjustment and fill layers.

Combining Images

In Chapter 7, you learned how to copy an image to a new file and then duplicate it so that it becomes a layer in a second image. You can also move images from one layer of a file to another layer of a different file in other ways.

Dragging and Dropping Images

When you have an image that's a layer in one file and you have the destination file also visible in the Photoshop Elements window, you can drag one selection into another window and drop it there (see Figure 8.1).

Use Move tool to drag image from one file to another
Drag handle to resize image if necessary

Figure 8.1

You can drag and drop a layer from one image to a new layer in another image.

Once the image is dropped into its new location, you'll notice eight selection handles along its perimeter. Drag the handles inward to make the image smaller; drag them outward to make the image bigger. But notice that simply clicking and dragging the handles changes the proportions of the image as well, which can distort it.

In Focus

If you want to retain the original proportions of an image while you resize it, hold down the Shift key while you drag one of the selection handles. You can also drag and drop an image by holding down the Ctrl key and dragging with any tool other than the Hand or Shape tools.

Try it now: Open the *flowers.psd* file from the Chapter 8 folder on this book's CD-ROM. Click and drag one of the four corner handles and notice that the flower becomes either flattened or elongated, depending on the direction in which you're dragging. Notice that you can also click and drag any of the dotted lines that surround the image when you click it with the Move tool. Click the Step Backward button in the shortcuts bar when you're done to restore the image to its original shape.

Next, hold down the Shift key while you drag one of the corner handles. This resizes the image equally in both height and width and enables you to retain the original proportions.

Pasting One Selection into Another Selection

Now it's time for you to try your own hand at creating a new layer by cutting and pasting. This time, though, try making a selection in one image and pasting it into a selection area in a second image. Follow these steps:

1. Start by opening the *flowers.psd* file located in the Chapter 8 folder on this book's CD-ROM, if it's not open already.

2. Choose File → Save As to open the Save As dialog box.

3. Save the file on your hard disk with a new name: *flowers-layers.psd*.

4. In the open space near the center of the image, draw a selection area with the Lasso tool. (You may want to refer to Figure 8.2 for an example.)

5. Open a second file, *dkredflower.tif*, in the Chapter 8 folder of this book's CD-ROM.

6. Click the Magic Wand tool. In the options bar, set the Tolerance to 92, and make sure the boxes next to Anti-Aliased and Contiguous are selected.

7. Click the dark red flower to select it. You will find that some areas of the image are not selected; click them with the Magic Wand tool until you've selected the entire flower.

8. Click the Move tool, Shift-click one of the handles around the dark red flower, and drag inward to make the flower approximately the size of the selection area you drew in the *flowers-layers.psd* image (see Figure 8.2).

9. Click the Rectangular Marquee tool, and then choose Edit → Copy. (Copy is not available as a menu option while the Move tool is active.)

10. Switch to the *flowers-layers.psd* image, and then choose Edit → Paste to paste the image into the selection area you drew.

When you've added the new red flower to the *flowers-layers.psd* image, save your changes and leave the file open so you can continue working with layers in the following sections.

Figure 8.2

You can paste a resized selection into a selection area in another file.

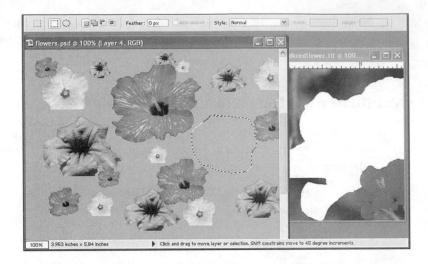

Scaling a New Layer

The flower you pasted into the image in the previous section was added to the file as Layer 5. Choose Window → Layers to display the Layers palette and click the eye icon next to each of the layers. You'll notice that Layer 2 contains the yellow flowers, Layer 3 the purple flowers, and Layer 4 the light red flowers.

Click the Magic Wand tool and select the dark red flower you just pasted. Press Ctrl+C (Windows) or Cmd+C (Mac) to copy the image. Choose Select → Deselect, and then press Ctrl+V (Windows) or Cmd+V (Mac) to paste the flower, which is added to another part of the image as Layer 6. Select the flower layer with the Move tool and Shift-drag one of the corner handles to resize the flower. Repeat these steps until you have added five or six new red flowers (and layers) to the image (see Figure 8.3).

Figure 8.3

Select a layer with the Move tool and drag a handle to resize it.

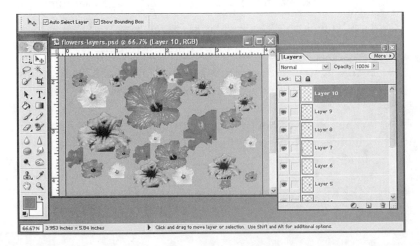

Shop Talk

Resizing and **scaling** are actually two different terms. Scaling is actually what you did in this section: You changed the size of the image while not actually changing the number or arrangement of pixels within it. Resizing means that you change the size while changing the number of pixels to maintain image quality as much as possible.

Checking Image Size

Once you have repeatedly copied and pasted a flower layer into the image we're using in this exercise, *flowers-layers.psd*, you'll see that you've added a corresponding number of layers to the image. Each of these layers makes the image's file size larger. If the image's size isn't already displayed, click the arrow in the status bar at the bottom of the Photoshop Elements window, and choose Document Sizes from the popup menu. The size appears in the status bar (see Figure 8.4). If the file size is too big, you can merge layers, as described in the next section.

It's Element-ary

The status bar shows two sizes for the active file that has layers. The one on the left indicates what the file size would be if you flattened all layers. The one on the right is the current file size with all layers intact. Left-click either size to see the image's physical dimensions.

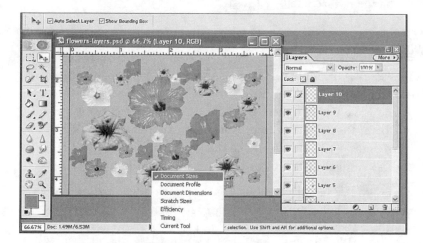

Figure 8.4

Ten layers, six megabytes! Time to merge layers to shrink the file size.

Merging Layers Down

Each of the layers in an image carries a price in disk real estate. To reduce the file's size, you can merge layers. Because each of the layers you added to *flowers-layers.psd* contains the same sort of image (a dark red flower), you can merge each image down to blend it with the previous layer. Follow these steps:

1. Choose Window → Layers to display the Layers palette if it isn't displayed already.

2. Select the topmost layer.

3. Choose Layer → Merge Down or press Ctrl+E (Windows) or Cmd+E (Mac). The layer is combined with the one beneath it.

4. Repeat Step 3 until the *flowers-layers.psd* image contains five layers—one layer for each color of flower, and one for the background.

Check the file size in the status bar; you'll most likely have some reduction once you've reduced the number of layers.

Changing a Layer's Appearance

In Chicago recently, there was a project in which groups of plants and bushes in public parks were spray-painted unusual colors, such as blue and pink. (It's called *art*.) Layers let you change colors and other features of objects all at once in much the same way. Poof! Quicker than you can wield a spray paint can, you can change a field of flowers from red to aquamarine. Springtime grass turns to winter white. Photoshop Elements gives you the ability to change nature itself in a flash.

Adjusting Image Attributes

One of the great advantages of working with layers is the ability to change parts of an image all at once. Try it yourself by opening the *flowers-layers.psd* image you saved earlier, selecting a layer in the Layers palette, and then choosing an option from the Image menu. The Transform, Resize, Crop, and Adjustment submenus are all available. Choose Image → Adjustments → Equalize to make the objects in the layer all equally luminous. Choose Image → Adjustments → Posterize for an even more vivid effect.

Most of the time, however, you're better off adjusting the appearance in a layer with one of the Enhance menu options: Enhance → Adjust Lighting, Enhance → Adjust Colors, or Enhance → Adjust Brightness/Contrast. For a really striking effect, select a layer and choose Enhance → Adjust Color → Replace Color. Adjust the Hue, Saturation, and Brightness sliders in the Replace Color dialog box. Make sure the Preview box is checked and that the Image button is selected; you can see the effect of your adjustments in the layer itself as you move the controls (see Figure 8.5).

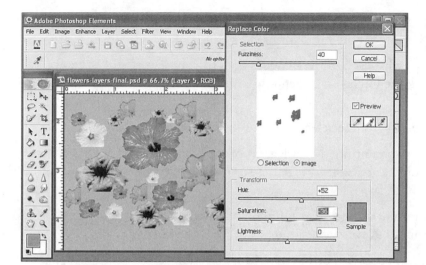

Figure 8.5

Adjust colors for all the objects in a layer.

Adjusting Opacity

Another adjustment you can make when you divide an image into layers—one that you can't make with a single-layer image—is making parts of the image more or less opaque than others. This can give your image a three-dimensional effect. Try setting the opacity for different layers to different values: Open the layer palette and select a layer, then click the arrow next to Opacity, and move the slider to the left to reduce the setting from the default 100 percent. Do this several times to make one layer 90 percent, one 80 percent, and so on, to give the image added depth and interest.

In Focus

You can also adjust the opacity for an individual layer with a keyboard shortcut. Select the layer, and make sure you've selected a tool that doesn't have its own Opacity setting (such as a selection marquee). Then just press a number key—1 equals 10 percent opacity, 2 equals 20 percent, and so on. Press 0 to return to 100 percent.

Choosing a Blend Mode

Another way to take advantage of the layers in an image is to control the way the contents of one layer interact—or *blend*—with another. You do this by specifying a blend mode. A *blend mode* is a way of making the pixels in one layer interact differently with the layers beneath it.

Click the Blend Mode drop-down menu in the upper left-hand corner of the Layers palette to find the mind-boggling (you might say mode-boggling) options available to you. (The Blend Mode list doesn't immediately look like it contains any modes, because the default setting simply says Normal.)

The best way to learn what each of these modes does to your layers is to open up *flowers-layers.psd*, click the top layer, and choose a blend mode from the list. Try out the most important ones:

- Choose Dissolve to give the selected layer a grainy appearance.

- Choose Multiply to multiply the dark areas of the selected layers and the layers beneath it. The dark areas blend together so that the selected layer blends into the one beneath it.

- Choose Screen if the selected area is light—It lightens the light parts both of the selected layer and the layers beneath it.

- Choose Overlay, Soft Light, or Hard Light if you want to blend layers by lightening up all the light areas and further darken the dark areas. These three commands all do pretty much the same thing.

- Choose Color Dodge or Color Burn if the pixels in the selected layer are especially light or dark. Choose Color Dodge if they are light: Color Dodge lightens the underlying layers and blends them with the lighter areas of the selected layer. Color Burn does the opposite: It darkens the underlying areas and blends them with parts of the selected layer that are already dark.

- Difference is one of the most interesting blend modes. It's also hard to explain. It takes the selected layer and the ones beneath it and inverts them based on their colors. It takes the lighter colored pixels in the layers and subtracts the darker colored pixels from the brighter ones. This works best when the colors are bright, such as in Layer 3 of the sample image *flowers-layers.psd* (see Figure 8.6).

Return to Normal, the default setting, if you don't want any blending between layers.

Figure 8.6

Play with different blend modes to get the effect you want.

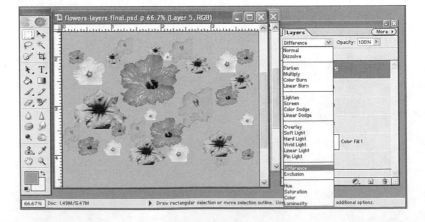

Arranging Layers

Once you've arranged a "layer cake" image, the temptation is to leave things just as they are. But when you avoid moving and grouping layers, you miss out on some striking effects. Photoshop Elements options for reordering and grouping layers enable you to create a new and improved set of flavors for your "cake."

You'll find the commands that enable layers to fall into line under the Arrange submenu of the Layer menu. Select the top layer and choose Layer → Arrange → Send Backward to move it down to the next layer in the set. Choose Layer → Arrange → Send To Back to move it to the layer just above the Background layer (which is always the bottom layer). Once it's on the bottom, choose Layer → Arrange → Bring Forward to move it back up one level; then choose Layer → Arrange → Bring To Front to move it back to the top level. You can also click and drag layers to move them up or down in the Layers palette.

The point of all this arranging is not to gain expertise with the Arrange submenu itself but to change the way layers interact with one another. It's like arranging the people in a class photo: You want to move the taller folks to the back and the shorter ones up front so everyone can be seen, and everyone has a place in the whole group.

Swatch Out!

Two options bar options for the Move tool are Auto Select Layer and Show Bounding Box. These options can cause you to make selections and achieve effects you weren't really looking for. Auto Select Layer causes you to switch to a layer when you click any part of it with the Move tool—you can easily select a layer you didn't want if you don't click carefully. Show Bounding Box automatically surrounds a layer with a box with selection handles. If you click and drag a box, you instantly transform (or, you might say, distort) a layer. Deselect either of these options to reduce the chance of trouble. The Show Bounding Box option also appears when the Shape Selection tool is active.

Grouping Layers

Another way to control the way layers are arranged in an image is to group them. Grouping layers is different than linking layers, which you learned about in Chapter 7. Linking simply enables you to move, copy, or paste layers together. But grouping enables layers to share the outline and opacity of the bottom most or base layer in the group.

Select a layer, and then select another layer and choose Layer → Group with Previous. The selected layer is grouped with the layer above it. Why would you want to group layers? Grouping enables you to change the color of several layers at once by placing an adjustment or fill layer above them, as described in the following section.

Adjustment and Fill Layers

Thus far, the changes you've made to the layers in the image you've been working with have involved menu commands on the Images and Layers menus. But you haven't actually made any color corrections as yet. By this time you may be asking how to actually change those green flowers to blue, white, or even (shudder) black?

You do it not by changing the color of the pixels in the layer itself, but by creating a new layer, called an *adjustment layer*, that contains the color correction. The colors in the adjustment layer change the colors of the underlying layer (and any layers that you have grouped with the selected layer by choosing Layer → Group With Previous). Because the adjustment colors are contained in a separate layer, you can delete or change them easily without changing the contents of the other layers.

A similar layer, called a *fill layer*, lets you fill underlying layers with color. Technically speaking, you fill the fill layer with the color, and the fill layer color colors the layer directly beneath the fill layer. Sound like a tongue twister? It's really just as simple as putting on colored sunglasses to change the appearance of what you see through them. As usual, it becomes clearer when you try it yourself.

In the Layers palette, click the layer that you want to color-correct to select it. Then choose Layer → New Adjustment Layer → Levels. In the New Layer dialog box, type a name for the layer (if you want to) in the Name text box, and select the Opacity level and Mode if you want. Then click OK. The adjustment layer is placed on top of the one you selected. Double-click the Layer thumbnail in the Adjustment layer in the Layers palette to display the Levels dialog box, where you can change colors by moving the three triangles (see Figure 8.7).

An adjustment or fill layer is like a piece of clear acetate you've placed over a layer (okay, they're not exactly sunglasses). If the acetate is colored, it colors the layer beneath it. The Levels dialog box lets you adjust the levels of color in the adjustment layer, which, in turn, changes the colors in the layer below.

The Levels dialog box can be complex and intimidating, but don't worry; you only need to check the Preview box and move the three triangles (see Figure 8.8) to the left or right and watch the color change in the image itself until you get exactly the color you want. (See Chapter 9 for more on changing color levels.)

Adjustment layer

Layer thumbnail

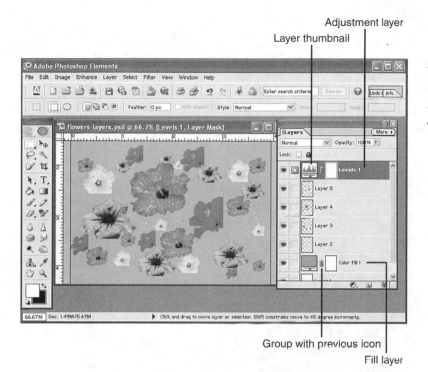

Figure 8.7

Change layer colors by placing an adjustment layer above it.

Group with previous icon

Fill layer

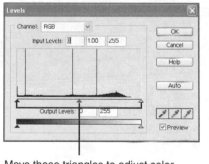

Figure 8.8

Move the triangles to adjust colors in the adjustment layer.

Move these triangles to adjust color

The Least You Need to Know

◆ You can drag and drop to combine images and create different layers.

◆ Merging layers simplifies an image and reduces file size.

◆ A blend mode controls the way a layer blends with the layers beneath it.

◆ To color-correct a layer, you create an adjustment or fill layer.

Part 3

Working with Photographs

Some day your prints will come, but not before you've done some fancy editing to make them even better than they were when they left your scanner or digital camera—or even the family photo album.

In this part of the book, you'll learn about the new QuickFix features that enable you to dramatically improve image quality with just a few mouse clicks. You'll learn how to use one of the single most effective image editing approaches—adjusting levels. You'll learn how to give yourself a face lift with retouching tools, and finally, how to save images in the right format based on how you plan to use them.

Quick Phixes for Phunky Photos

In This Chapter

- Diagnosing photo problems

- Straightening out crooked scans

- Focusing on what's important by cropping

- Doing a quick brightness or contrast tune-up

- Quick-fixing color problems

Maybe it was the photo lab's fault. Or maybe it was that cheap digital camera that seems to deal in mini- rather than mega-pixels. Whatever the cause (it couldn't possibly be you, the photographer), that image has you reaching for the Recycle Bin, the Trash—maybe even that garbage can under the kitchen sink. But wait. Don't toss that subpar image just yet. Let Photoshop Elements open its box of image editing tools and quickly perform some magic.

Photoshop Elements is an ideal application for casual users who want to take advantage of powerful image editing tools but who don't want to get their hands dirty by having to learn the technical details of image editing. In this chapter, you'll learn how fix the obvious problems digital photo images sometimes have. In fact, this book's CD-ROM includes an especially "troubled" image for you to doctor up. You'll crop and straighten images, and then learn what the QuickFix tools can do to correct problems with color and contrast. Those of you who want to get into image retouching can also use the tools described in Chapters 10 and 11.

Straightening a Crooked Image

Sometimes, you're not interested in retouching, adjusting levels, and making other subtle changes to photos. You just want to fix the obvious things, print the image, and move on to the next one. In this section, you'll get a chance to practice one of the simplest and most obvious problems: straightening a crooked image.

Perhaps you put the photo in the scanner crooked; perhaps you stumbled when you pushed the shutter on your digital camera. Whatever the reason, you're faced with two options:

- Rescan the image (if it was scanned).

- Take a new photo (if it was snapped with a camera).

Unless, of course, you've got Photoshop Elements at your disposal, with its powerful and whimsical menu choice Image → Rotate → Straighten Image. A related command, Straighten and Crop Image, gives even more dramatic improvement.

In Focus

In case you scanned your image horizontally when you should have gone vertical, don't fret. Turn to the Image → Rotate submenu, which lets you reorient your image in 90-degree increments. You can even flip your image horizontally or vertically using different options on the same submenu.

Open the *badscan.tif* file in the Chapter 9 folder on this book's CD-ROM, choose File → Save As to give the file a different name (such as *badscan2.tif*) so you can save it to your hard disk. With *badscan2.tif* open in all of its crooked glory, choose Image → Rotate → Straighten and Crop Image. Photoshop Elements attempts to reorient your image to make your image as vertically straight as possible, and crops some (though not all) of the crooked edges. It looks for major features in your picture and aligns them with the *x* and *y* axes. Figure 9.1 shows this in action. The picture on the left is the original. The one on the right shows the results of the Straighten and Crop Image command.

Figure 9.1

The Straighten and Crop Image command takes a crooked image (left) and brings it into line (right).

Cropping to Improve Bad Images

As you can see once you've applied the Straighten and Crop Image command, some more cropping is needed on the poor-quality image you're trying to improve. Cropping is a way of selecting the parts of an image you want to preserve; the software tool you're using deletes the rest of the image. Cropping is a simple and highly effective way of improving images: just focus in on the part of the image that's most important to you.

In *badscan.tif*, the part of the image you want to preserve is the father who's greeting his daughter. The crowd in the background is just a distraction. Follow these steps to crop the image:

1. Open *badscan.tif* if it is not still open.

2. Choose the Crop tool in the toolbox (it's third from the top and on the right side of the toolbox).

3. Using the mouse, move the cursor to the start of the area you want to crop. Press the mouse button and drag to outline the portion you want to preserve. When you release the mouse, the unselected portion of the image will darken, as Figure 9.2 shows.

4. If you desire, adjust the selection outline. Use any of the eight square handles that surround your selection to change the selected area.

5. When you're completely satisfied with the area to crop, press the Enter or Return key. To cancel the operation without cropping, press the Esc key instead.

After you select the crop area and press Enter or Return, Photoshop Elements crops your image to the chosen dimensions. Your newly cropped image replaces the original in the image window (see Figure 9.3).

Crop tool

Click and drag on handle
to resize crop area

Figure 9.2

*Improve image composition
by cropping your pictures.*

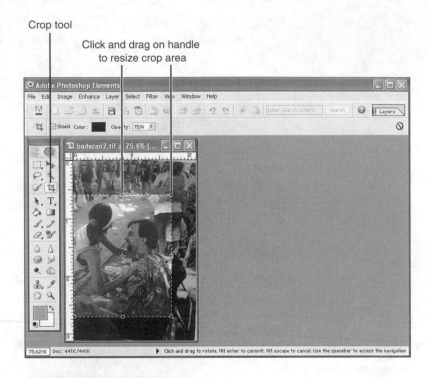

Figure 9.3

*Cropping can improve an
image by focusing on the best
part.*

Finding a Quick Fix

Once you've repaired an image's obvious problems (crookedness, wrong orientation, or cropping), you may need to deal with issues involving color and lighting. Here, as elsewhere, Photoshop Elements lets you accomplish complex effects without requiring you to climb a steep learning curve.

The QuickFix dialog box gives you a way to fix your pix with just one or two mouse clicks. It provides a centralized control panel with all the functionality needed to adjust lighting, color, and sharpness. You can launch QuickFix in any of several ways. With *badscan.tif* open, choose one of the following options:

- ◆ Select Enhance → QuickFix.

- ◆ Click the QuickFix icon on the shortcuts bar.

The QuickFix dialog box, shown in Figure 9.4, enables you to correct your image in any of the following four different categories of fixes:

- ◆ **Brightness**   This adjustment category offers fixes for contrast, levels, and brightness/contrast, as well as fill flash and adjust backlighting.

- ◆ **Color Correction**   Here you'll find adjustments for Auto Color (same as Enhance → Auto Color Correction) or user-adjusted hue and saturation.

- ◆ **Focus**   This category includes Auto Focus and Blur and enables you to sharpen or blur your image as needed.

- ◆ **Rotate**   With this tool, you can rotate your image 90 degrees in either direction, 180 degrees, and mirror it both vertically and horizontally.

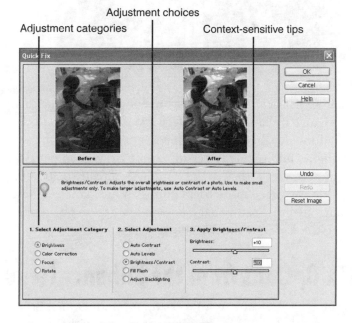

Figure 9.4

Fix all your image problems at once with the Photoshop Elements QuickFix dialog box.

Each feature of the QuickFix dialog box helps make image correction a snap. You can instantly see the effect of a change, and either accept it by clicking OK or clicking Undo to reject it.

Play around with *badscan.tif* using the controls in the QuickFix dialog box. First, choose Brightness, choose Auto Contrast, and click Apply. You'll see an instant improvement in the After box at the top of the QuickFix dialog box.

Next, choose Auto Levels. For now, don't worry about what levels actually are. Click Apply, and see how the colors in the image brighten dramatically. Choose Brightness/ Contrast, and move the sliders up by a factor of 10. The image suddenly seems to come out into the sunshine.

Once you can see the figures in your image, you can make the colors in the image look more vivid. Click Color Correction, choose Auto Color, and click Apply. Finally, click Focus, choose Auto Focus, and click Apply. When you've made these changes, click OK; the QuickFix dialog box closes. Choose File → Save As to save your new and quickly fixed image on your hard disk (see Figure 9.5).

Figure 9.5

QuickFix can instantly improve the lighting and color of an image.

 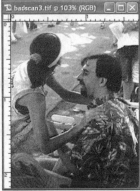

The advantage of using QuickFix is that it gives you control over your changes. You can see the effect of a change instantly in the Before and After boxes, and choose Undo if you do not want to adopt a change. Some changes, after all, just don't work; if you try to apply backlighting or fill lighting to repair *badscan.tif*, you only make the image muddier and darker (in part, that's because the lighting is already behind the figures shown in the image; it doesn't need more backlighting). Once you use QuickFix to make changes in a controlled manner, you'll gain enough experience to instantly apply corrections using the Enhance menu options.

Using Instant Fix Options from the Enhance Menu

The Enhance menu provides the same set of tools found in the QuickFix dialog box. These menu options instantly fix picture tone in your images without any further need for dialog boxes or interactive decisions. They provide "even quicker fix" solutions for images that look nearly right to begin with but are slightly off in tone. These commands automatically correct tonal errors and help restore your picture to all it can be.

The big difference between whether you use the Enhance menu or the QuickFix dialog box is that some of the Enhance menu options are applied instantly, without the control that Before and After images give you. To use any of the Enhance menu options, follow these general steps. First, determine if you want to correct all or part of your picture. If you want to correct just part, select that part. Otherwise, choose Select → Deselect or press Ctrl+D (Windows) or Cmd+D (Mac) and remove any current selection. Then choose the appropriate auto-correct tool from the Enhance menu. Your options include the following:

- **Auto Levels** The Auto Levels quick fix determines the lightest and darkest pixels in your image for each of your color channels (red, green, and blue for RGB images). It then redistributes the rest of the picture's pixels to provide a proportional range of colors—with a better distribution of light and color. This makes your picture look clearer and more realistic. Open *reallybad.tif* from the Chapter 9 folder of this book's CD-ROM and save it to your hard disk with the file name *reallybad2.tif*. Select the bottom half of *reallybad.tif* by drawing a rectangular marquee around it. Then choose Enhance → Auto Levels. The girls depicted in the bottom half become more visible. Keep the bottom half selected so you can try the next command.

> **CAUTION**
>
> **Swatch Out!**
>
> Auto Levels works with each color channel individually. Because of this, it can sometimes introduce an undesired color cast. When this happens, you can either undo the fix and try again with Auto Contrast instead or use Color Variations or Auto Color Correction to remove the cast.

- **Auto Contrast** This command does pretty much what you'd expect: It adjusts the overall contrast within your picture to create a better mixture of tones. Unlike Auto Levels, it does not adjust each color channel individually. Instead, it looks at your image as a whole. Keep the bottom half of *reallybad2.tif* selected (or, if you have deselected it, select it again). Then choose Enhance → Auto Contrast. Can you see any result? No dramatic change occurs; the image has dramatic contrast already.

- **Auto Color Correction** The Auto Color Correction fix adjusts the contrast and color of your image. It works by neutralizing midtones (the main colors of your image, as opposed to the deep shadows or highlights) and reducing extreme values of very bright and very dark pixels. Unfortunately, this effect is very hard to show in a black-and-white book, but give it a try with *reallybad2.tif*. In this case the results are more noticeable, because the colors in the image are so reddish to begin with. For many images, the Auto Color Correction command improves skin-tones and provides more natural-looking colors in your images.

Keep *reallybad.tif* open with the bottom half selected, so you can try some quick lighting repairs as described in the following section.

Fixing Fill and Backlights

Photoshop Elements offers another set of fixes with its fill and backlight commands. These options enable you to correct common lighting mistakes in your images such as a background that is too light or a subject that is too dark. To get to these commands, choose Enhance → Adjust Lighting → Adjust Backlighting or Fill Flash. If you want to make both corrections, you should probably first start with Fill Flash and then Adjust Backlighting. These two options are worth getting acquainted with:

◆ **Fill Flash**   This option applies a very slight change (such as at a setting of +3). Fill Flash enables you to reveal detail that would otherwise be hidden in shadows. This command lightens part, or all, of your image to enhance shadowed portions.

◆ **Adjust Backlighting**   After adding a bit of fill flash, choose Adjust Backlighting from the Enhance → Adjust Lighting submenu to improve the backlighting in the bottom half of *reallybad2.tif*. Make a slight adjustment, moving the slider up to the +6 setting. Select the Preview check box (if it isn't selected already), so you can instantly see the improvement. Backlighting occurs when the source of light lies behind rather than in front of your subject. Photoshop Elements enables you to correct overly bright backgrounds and restore detail to your images. In Figure 9.6, you can see the results in action. The inset rectangle shows the Adjust Backlighting command applied to just a portion of the picture. Notice how more mountain detail is revealed.

Figure 9.6

Backlighting brings washed-out details into prominence.

Adjusting Brightness and Contrast

Sometimes, you may have an image that looks perfectly fine on glossy photo paper. It's well composed, the lighting is terrific, the colors are smashing. But when you scan the image and open it in Photoshop Elements, it just looks dark and less contrasty than you expect. Such deficiencies commonly occur with poor-quality scanners, but you can fix them quickly with some enhancements of brightness and contrast.

Try it yourself by opening the *lakescene.tif* image from the Chapter 9 folder of this book's CD-ROM. Choose File → Save As to save the file on your hard disk with the name *lakescene2.tif*. Then Choose Enhance → Adjust Brightness/Contrast →

Brightness/Contrast, select Preview, and drag the Brightness and Contrast sliders to the right to increase the associated values. Move the Brightness slider to a setting of +19, and the Contrast slider to a setting of +16. Because you've selected Preview, Photoshop Elements shows you how your results will look, before you confirm your changes. The results look bright and sunny again, as shown on the right in Figure 9.7, next to the original version on the left. Click OK.

In Focus

Does the Brightness/ Contrast dialog box obscure your view of your original image? If you want, you can simply click its blue title bar and drag it around your window to reveal any portions of your picture obscured beneath it.

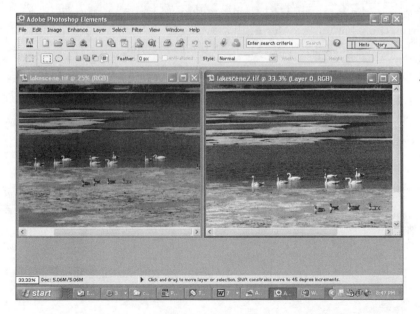

Figure 9.7

Brightness/Contrast adjustments work well for good images.

Adjusting Colors

Brightness/Contrast adjustments are good for making an image look brighter and more lively. But they don't change the image's colors. When you corrected *lakescene2. tif* by changing the brightness and contrast, the water lilies and other plants floating in the water came out looking pretty yellow. You can brighten the image while changing the color (or, as it's sometimes known, the *hue*) by choosing Enhance → Adjust Color and choosing one of the submenu options.

When you choose Enhance → Adjust Color → Hue/Saturation, for instance, you view the Hue and Saturation dialog box, which enables you to interactively adjust the colors within your image.

Hue/Saturation

The power and flexibility of the Hue/Saturation dialog box comes from its capability to adjust colors while changing brightness as well. Whenever you select (or remove) colors from this set of colors, you change the portions that Photoshop Elements adjusts for changes in hue, saturation, and lightness. This enables you to enhance the presentation of, for example, just the reds in your image, or soften just the blues—a powerful option when you want to add strong artistic touches to your pictures.

Follow these steps to adjust the colors in the same image you worked on previously. Keep *lakescene2.tif* open in the Photoshop Elements window. Open the original *lakescene.tif* image from the Chapter 9 folder of this book's CD-ROM again, and save it to disk with the file name of *lakescene3.tif*. Then do the following:

1. Choose Enhance → Adjust Color → Hue/Saturation.

2. Leave Master selected in the Range drop-down list.

3. Move the Hue slider to the right to the +9 setting and watch the lilies grow green again.

4. Move the Saturation slider to the right to the +5 setting to increase the intensity of colors.

5. Move the Lightness slider to the +12 setting to brighten the lake scene.

6. To apply your changes, click OK.

After you click OK, Photoshop Elements applies the changes to your brighter, greener picture.

Color Variations

There's another excellent choice for beginners lurking at the bottom of the Adjust Color submenu: Color Variations.

When you choose Enhance → Adjust Color → Color Variations, you open the Color Variations dialog box, which provides those of us who aren't familiar with blending colors with a way to visually adjust color in an image.

Like the QuickFix dialog box, Color Variations gives you a Before and After view of the image you're working on. First, select a characteristic of the image that you want to work with (midtones, shadows, highlights, or saturation). Then click one of the thumbnail images to alter the image. The effect is displayed instantly in the After box at the top. For *reallybad.tif*, it turns out that if you consistently lighten the midtones, shadows, and highlights, and choose less saturation, the bottom half of the image is clearly improved over the top (see Figure 9.8).

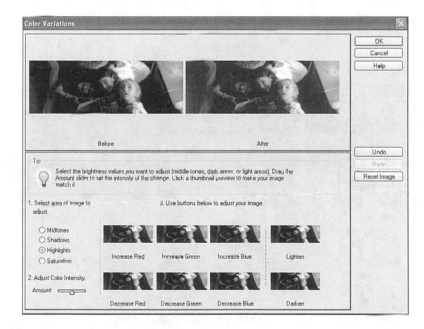

Figure 9.8

Color Variations visually guides you through color corrections.

Getting the Red Out

"Smile! Look at the camera!" With these words, your subject turns right towards your camera lens and, in a flash—literally, an electronic flash—his or her photo is taken. The problem is, the subject has fallen victim to the dreaded red-eye syndrome; when you view the photo, the subject's pupils seem to be red rather than their natural color.

Red eye results when the flash is reflected directly off the eye's retina. Photoshop Elements has a quick fix for red eye that can remove the red with just a few clicks. To try it out for yourself, follow these steps:

1. Open the *redeye.tif* file from the Chapter 9 folder on this book's CD-ROM. Choose File → Save As to save the file on your hard disk with the file name *redeye2.tif*.

2. Click the Zoom tool in the toolbox (it's in the bottom row of tools on the right).

3. With the Zoom tool, click the eyes of the child in the photo. Click two or three times until you can clearly see the pupils of the red eyes.

4. Click the Red Eye Brush in the toolbox (it's the seventh tool from the top on the right).

5. In the Red Eye Brush tool's options bar (see Figure 9.9), click the Size drop-down list. Move the slider to the left and select 10px (10 pixels). You want a brush size that covers the red pupil in the image.

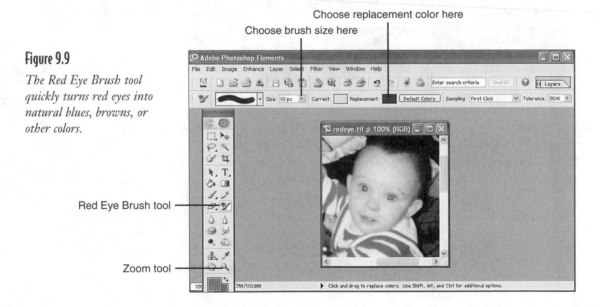

Figure 9.9

The Red Eye Brush tool quickly turns red eyes into natural blues, browns, or other colors.

6. Move the Red Eye Brush tool over the red area and notice that the red color appears in the Current Color box.

7. Do one of two things to select a replacement color: Click Default Colors to choose black, or click the color box next to Replacement to display the Color Picker. Click a color in the Color Picker and click OK.

8. Click over the center of one red eye with the Red Eye Brush tool, and then click over the second eye.

9. Click Save to save your changes. If you want, reopen the original *redeye.tif* file to compare the change in eye color.

In Focus _____

If you have a printed photo with a red-eye problem you want to correct, scan the image at a high resolution such as 200 or 300 dpi. The higher the resolution, the more easily you'll be able to focus in on the eyes you need to recolor.

In this chapter you have seen how to apply some quick fixes to your pictures in ways that don't require you to sweat a lot. In the following chapter, you'll learn how to apply more detailed changes in a more controlled way.

The Least You Need to Know

◆ The QuickFix dialog box repairs images more quickly than many individual menu commands.

◆ The Straighten and Crop Image QuickFix command can correct crooked scans instantly.

◆ The brightness and contrast adjustments can improve good photo scans that were too dark.

◆ The hue and saturation adjustments make an image brighter while adjusting the color at the same time.

◆ The Red Eye Brush tool instantly changes red eyes to more natural colors.

Chapter 10

Working with Colors

In This Chapter

- ◆ Redistributing an image's range of colors
- ◆ Brightening or darkening an image
- ◆ Boosting color saturation
- ◆ Removing a color cast from an image
- ◆ Replacing colors within an image

Photoshop Elements is great for providing instant fixes you can apply to an image with just a couple of mouse clicks—like the "QuickFix" options described in Chapter 9. But sometimes those quick Enhance menu options—Auto Levels, Auto Contrast, and Auto Color Correction—aren't enough to breathe life into dreary, muddy images that just leave you feeling down in the dumps.

In this chapter, you'll learn some approaches to color correction that are guaranteed to pick up your spirits and make you a better—not to mention smarter—image editor. First, though, we provide an overview of the color models you can work with in Photoshop Elements. The theory is that, once you know how digital images get their colors, you can apply some intelligent corrections to them.

You'll also learn how to choose foreground and background colors and adjust your monitor to display colors accurately. Then you'll use the powerful Levels command to redistribute the colors within an image, and use Variations to adjust the intensity of colors. Finally, you'll learn how to change the hue-saturation-brightness qualities within an image as well as blending colors. By the time you've tried this chapter's exercises, you may just want to abandon the "quick fix" route and take charge of the colors in your images.

Color Modes

As you learned in Chapter 4, most images you are likely to work with in Photoshop Elements are made up of bits of digital information called *pixels*. You're probably wondering how, exactly, those tiny little pixels, crammed 150 or 300 in a single inch, convey the rich variety of colors in a photo. A single digital photo can have a million or more distinct colors in it.

How is it possible to reproduce that number of colors? Your printer doesn't have a million different ink containers in it—rather, you have three or four or more different ink colors, and your printer uses these colors in different color combinations. The combination of inks is called a *color mode*. The following sections describe color modes you can use with Photoshop Elements. You can get a quick look at them by choosing Image → Mode from the Photoshop Elements menu bar. As Figure 10.1 shows, a popup menu appears with the color modes listed.

Figure 10.1

Color modes are ways of reproducing color in an image.

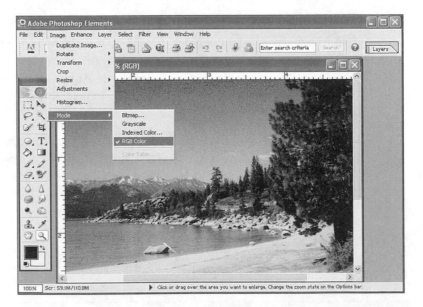

RGB

Click File → Open from the Photoshop Elements menu bar. In the Open dialog box, click the Look In drop-down menu and open the Chapter 10 folder on this book's CD-ROM. Double-click the *lake.tif* file to open it. Look at the image's blue title bar.

The term "RGB" appears there to tell you that the image uses a *color mode* called RGB, which means that all the colors in the image come from different combinations of red, green, and blue light.

Because they are the primary colors in the color spectrum, red, green, and blue can reproduce everything from white to black. If you combine all three colors at 100-percent intensity, you get white; turn off all three colors and you get the absence of color: black. For images you intend to view onscreen, print on your printer, or e-mail to friends, RGB is the color mode to choose.

Shop Talk

Does the term **color mode** sound confusing? Think of a combination of colors as a *color model*: a method of reproducing a real-world object with an infinite variety of colors on a device that only has a few primary colors to work with. That "device" might be a monitor, scanner, or a printer.

CMYK

The color catalogs you get in the mail, the brochures you pick up at museums, or the color photo books you purchase at bookstores all use a different color model: CMYK. CMYK uses combinations of four printers' inks: cyan, magenta, yellow, and black (a K represents black rather than B, so B isn't misunderstood as blue).

Printers typically print color booklets by first separating color images into the four colors and making plates of them. The cyan plate contains only the cyan parts of the image; the magenta plate contains only magenta, and so on. The four plates are attached to printing presses that print the four colors onto paper. This is called four-color process printing, and it's the standard way of printing color publications.

What does all this mean for you, the Photoshop Elements user? If you are planning to send your images to a printer to have a brochure or other publication printed, use CMYK mode. Otherwise, stick with RGB.

Indexed Color

Color images that are intended for reproduction on web pages need to have special qualities. For one thing, they need to be compressed. File compression keeps the file size small, which means they appear more quickly in a Web browser window. They also need to be saved in one of three file formats specially designed for the web: Joint Photographic Experts Group (JPEG), Graphics Interchange Format (GIF), or Portable Network Graphics (PNG).

Of the three web formats, GIF and PNG support a special "stripped-down" variety of color model called indexed color. Indexed color uses only a fixed palette of colors (such as 256 or 216) in an image. By limiting the number of colors in the image, the file size is greatly reduced. GIF and PNG are excellent formats for preparing line art for the web because such drawings don't need as many different colors as photos. For photos, you should use JPEG, which uses the RGB model and can have millions of colors.

You can get a look at an image's color palette by opening a file in Chapter 10 folder on this book's CD-ROM, *gargoyle.tif*. Choose Image → Mode → Color Table, and the color palette (Photoshop Elements uses the term "table" instead of "palette") appears, as Figure 10.2 shows.

Figure 10.2

Indexed color draws colors from a simplified palette/table.

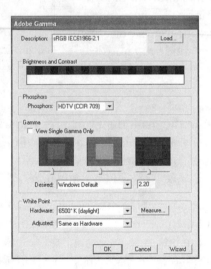

Grayscale

You probably call photos that aren't in color "black and white" images. But if you take a magnifying glass and look at one of these photos closely, how much black and white do you really see? Probably not much. Rather, you see many shades of gray, and that's why graphic designers call these grayscale images.

You can convert the color image *gargoyle.tif* or *lake.tif* instantly to grayscale: Just choose Image → Mode → Grayscale. A dialog box appears, asking you to confirm that you really want to discard the color information in the image. Click OK, and the colors are changed to shades of gray. Click Step Backward (or press Ctrl+Z on Windows, Cmd+Z on a Mac) to undo the change.

Managing Color

Now that you have a basic overview of the different types of color models supported by Photoshop Elements, you can learn exactly how to work with these colors. Remember, though, that it's pretty much impossible to perfectly reproduce real-world colors because monitors can't display them adequately and software programs can only work with a finite number of colors. Your goal, therefore, is to use get the most accurate color reproduction you can, so you can make the best images possible.

Gamma

While most of this book focuses on Photoshop Elements for obvious reasons, there's a "silent partner" that you depend on every step of the way as you open, edit, and save digital images. It's that big screen you look at all the time: your computer monitor.

When you install Photoshop Elements, you get a tool for calibrating your monitor so it can interpret and display colors accurately. It's called the Adobe Gamma Control Panel, and you use it by following these steps:

1. In Windows, choose Start → Control Panel and, when the Control Panel window opens, double-click Adobe Gamma. On a Mac, choose Apple → Control Panels → Adobe Gamma.

2. When the Adobe Gamma window appears, click Control Panel, and then click Next.

3. In the next Adobe Gamma window, uncheck the box next to View Single Gamma Only. Three color swatches appear in red, green, and blue.

4. Move each of the sliders to the left or right so that the inner section of each color swatch matches the outer section. (The inner section of each color swatch should almost disappear.)

5. Click OK.

6. When the Save As dialog box appears, click Save to save the color information you created on your hard disk.

In Focus

Click the Wizard button at the bottom of the Adobe Gamma window if you want to be led step-by-step through the process of creating a color profile that your monitor can use.

What you've just done is provide Photoshop Elements with information about your monitor's color profile. Photoshop Elements can then adjust the display of images accordingly so the colors in those images are more accurate.

Picking Colors

Once you've calibrated your monitor and absorbed some general introductory information about color modes, you can finally go about picking colors.

The first thing you need to know about colors in Photoshop Elements is that you have two general types of colors you can work with: a foreground color and a background color. The tools that control these colors are located at the bottom of the toolbox, as shown in Figure 10.3.

Figure 10.3

These icons let you choose foreground or background colors for an image.

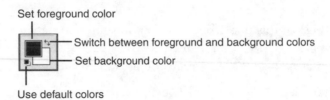

Set foreground color

Switch between foreground and background colors

Set background color

Use default colors

Open *lake.tif* in the Photoshop Elements window, and click the background color. (By default, the background color is white, and the foreground color is black.) The background color icon jumps to the front. Click the Switch foreground and background colors arrows, and the two icons switch places.

Next, click the Set Foreground Color icon. The Color Picker dialog box appears (see Figure 10.4).

Figure 10.4

The Color Picker gives you a way to select colors you can apply to an image.

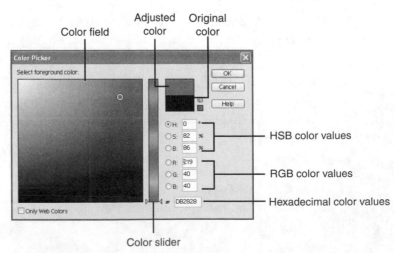

Color field

Adjusted color

Original color

HSB color values

RGB color values

Hexadecimal color values

Color slider

Move the mouse pointer over the Color field (the large box that contains a rainbow of colors); it turns into a circle. Click in the Color field to select a color; the color you select appears in the Adjusted Color box. In addition, notice that a wealth of information about the selected color appears, including numbers in the R, G, and B boxes that represent exactly how much red, green, and blue are contained in this color (the numbers vary from 0 to 255).

Click OK to close the Color Picker and return to the Photoshop Elements window. The selected color appears in the Set foreground color box at the bottom of the toolbox. You can now apply this color to an image. Click the Brush tool and draw with it directly on the open image *lake.tif*. When you're done, click Cancel. Once you've picked a color, you can apply it to an image with many of the toolbox tools, including the Brush, Pencil, and Paint Bucket tool. They, and other more advanced tools such as the Eyedropper and Clone Stamp tools, are discussed later in this book.

> **It's Element-ary**
>
> It's easy to apply foreground colors to an image. But what about the background colors? The background doesn't appear in a digital photo, but it is an essential part of vector drawings you create with Photoshop Elements. When you use the Eraser tool, you're painting on the background color in order to remove details from the foreground.

> **It's Element-ary**
>
> The color adjustments in this chapter assume that you have some basic knowledge of the two color modes, red-green-blue (RGB) and cyan-magenta-yellow-black (CMYK). If you need a refresher course, refer to Chapter 4.

Getting Your Images on the Level

Even though an image can have millions of different colors distributed in one of a number of color modes, these colors may not be distributed along the full spectrum of white to black. If you use an older or primitive scanner, for instance, you may run into this problem—the scanner is able to capture millions of colors, but it doesn't distribute those colors evenly. The result is that scanned images that appear darker, more bland, less lively, and *blah*—you choose the descriptive term. The solution is to turn to the Levels dialog box to redistribute colors the way they were meant to be.

Why Adjust Levels Yourself?

You've probably had the following experience: You come up with a terrific photo from your vacation by the ocean that you're eager to e-mail to your sister across the country. You plop the image onto the scanner, run it through, save it up, and open it in

Photoshop Elements. Your jaw drops: What happened to those bright sparkling whites and rich deep blacks in your image?

You'll find an example image in the Chapter 10 folder on this book's CD-ROM; open up the scanned file *heron.tif* and save it to your hard disk so you can adjust it. (By saving it to your hard disk you preserve the original version so you can compare it later.) This file might look good all by itself, as long as you don't know that it was taken on a bright, sunny day in Florida rather than a cloudy and increasingly overcast afternoon in, say, New Jersey. Figure 10.5 shows the *heron.tif* file.

Figure 10.5

Scanners can take the life out of photos, but you can revive them by adjusting Levels.

You could apply a QuickFix to this image: Try it now by choosing Enhance → Auto Levels. This brightens up the image considerably, but leaves it with an unnatural bluish cast. The reason is that Auto Levels applies the same level of correction evenly to each of the image's color channels. The problem in this case is that the blue channel didn't need as much correction as red and green. By changing all the levels automatically, the color balance has been tipped toward blue.

You could also try Enhance → Auto Color Correction. Try it now; the colors are improved considerably and without adding a bluish color cast. But they're not as vibrant as the original. Click Step Backward in the shortcuts bar to undo Auto Levels. To gain control over color correction, you need to adjust levels on your own using the Levels dialog box.

> **Shop Talk**
>
> When the balance of colors in an image tips toward one color predominantly, the image is said to have a color cast. This chapter encourages you to change colors in a balanced, natural way so you don't have a cast. You'll learn about fixing color casts later in this chapter in the section named (surprise!) "Removing a Color Cast."

In Focus

See this book's color insert for examples of the heron image described in this section. You'll see the original, the Auto Levels fix, and the Levels dialog box adjustment all together so you can compare different color correction methods for yourself.

The Levels Dialog Box

To change color levels in a more controlled way and venture boldly into the world of professional color correction, open the Levels dialog box by using either of the following methods:

◆ Choose Enhance → Adjust Brightness/Contrast → Levels.

◆ Press Ctrl+L.

When you open the Levels dialog box for the first time (see Figure 10.6), you're likely to be a little intimidated by it. Don't be. You don't need to learn to use every button, box, or drop-down menu option in the dialog box. You can achieve good color correction results by just using a few of the most important tools.

It's Element-ary

You also open the Levels dialog box when you create an Adjustment layer to change colors in a multilayered image, as described in Chapter 9.

Histogram

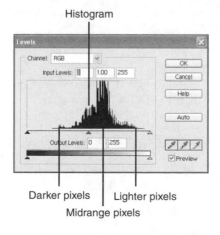

Figure 10.6

Levels redistribute colors to improve brightness and contrast.

Darker pixels   Lighter pixels

Midrange pixels

That big black blob in the middle of the dialog box that looks either like a mountain range or something vaguely medical has a medical-sounding name: *histogram*. It's a visual map of the image's colors. The shapes on the left show the darker pixels in the range of colors; the shapes on the right are the lighter pixels. In the middle are the midtones.

Play doctor for a moment and diagnose what's wrong with this image. For one thing, you'll notice that the range of colors is very narrow—the colors are all bunched in the large peaks in the center. The colors don't extend all the way out to the edge as they would if they were more evenly distributed. By making colors extend farther into the lighter and darker pixels, you'll improve the contrast and balance of your colors dramatically.

If you want to see a more balanced histogram, one in which the colors are distributed more evenly across the full color spectrum, click OK to close the Levels dialog box, then click the Open button in the Photoshop Elements shortcuts bar. Then navigate to *carp.psd*, one of the sample files that come with the program (it's in C:\Program Files\ Adobe\Photoshop Elements 2\Samples). Figure 10.7 shows this image's histogram.

Figure 10.7

This screen shot shows a more balanced color histogram.

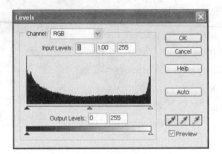

Swatch Out!

Don't get the impression that every histogram has to look exactly like *carp.psd*'s. If, for example, you open the other sample image files that come with Photoshop Elements, you'll see a wide range of histogram shapes. Every image has to be judged on its own visual merits. Only if you feel that more contrast and brightness are needed should you turn to the Levels dialog box.

Also, because the file *carp.psd* contains text, you may see a warning message if you don't have a font installed in your system. Don't worry; just click OK and Photoshop Elements will substitute a font you do have available.

Adjusting Levels

The other important parts of the Levels dialog box that you need to know about are as follows:

- The three triangles just beneath the histogram are sliders that you move to the left and right to map the image's actual colors to the full range of white-to-black colors.

- The three Input Levels boxes just above the histogram give you a measurement so you can evaluate the distribution of the lightest, medium, and darkest pixels in your image.

- The Preview check box is best left checked so that, as you make adjustments by moving the sliders, you can see the effect in your image.

Adjusting levels is a difficult concept to understand, because you don't actually take parts of the image's histogram and reshape it to redistribute the colors. Rather, you move the three triangular sliders so that the image's lighter pixels are closer to the white end of the spectrum (as represented by the slider on the right) the image's darker pixels are closer to the dark end of the spectrum (as represented by the slider on the left) and the image's midtones are either lighter or darker. As usual, such a concept becomes clearer when you actually do it yourself:

1. Drag the triangle on the left toward the right until it intersects with the point where colors begin to peak, which represents the darker colors in your image.

2. Drag the triangle on the right toward the left until it intersects with the right edge of the histogram.

3. Drag the slider in the middle if you feel you need to adjust the midtones of the image. It's often a good idea to leave this alone and move the other two triangles first.

Figure 10.8 shows the arrangement of triangles. You'll find Levels adjustments easier to understand if you make believe that the triangle on the left represents absolute bright white (which has full complements of red, green, and blue) and the one on the right represents absolute black (or the absence of red, green, and blue).

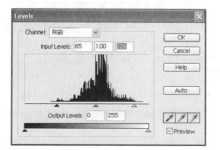

Figure 10.8

By adjusting levels, you make an image's existing colors more evenly distrib-uted.

A box showing gradations from white to black has been added beneath the sliders. This box doesn't actually appear in the Levels dialog box, which has had its confusing Output Levels and slider removed for greater clarity. Hopefully, the additional box helps you understand what you're doing when you move the triangles—you're mapping the colors in the image closer to the full range of tones rather than being stuck mostly in the middle of the full range of tones.

After you move the "Black" and "White" sliders you can move the middle slider to make the image's midrange (or medium) colors darker or lighter. This often produces the most satisfying changes, so take some time with it. A darker effect is shown on the left in Figure 10.9; a lighter one is shown on the right.

Figure 10.9

Move the middle slider to lighten or darken midrange colors.

Move slider to left   Move slider to right

As you move the sliders, notice that the numbers in the Input Levels boxes change accordingly—0 represents black and 255 represents white. There isn't any exact science to how much you should change the levels to produce an image you want; it is a matter of trial and error, and you should feel free to experiment with the controls until you achieve the result you want.

When you're satisfied with the corrected image, click OK to close the Levels dialog box and view the result. Figure 10.10 compares the original with the improved version.

Figure 10.10

A lifeless scan is quickly revived by a few Levels corrections.

Changing Color Variations to Boost Saturation

In many cases, simply changing the levels of brightness and contrast in an image can make a dramatic change in its range of colors. But remember that, when you adjust levels, you're not directly adjusting the colors—you're making the existing colors more vibrant and, for want of a better word, contrasty. When you move the midrange slider to the left, you make the midrange colors lighter, and they lose their intensity—which is also called *saturation*.

If you find that some of the colors in your image are more muted after making adjustments in the Levels dialog box, try adjusting Color Variations to boost their intensity:

Shop Talk

Saturation is the technical term used to describe the intensity of colors. If you want to sound like a real graphic designer, don't say colors are more intense; say they're more saturated.

1. Open the corrected version of *heron.tif* in the Photoshop Elements window if it isn't already open.

2. Choose Enhance → Adjust Color → Color Variations to make the Color Variations dialog box take over practically your entire screen (see Figure 10.11).

Figure 10.11

You can use Color Variations to fix a color cast.

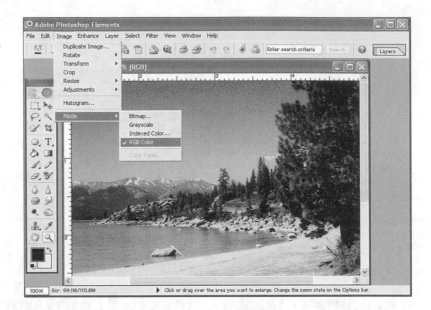

3. Click the Saturation radio button to make most of the preview images disappear. The ones that remain represent different levels of color intensity—that is, saturation.

4. Click the bottom image (the one labeled "More Saturation"). The After image near the top of the Color Variations dialog box shows how the image will look with more saturation.

5. Click OK to close Color Variations and apply the change. A livelier and considerably happier-looking heron appears.

You can use the Adjust Color Intensity slider near the bottom left-hand corner of the Color Variations dialog box if you want even more or less saturation than the preview images show, but it doesn't always give you a large amount of control—the changes are often too coarse to be realistic.

Removing a Color Cast

Like a cast that you wear on your arm or leg, a color cast in an image seems to weigh it down and obscure what's really underneath. You often encounter color casts when working with old family photos that have been lying around in albums growing yellow with age. Photoshop Elements gives you an excellent way to throw off that old color cast to give your old images a new lease on life.

Color Cast Repair: The Express Way

As usual, Photoshop Elements provides a couple of options for repairing a color cast—an "express" route and a roundabout "scenic" route that takes longer but is ultimately more rewarding.

First, the express route. Open the file with a pronounced color cast that is provided for you on this book's CD-ROM and that has the obvious file name *colorcast.tif*. This is a family photo showing one of this book's authors in his younger and more vulnerable years sitting on his mother's lap. Your job is to get rid of the apparent sunburn afflicting both mother and child (and the wall and couch, for that matter) while preserving the bright red of the baby outfit and hopefully bringing out some more green in the Christmas tree in the background.

In Focus

If you select, in error, a portion of your image that is not black/white/gray, choose Edit → Undo Color Sample. To revert your image entirely, click the Reset button on the dialog box.

First, save the file to your hard disk so you can work on it while preserving the original version. Next, choose Enhance → Adjust Color → Color Cast. The Color Cast Correction dialog box appears (see Figure 10.12).

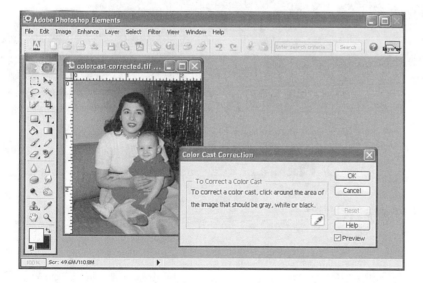

Figure 10.12

Photoshop Elements leads you interactively through the steps involved in correcting a color cast.

As instructed, while the Color Cast Correction dialog box is open, pass your mouse pointer over the image (you'll notice that it appears as an Eyedropper tool). Click the part of the image that you want to be black. In *colorcast.tif*, the obvious choice is mama's hair. When you do this you are identifying one end of the color spectrum (black) so you can reset the range of colors in the image.

In Focus

You don't have to color-correct an entire image when fixing a color cast. If you only want to correct part of an image, select that portion using one of the selection tools, and then choose Enhance → Adjust Color → Color Cast.

Next, click a part of the image that should be pure white so you can identify the end of the color spectrum. In *colorcast.tif*, that means clicking mama's white sweater. A miraculous change occurs. If an area existed in this image that should obviously be gray to identify a midtone color—but there isn't one, so just stick with black and white for this image. Click OK to close the Color Cast Correction dialog box and enjoy the new and improved image—but just for a moment. Click Step Backward in the shortcuts bar to restore the image to its original state so you can try another way to correct it.

Color Cast Repair: The Do-It-Yourself Way

Quick methods don't always work. If you don't like the "express" way of correcting a color cast, you can use the Variations dialog box, which enables you to correct one color at a time instead of all colors at once.

To use this method, open the uncorrected version of *colorcast.tif* and choose Enhance → Adjust Colors → Color Variations. The Color Variations dialog box appears. You've got a dizzying array of options: Which one do you choose? The image seems bright enough, so you don't need to change highlights or shadows. The red in the baby suit indicates that colors have sufficient saturation, too. Click Midtones to focus on the image's medium tones.

In Focus

Sometimes you don't want to adjust colors. Instead, you want to remove them entirely and turn your picture into a black-and-white image. To do this, choose Enhance → Adjust Color → Remove Color. Photoshop Elements re-moves all color from your image.

Click each of the variations in turn to see its effect in the After box. If the After box becomes muddled or you're unclear as to just how many color changes have been made, click Reset Image. In our opinion, the most obvious option is the only one you need to choose: Reduce Red. Click Reduce Red and then click OK to remove the color cast while preserving the current saturation levels in the image.

Chances are you'll get better results by using Variations to remove a color cast than the Color Cast menu option. Figure 10.13 shows a comparison of the various results (also refer to this book's color insert section for a comparison). (Focus on the Christmas tree in the background—you'll see that it's far less red, and more realistically green, in the version corrected with Color Variations.)

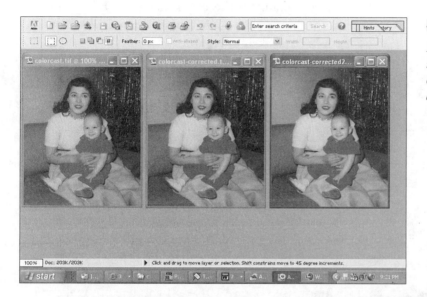

Figure 10.13

From the left: The original image, the Color Cast menu option, and Color Variations *correction results compared.*

It's Element-ary

As a newbie to image editing, you're likely to jump to the Brightness/Contrast dialog box (Enhance → Adjust Brightness/Contrast → Brightness/Contrast). The Levels dialog box gives you a far more sophisticated way to adjust the brightness and contrast in color and black-and-white images.

The Hue/Saturation dialog box (Enhance → Adjust Color → Hue/Saturation) is just too complex for casual users—and besides, much of its functionality is covered by the Variations and Replace Color commands, which this chapter discusses elsewhere.

If you're skeptical, open the original version of *colorcast.tif* and try to color-correct it using Brightness/Contrast or Hue/Saturation. Chances are you'll be running quickly back to the Color Variations dialog box, which gives you visual cues to how to correct colors that are far easier to use.

Replacing Colors

Sometimes, all the corrections in the world can make an image look better overall but fail to change one color that needs to be different. In *colorcast.tif*, for instance, you can use the Color Variations dialog box to change the colors overall, but there's the nagging problem of the mother's sweater, which appears far yellower than she would have liked in real life.

You can "launder" the sweater—or change any single color to a different color—by using the Replace Color command. Replacing a color is a two-part process: First you select what you want to replace, and then you transform it. To apply the process to an image yourself, open the color-corrected version of *colorcast.tif*, and select the sweater.

Once you select the sweater, choose Enhance → Adjust Color → Replace Color to display the Replace Color dialog box. Make sure the Selection radio button is clicked. Click anywhere on the sweater, either within the Replace Color dialog box or the image window (see Figure 10.14). If you need to make your selection area either larger or smaller, move the Fuzziness slider (move it to the right to make the selection bigger or move it to the left to shrink it).

Once the area you want is selected, move the Saturation and Lightness sliders in the Transform section of the Replace Color dialog box to the right to change the color of the selected area to something whiter (don't move them all the way, or you'll end up with an unnaturally bright white). (Notice that the selected color appears in the Foreground Color box, too, in case you want to use it elsewhere.) When you're satisfied, click OK.

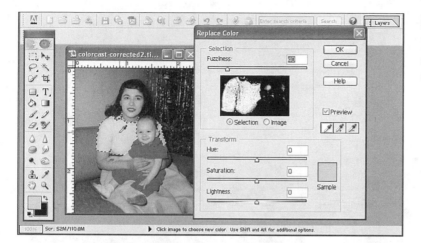

Figure 10.14

This dialog box lets you instantly replace a single color.

The Least You Need to Know

◆ The Levels command is one of the most effective ways to color-correct an image.

◆ The three triangular sliders in the Levels dialog box let you redistribute an image's range of colors.

◆ Auto Levels adjusts all color levels equally, which can produce a color cast.

◆ You can use Color Variations to boost the saturation of colors and to remove a color cast.

◆ The Replace Colors command lets you select a color and then replace it with another.

Retouching and Editing Images

In This Chapter

- ◆ Improving lighting problems by dodging and burning
- ◆ Changing color intensity by sponging selected areas
- ◆ Smoothing out rough spots by smudging
- ◆ Focusing in on selected areas by sharpening
- ◆ Helping colors blend smoothly by blurring

Sometimes it seems like everybody's getting a digital face-lift these days. Supermodel Cindy Crawford had her belly button erased on the cover of *Elle* magazine in 1998; actor Harrison Ford had the famous scar on his chin removed on the cover of *Premiere* magazine.

You, too, can get some wrinkles tucked or some strands of thinning hair added in with the magic of the Photoshop Elements image-editing tools. The process of altering photos by actually touching the surface of the image is called *retouching*. Retouching used to be something only trained professionals could do, and they only had tools like airbrushes available that seem crude compared to what Photoshop Elements provides you.

Shop Talk

Retouching is the process of changing the appearance of selected areas within a photograph. Lightening areas that seem too dark, blurring colors so they blend more smoothly, and erasing or adding details are all examples of retouching.

This chapter gives you hands-on experience altering photos using editing tools with the descriptive names of Smudge, Blur, Sharpen, Dodge, Burn, and Sponge. Each of these tools either lets you move pixels around or change the color of individual pixels—often, using colors borrowed from the image itself so you can make flaws or other features seem to disappear. You don't *have* to retouch images, of course, and if you don't like what you've done, Photoshop Elements always gives you the chance to back out and undo your work. But if the occasion calls for it, there's no cosmetic problem you can't solve with the help of the Photoshop Elements retouching tools.

Retouching to Solve Lighting Problems

One of the problems that most commonly leads to photos being tossed in the garbage is backlighting—you point the camera directly into the sun, and you don't adjust for the bright light shining directly at you, so the details you want to see in the foreground are left in shadow.

The opposite can also occur—too much light leaves someone looking unrealistically pale or even featureless. The Dodge and Burn tools can help you bring life back to over- or underexposed parts of an image.

Dodging to Lighten the Dark Areas

Dodging is a term that comes from traditional photo developing. It was commonly done in newspaper photography; as a print was being exposed to light in the darkroom, the technician would constantly wave (or "dodge") a little tool over part of the image that needed to be lightened. The part of the image beneath the tool would be exposed to less light and thus turn out lighter than the rest of the image.

You'll now use the Photoshop Elements Dodge tool to lighten part of a photo by following these steps:

1. Open the *dodge.tif* file located in the Chapter 11 folder on the CD-ROM that comes with this book.

2. Choose File → Save As and save the file to your hard disk with a different file name.

3. Click the Dodge tool in the toolbox. You'll find the Dodge tool in the third section from the top, along with the software's other retouching tools (see Figure 11.1).

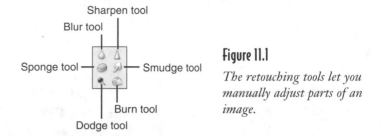

Figure 11.1

The retouching tools let you manually adjust parts of an image.

4. Choose View → Zoom In to zoom in on the face of the girl in *dodge.tif*. (You may want to zoom in more than once.)

5. Set the Dodge tool options in the options bar. Click the arrow next to Size and adjust the size to 20px (20 pixels); choose Shadows from the Range drop-down list; choose 5% from the Exposure drop-down list.

6. Click and hold down the mouse button over the face of the girl in the lower left. Do this quickly—move in a circular motion around the girl's head for a count of three and then release the mouse. Click Step Backward in the shortcuts bar if you're unhappy with the result and want to try again.

7. Move the Dodge tool across the left side of the face of the girl with the dark hair. The faces of the two girls in the middle of the group should begin to emerge. Figure 11.2 shows the original on the left, and the corrected version on the right.

CAUTION

Swatch Out!

Use the Dodge tool sparingly. It's easy to overuse it so that part of an image turns out looking washed-out and unrealistically light in relation to its surroundings. The lower the Exposure setting, the more subtle the dodging effect.

Figure 11.2

Dodging can bring out parts of an image that are in shadow.

The Dodge tool options give you more control over the effect. Choosing Midtones or Highlights lets you lighten parts of an image that aren't in shadow. Setting the Exposure to a higher level lightens more quickly—though you should probably start with a lower setting and move up to a higher one gradually.

Burning in More Detail

Burning is the opposite of dodging: You take part of an image that's washed-out and overexposed and create more definition by giving it more contrast and making it darker.

Try out the Burn tool yourself by opening *burn.tif* from the Chapter 11 folder on this book's CD-ROM, saving it to your hard disk, and clicking the Burn tool in the toolbox. Click View → Zoom In a couple of times so you can zoom in on the pale-faced little girl. Click, hold down, and move the Burn tool around the girl's face. Choose a size of 20–25 pixels for the tool, and set the Exposure to about 10 percent. This time choose High-lights from the Range drop-down list.

Make your movements in short, one- or two-second bursts—this way, if you are unhappy with your work (and you might be, the first time you try it), you can click Step Backward to undo the correction in stages.

In Focus

With Burn and all retouching tools, it pays to be subtle and gentle. Choose an extra-low Exposure setting, such as 3 to 5 percent, to make subtle changes. Otherwise, you'll be drawing stripes across the light parts of your image.

For added practice, try to add some texture to the girl's dress. Choose Midtones from the drop-down list, and make the tool size 40 pixels (a larger tool means the movements across the dress will be less visible).

It's a good idea to open the original version of the image from this book's CD-ROM and have its image window open next to the image window of the version you are retouching. This way, you can compare the "before" and "after" effects, as Figure 11.3 shows.

Figure 11.3

The Burn tool lets you add details to a selected part of an image.

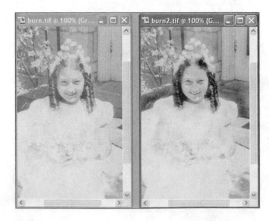

Sponging to Change Saturation

The Sponge tool gives you another way to make selected areas of an image lighter or darker. The Sponge tool, unlike the Dodge or Burn tools, either removes or adds color from the area you're working on (it doesn't work on grayscale images). It takes the existing colors and either makes them lighter or darker. If you add color to part of an image, you can use the Sponge tool to make slight adjustments rather than undoing and then colorizing all over again.

The Sponge tool is especially good when you want to make, for example, an individual person stand out from his or her surroundings in a color photo. You can either make the person more or less colorful, depending on the option you choose in the Sponge tool's options bar settings.

Open the *sponge.tif* image from this book's CD-ROM, save it on your hard disk, and click the Sponge tool. Choose 40px by clicking the down arrow and then moving the Size slider. Then choose Desaturate from the Mode drop-down list in the options bar to make the colors in this image less saturated—you could hardly make them more saturated. (As you might expect, choosing Saturate would make the existing colors even more pronounced.) Make the Flow setting 50 percent. (The Flow setting controls the rate at which the saturation changes.)

Click, hold down, and move the Sponge tool around the girl at the top of the image to make her stand out from the others by being less red. Remember to move the Sponge tool in short bursts so you can undo your work in stages. Figure 11.4 shows the change.

Figure 11.4

The Sponge tool makes selected colors either more or less saturated.

Retouching to Adjust Texture

One of the most popular reasons to retouch photos is to smooth out skin texture or other kinds of surface problems. Photoshop Elements gives you one retouching tool that's specially designed to smooth out rough edges wherever they occur—the Smudge tool.

Smudging Out the Rough Spots

You might think of smudging as resembling the process patching a plaster wall that has nail holes and hairline cracks in it. You take some spackle or plaster mix and smooth over the imperfections with the paste until the problem areas are covered up. Then after the plaster dries you sand the surface so it's extra smooth.

It's far easier to use Photoshop Elements' Smudge tool to smooth out areas of an image. Find out for yourself by opening the *smudge.tif* file from the Chapter 11 folder on this book's CD-ROM and saving it to your hard disk. Then follow these steps:

1. Click the Smudge tool in the toolbox.

2. Click View → Zoom In or press Ctrl++ (Ctrl plus the plus sign key) (Windows) or Cmd++ (Cmd plus the plus sign key) (Mac) three times to zoom in on the gargoyle's face. The gargoyle has a reason for his complexion problem; he's made of stone and he's been sitting on the side of a building for more than a century. Your job is to make his face look nice and smooth.

3. Set the options for the Smudge tool. Try a Brush size of 25px, choose Lighten from the Mode drop-down list, and set the Pressure to 30 percent.

4. Click the gargoyle's face and rub along it. Try to move with the direction of the folds and bends in the face, as though you're giving the gargoyle a shave—it's more effective to smudge in the direction of imperfections rather than against the grain.

5. After you've gone over the entire face once, choose Midtones from the Range list and repeat Step 4.

6. Make the Smudge tool's size smaller so you can smooth out the dark spot under the gargoyle's nose and any other spots you want to erase.

When you're done, you should have a clean-shaven and happy gargoyle. The corrected version is shown on the right in Figure 11.5.

Figure 11.5

Smudging smoothes out areas of an image that appear rough.

After you've gotten a little experience with the Smudge tool, check out the different settings in its options bar:

◆ Use All Layers is great if you're retouching a multilayered image. Checking this option gives you the ability to choose colors from any of the layers so you can smudge with them.

◆ Finger Painting has nothing to do with that digit next to your thumb. Checking this option causes the Smudge tool to pick up a bit of the current Foreground color at the beginning of your stroke, and then blends that color with the rest of the colors you are retouching.

In Focus

Remember to move in short, controlled segments. Try to release your mouse button periodically. This way, if you make a mistake and smudge more of the image than you wanted, you can click Step Backward and undo only a single change rather than erasing all your work and having to start over from the beginning.

In addition, the settings in the Mode drop-down list let you darken or lighten when you retouch, and give you the chance to change the hue, saturation, or luminosity of the area you are retouching as well.

Retouching to Adjust Clarity

Another set of retouching tools gives you the ability to manually make parts of an image either sharper or less focused. Use them when you need to change one or more parts of the image rather than an entire image. For example, the Sharpen tool comes in handy when you need to sharpen a small area of an image that you can isolate by hand—though, frankly, if you've got a large area or even an entire image you want to sharpen up, you'll probably be better off with one of the sharpening filters described in Chapter 17.

In Focus

The settings given here for strength and size are only suggestions. Sharpening, as with other types of retouching, isn't an exact science. You'll learn the best settings over time by trial and error. Don't be afraid to try different settings and press Ctrl+Z (Windows) or Cmd+Z (Mac) if you want to undo your work and change the settings.

Sharpening Up Fuzzy Spots

To literally get hands-on experience with the Sharpen tool, open the exceedingly blurry photo *sharpen.tif* from the Chapter 11 folder on this book's CD-ROM and save it to your hard disk.

Suppose you only want to sharpen up the faces of the woman and the little boy. Click the Sharpen tool and zoom in on the faces by choosing View → Zoom In or pressing Ctrl++ one or more times. Because this image is very light as well as blurry, choose Darken from the Mode drop-down list to darken it as you sharpen it. Set the Strength to 85 percent, and set the tool size to 6 pixels.

Carefully (this will take a steady hand) draw over the features of the woman's hat and face as though you're tracing it. Pay attention to the eyes, nose, and mouth, and the outline of the face and hat. Then outline the little boy's face. It probably looks, close-up, as though you're damaging the image by adding dark pixels to it. But when you view the images at normal size you can see an improvement—though only a slight one (see Figure 11.6).

Figure 11.6

The Sharpen tool can help darken as well as sharpen selected areas.

To get some experience with some of the other options that Photoshop Elements gives you for sharpening up images, open the original version of *sharpen.tif* and save it with the file name *sharpen-SharpenFilter.tif*. Choose Filter → Sharpen → Sharpen to sharpen the image and compare it to what you did with the Sharpen tool. You can repeat these steps for Sharpen Edges, Sharpen More, and the strongest sharpening filter of all, Unsharp Mask. These options are all compared in Figure 11.7.

Figure 11.7

The Sharpen tool doesn't sharpen as effectively as sharpening filters.

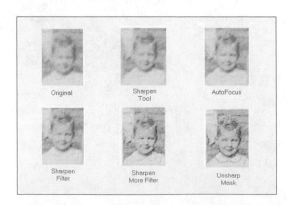

Blurring Distinctions

Having spent a considerable amount of time trying to sharpen the incredibly blurry image in the previous section, you're probably wondering why you'd ever want to *intentionally* blur parts of an image.

The answer is easier to understand if you think about color images and how the colors interact with one another: Blurring becomes useful when you want to soften the area where one color meets another one.

Suppose you copy a piece of one image and paste it so that it's a new layer in a second, completely different, image. That's what was done with the *lake-layers.psd* image, which you'll find with the Chapter 7 files on this book's CD-ROM.

> **It's Element-ary**
>
> If you want to make an entire image more blurry, use one of the software's many blur filters, as described in Chapter 17.

Open *lake-layers.psd*, click the Blur tool, and set the options bar settings as follows: Size: 7 px; Mode: Color; Strength: 85 percent. Then brush around the outline of the hair of the girl on the right. By going around the edge of her hair a few times, you blur the sharp edge where the two images meet, so they blend together more easily. Figure 11.8 shows the original image on the left and one with blurred hair on the right.

Figure 11.8

Blurring helps colors blend together more smoothly.

The Least You Need to Know

◆ Retouching tools enable you to change one area of an image while leaving the rest unaffected.

◆ Retouching requires you to manually move tools over the surface of an image to change it.

◆ Dodging lightens areas of an image, whereas burning darkens selected areas.

◆ Sponging either increases or decreases the saturation of the area you're working on.

◆ Blurring and sharpening let you change the clarity of isolated areas; use a filter to change a whole image.

Saving Early, Often, and in the Right Format

In This Chapter

◆ Learning how saving files can save your work

◆ Saving files with new file names and formats

◆ Compressing your images for e-mail

◆ Transforming an image into a PDF file

◆ Optimizing your work for the World Wide Web

Saving your work is simple when you're working on a text file. But when you've spent considerable time and effort editing, color-correcting, and transforming images using the many powerful tools provided by Photoshop Elements, it's essential to save your work early, often, and in the right format. In this chapter, you'll learn about special considerations when saving image files, including how to optimize images for e-mail, for Adobe Acrobat, and for the World Wide Web.

File-Saving Basics

At its simplest level, saving a copy of an image file in Photoshop Elements is the same as any other program—you save the file to preserve any changes you've made to the file on disk. However, some additional qualities of digital images are associated with how you save the file, and you should know about them:

- **File format**   A format is a standard set of instructions used to save the individual bits of data so that it appears as a digital image. The Photoshop Elements *native* file format is PSD (Photoshop Data). Images saved in PSD format have the file extension *.psd* as well as the capability to save layers.

- **File size**   Image file formats differ in how much space they require to store your picture. The more disk space used, the harder it becomes to transfer your picture over the Internet or store it on traditional computer media.

- **File compression**   This refers to the way that a file format shrinks the size of an image in order to conserve storage space. As file compression increases, file size decreases.

- **Image fidelity**   This refers to the way a picture remains true to the original. Often file compression decreases image fidelity and produces pictures with subtle visual flaws.

- **Artifacts**   An artifact is a portion of an image that did not appear in the original. Artifacts are generally produced by compression that results in the loss of parts of an image and include such features as overall blockiness, graininess, or stray color variations.

As you can see from the preceding list of terms, you have quite a few things to think about when you choose how to save your image files.

In Focus

Compression becomes important whenever digital images need to be transported from one computer or disk to another. But compression schemes differ in how they affect the digital information in an image.

A common side effect of file compression is loss of image fidelity. A *lossy* image compression scheme like the one used by the Joint Photographic Experts Group (JPEG) produces a picture that loses image fidelity. On the other hand, *lossless* compression such as that used by the Tagged Image File Format (TIFF), retains full image fidelity when saved.

Also, it's a good idea to save your work every ten or fifteen minutes or so. This way you won't lose your work in case the power goes out suddenly or your computer crashes for some reason. If you have a file on which you've been working for many hours, create a backup on a Zip or Jaz disk or on another computer for extra protection.

Ready, Set, Save!

If you want to save your work in Photoshop Elements, you can choose from any of the following saving options, using the current default file type:

- ◆ Choose File > Save.
- ◆ Press Ctrl+S (Windows) or Cmd+S (Mac).
- ◆ Click the Save icon on the shortcuts bar.
- ◆ Choose File → Save As if you want to save the file with a different name or in a different format (or both).

Performing any of these operations tells Photoshop Elements to update your image file on disk with any recent changes you've made.

Switching File Types or Names with Save As

You never have to stick with any current file type—or file name, for that matter—if you want to switch to a new one. To save to a new file type or name, first save any changes to your original file by clicking the Save button in the shortcuts bar, and then follow these steps.

1. Choose File → Save As to display the Save As dialog box.

2. Click the arrow next to Save In and choose a location from the drop-down list to locate a directory, disk drive, or network computer where you want to save your file.

3. Enter a new name for your file in the File Name box. (You don't have to change the

It's Element-ary

The Save button is only lit up or "clickable" when you've made changes to a file.

In Focus

In theory, PC users can enter file names up to 255 characters in length, while Mac users can enter names that have as many as 31 characters. In practice, short and recognizable file names work best—they help you quickly find the file you want in a list of files.

file name; you can save with the same name but choose a different file format, as indicated in the next step.)

4. Choose a new file format from the Format drop-down list, as shown in Figure 12.1.

Figure 12.1

Use the Save As dialog box to save your work in a new file type.

5. Click Save.

6. Depending on the file format you chose in Step 4, an options window may appear. If so, set your choices for the options presented to you and click OK.

7. Wait as Photoshop Elements writes your file to disk using the new file format you selected.

After following these steps, you will have converted your file from its original type to a format that you picked.

Understanding File Formats

After viewing the alphabet soup that appears when you click the arrow next to the File Type drop-down list in the Save As dialog box, you might ask yourself, what are all those image file formats, and which is best for me? Here are some descriptions of the formats you're likely to use most often and (in parentheses) the file name extensions that correspond to each one. (Keep in mind, though, that file name extensions are not used on the Mac by default; the Mac doesn't use them unless you transfer files from one computer to another.)

- ◆ **Photoshop Data** (PSD, file name extension *.psd*), the Photoshop Elements native format, is a good choice if you plan to work on the file only in Photoshop Elements, or if you want the image to contain multiple layers (see Chapter 7).

- ◆ **Tagged Image File Format** (TIFF, file name extension *.tif* on Windows, *.tiff* on the Mac) is an excellent choice for high-quality images. When you choose TIFF, Photoshop Elements gives you the option to choose a lossless compression format called LZW, which keeps file sizes smaller. Both options preserve any layers within an image.

- ◆ **Macintosh PICT format** (file name extension *.pct* on Windows, *.pict* on a Mac) is the Macintosh's native image file format, and a good choice if you plan to work with the image only on a Mac.

- ◆ **Windows Bitmap** (BMP, file name extension *.bmp*) is a good choice only if you plan to work with your image in Windows—it tends to produce large files.

- ◆ **Portable Document Format** (PDF, file name extension *.pdf*) is Adobe's format for highly compressed page layout files that you want to make viewable on the web.

Two other popular formats, Joint Photographic Experts Group (JPEG) and Graphics Interchange Format (GIF), plus the less frequently used Portable Network Graphics (PNG) are discussed in the "Saving for the Web" section in Chapter 23.

Saving to PDF

Photoshop Elements offers two different ways to save your images to Adobe's proprietary Portable Document Format (PDF). PDF enables you to share your pictures more freely across a wide variety of computing platforms. Any user with a copy of Adobe Acrobat's free Reader software will be able to see a PDF image—no matter what format you used originally to save it. And because Acrobat Reader now runs on many platforms from Windows to Macintosh, from palmtops to cell phones, this handy feature lets you expand your range of sharing in a novel way.

In Focus

Normally, to create a PDF file, you need to either purchase and install Adobe's Acrobat Distiller software or use the PDF creation utility on Adobe's Web site (https://createpdf.adobe.com). Consider scanning your documents, opening them in Photoshop Elements, and saving them in PDF format to save time and trouble.

Basic PDF Saves

The simplest way to convert your image to PDF is as follows:

1. Click the bar at the top of the image window to make it the frontmost, active image.

2. Follow Steps 1 through 3 as listed previously in the section on "Switching File Types or Names with Save As."

3. Select Photoshop PDF from the Format drop-down list.

4. Click Save to open the PDF Options dialog box, shown in Figure 12.2.

Figure 12.2

Saving as PDF makes an image viewable on many different operating systems.

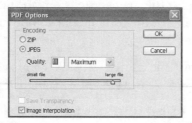

5. Select JPEG to compress the file to a smaller size using the JPEG encoding method (choose ZIP for a larger but higher-quality image). JPEG is an optimal file format for photos, while ZIP is great for text files. Either format works well with line art.

6. Move the slider to the right or left to choose your desired quality (Low, Medium, High, Maximum). The higher the quality, the bigger the file size. As quality decreases, so will size. The settings you've chosen appear in the Quality box and drop-down list as you move the slider.

7. Uncheck the Image Interpolation box; this smoothes out low-resolution parts of your PDF images, but tends to make them look fuzzy.

8. Click OK.

Once you save your PDF file, you can use your copy of Acrobat Reader to open it, or you can send the file to a friend who has this popular free software.

PDF Slideshows

Photoshop Elements enables you to do more than just store single images as PDF files. It lets you create entire slideshows from your collection of pictures. In essence, slideshows let you jump beyond the concept of sharing single pictures. With a slideshow, you can share an entire event.

Creating your own slideshow couldn't be easier. You don't even have to save your images in PDF format beforehand; they don't even have to be located in the same directory. Follow these steps:

1. Choose File → Automation Tools → PDF Slideshow to display the PDF Slideshow dialog box.

2. Click Browse.

3. In the Open dialog box, click the arrow next to the Look In drop-down list to navigate to where your images reside. Click to select those pictures you want to add to the slideshow.

4. When you've chosen all your images, click Open. The Open dialog box closes, and the selected images appear in the Open Files list in the PDF Slideshow dialog box. To reorder your set, drag any file name into a new position.

5. To add files that are already open in Photoshop image windows, check Add Open Files.

In Focus

Shift+click with your mouse to select contiguous files; press Ctrl+click (Windows) or Cmd+click (Mac) to add a noncontiguous file to your selection of slideshow images. You can press Ctrl+click or Cmd+click a second time to deselect a file. If you've included any file in error, simply select it and click Remove. Photoshop Elements will remove it from the list of Open Files.

6. After finishing your file selections, you can choose options from the Slideshow Options section:

    ◆ If you want your slideshow to repeat continuously, check the Loop After Last Page box.

    ◆ Choose an option from the Transition drop-down list to change the transition used to move from one image to the next. (You can also select Random Transition for more variety.)

7. In the Output File area, click Choose.

8. In the Save dialog box, navigate to where you want to save your file, enter a name in the File Name box, and click Save. The Save dialog box closes and you return to the PDF Slideshow dialog box.

9. After checking to make sure you've included all the files you want, that they appear in the proper order, and that you've set all the slideshow options as you desire, click OK.

10. Wait as Photoshop Elements opens each image and adds it to your slideshow. This may take several seconds or a minute or two.

After compiling your slideshow, a dialog box appears announcing that the PDF slideshow was successfully created. Press the Escape key (Windows) or Cmd+. (Mac) to end the show. You can now open this PDF document in Acrobat Reader for a full-screen treat, or you can e-mail the show to a friend.

In Focus

Some of your image-editing work is likely to consist of preparing images for presentation on the web. Files intended to appear online need to be compressed as much as possible, and special file-naming considerations come into play for web images, too. Luckily, Photoshop Elements has some tools that help you save files in one of several optimal formats for a web presentation.

For example, the Save As dialog box enables you to save images in an exciting new format designed especially for the web: JPEG2000. Photoshop Elements is one of the first programs to support this format. In addition, the Save for Web dialog box gives you the ability to preview images and calculate how long they'll take to appear in someone's web browser window based on their file size. You can then adjust the file size to make sure they'll appear more quickly. See Chapter 23 for an in-depth examination of web formats and how to save an image in the right format for your needs.

Optimizing an Image for E-mail

The same qualities that make an image optimal for the web—a highly compressed file size and a file format that can be viewed by software on a variety of operating systems and computers—also make an image optimal for e-mail. Where e-mail message attachments are concerned, the smaller the file size, the better.

Photoshop Elements streamlines the process of attaching an image to an e-mail message. The process involves some file-saving activities, too.

To attach an image to an e-mail message and have Photoshop optimize it for e-mail, follow these steps:

1. Open *pelican2.tif* from the Chapter 12 folder on this book's CD-ROM.

2. Choose File → Attach to E-mail or click the Attach to E-mail icon on the short-cuts bar. An alert dialog box appears. When your image attachment is too big in size or not in a format that can be viewed on the web (such as TIFF), Photo-shop Elements displays an alert window such as the one shown in Figure 12.3.

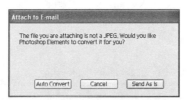

Figure 12.3

Photoshop Elements can help optimize images before you e-mail them.

3. Click Auto Convert. Photoshop Elements creates a lower-resolution copy of your image in JPEG format and attaches it to your e-mail message so you can send it.

The Least You Need to Know

- ◆ Choosing File → Save preserves any changes you've made to an image.

- ◆ Choosing File → Save As enables you to save an image with a new file name, in a new file format—or both.

- ◆ Saving an image in PSD or TIFF format lets you save multiple layers if your image has them.

- ◆ Saving a file in a new format requires you to balance file size with image quality when saving a file in a new format.

- ◆ Adobe PDF files and slideshows enable you to share individual images as well as collections of related pictures.

- ◆ Photoshop Elements automatically converts and compresses files that aren't yet optimized for e-mail attachments.

Part 4

Getting Creative with Text and Graphics

In this part of the book, you take a step beyond quick fixes and retouching photos. You learn how to add content to your images, such as text. You also get the chance to do some manual artwork with brushes, pencils, and erasers.

Here you'll transform a photo of the kids into a "Wanted" poster, add a cartoon balloon and some text to create a funny holiday card, or create your own flyer to locate the lost family dog. Whatever the task, all you need is a little imagination and a little experience with Photoshop Elements.

13

Adding Text to Your Images

In This Chapter

- ◆ Adding text to an image
- ◆ Applying changes to text attributes
- ◆ Using anti-aliasing
- ◆ Applying special effects

When working with your images, you may not only want a sharp photo image with just the right amount of contrast, backlighting, brightness, and hue; you may also want to add text—especially if you are e-mailing a wedding photo you took of your crazy uncle wearing a lampshade on his head!

This chapter shows you how to add text to an image, and how to change the font, color, and spacing attributes of your text to make it just right. You can also use anti-aliasing features, which enable you to smooth the edges of the fonts you have chosen, and you can add special effects to text such as warping, outlining, shadowing, and more.

Adding a Caption to an Image

Your tool of choice for adding text to an image is the Type tool, located in the toolbox (see Figure 13.1). The four Type tools available are the

Horizontal Type tool, the Vertical Type tool, the Horizontal Type Mask tool, and the Vertical Type Mask tool.

Figure 13.1

Use the Type tool to add text to your images.

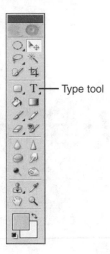

Type tool

You'll use horizontal type when you need the text to run across the page from left to right. You'll choose vertical type when you need the text to run up and down. Vertical type shows the text on the page as if you've pressed the Return or Enter key after inserting each letter. You can use the Type Mask tools for both horizontal and vertical type to create a border around the text entered, which can then be filled with a color, gradient, or pattern, or can be cut from the selection to create other effects. You can see an example of this in the full color insert (Figures i3 and i4).

To add horizontal or vertical text to an image, follow these steps:

1. Open or acquire the photo or image to which you want to add text and maximize the photo, or choose Open → New if you are making a logo or other non-photo image.

2. Click the Type tool and hold down the mouse button to open the menu choices. Choose the Horizontal Type tool if you want to add text horizontally; choose the Vertical Type tool to add text vertically. (Later, you'll learn how to use the Type Mask tools.)

3. Click inside the photo where you'd like to add the text.

4. Using the Type toolbar above the photo, change the font from its smaller default size to 72 pt. so that you can see what you are typing. (Otherwise, you might need a pair of reading glasses!)

Vectors and Bitmaps

A vector image like the one at top consists of shapes called paths, which create areas that can be filled with color. Bitmaps consist of little squares called pixels. *(Images courtesy of Scott Wills.)*

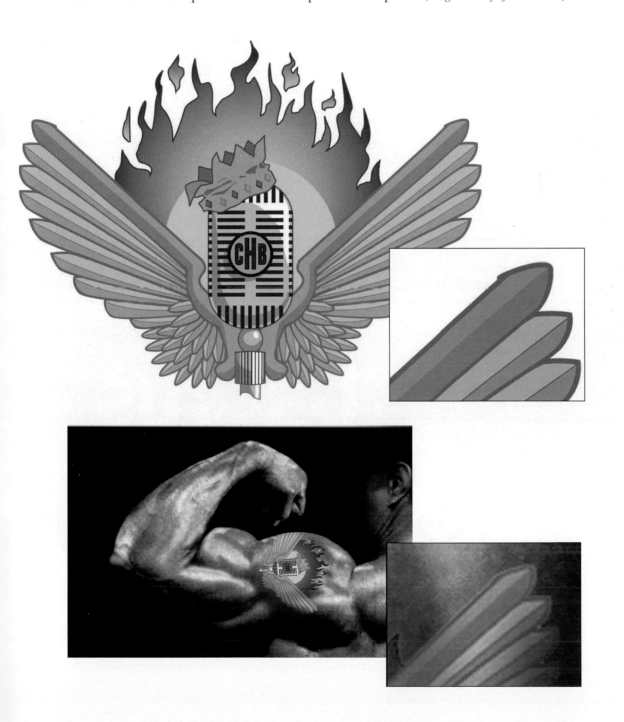

The Horizontal Type Mask Tool

The Horizontal Type Mask tool enables you to make a selection in the shape of the type on a page. Once you select the type, you can copy, move, or reuse it to your heart's content.

The Eyedropper Tool

The Eyedropper tool lets you select a color from the active image and make it the default foreground color. You can then reapply the color to other parts of the image with other tools—such as the Brush tool, which is used here.

Removing a Color Cast

Photoshop Elements gives you a variety of options for removing a color cast from an image. The original family photo is shown at top left. The version at top right shows the effect of choosing Enhance → Auto Color Correction. The version at lower left shows the effect of Enhance → Adjust Color → Color Cast. The version at lower right shows the effect of Enhance → Adjust Color → Color Variations.

Adjusting Levels

One of the most effective ways to correct the color in the image is by adjusting the levels of brightness and contrast. The original is at top left. At top right, the effect of Enhance → Auto Levels. At bottom left, the effect of Enhance → Adjust Brightness/Contrast → Levels. At bottom right, the effect of Enhance → Adjust Color → Color Variations. *(Photo courtesy Thayer Lindner.)*

Filters

Filters can be used to apply special effects to an image. The image at the top left is the original; the effects rendered to it (clockwise from the original) include Watercolor, Pointillize, Dry Brush, Mosaic Tiles, and Chalk & Charcoal. *(Photo courtesy Thayer Lindner.)*

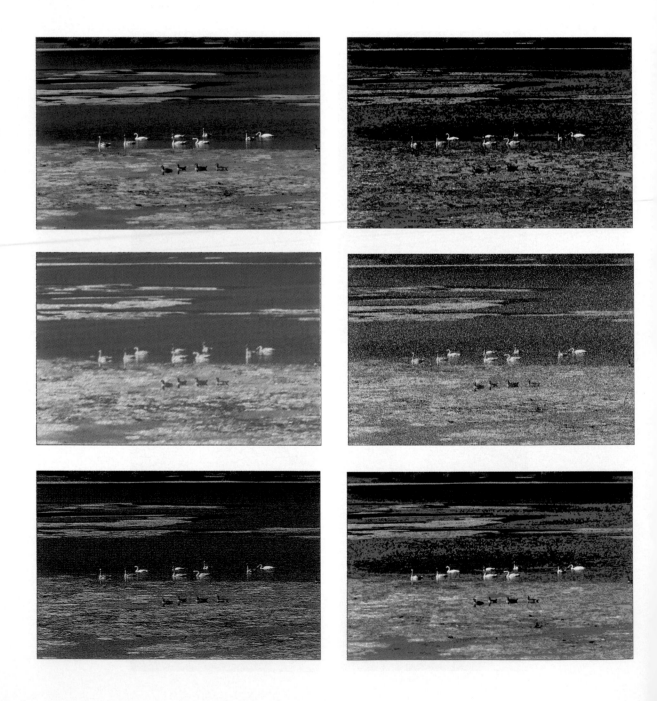

Quick Fixes

The Quick Fix options under the Enhance menu are new features in version 2.0 of Photoshop Elements. With just a handful of menu selections and mouse clicks, you can dramatically transform even the poorest quality photo. The original photo is at top left. Following clockwise are these transformations: Auto Contrast, Auto Levels, Auto Focus, Auto Color, and Boost Brightness.

Create a Photomerge

Another feature new to version 2.0, Photomerge, enables you to take a series of photos of a scene and have Photoshop Elements turn them into a single panoramic image. Only four images were used to create this panorama; more images would have created a smoother blend.

5. Type in the text you wish to add. Use the text justification buttons to center, left justify, or right justify the text, and/or use the other word-processing options such as strikethrough, faux italic, bold, or underline to change the look of the text.

6. With the text added and these options set, you can now change the text's characteristics. In the section "Tweaking Type Attributes," coming up soon, you'll change the font, the color, and other attributes using the Text toolbar.

Adding horizontal and vertical type to a picture is pretty easy. Just choose the tool and type. You can set the type attributes while typing, or you can set or change them after typing. Before we begin changing attributes such as color, font, and fill, let's look at the two remaining Type tools.

In Focus

When you add text using the Horizontal or Vertical Type tool, the program creates a new layer. This layer is shown in the Layers palette by a large capital T.

Understanding the Type Mask Tools

The titles of the tools say it all; the Type Mask tools are "type masks" you use to change the look of the type (or text) in your file. A mask is a cover, façade, or disguise, which hides what's underneath, much like a Halloween mask that conceals (or changes the look of) the person wearing it. Type masks are used similarly; they change the underlying characteristics of the text.

You can use these masks to place a border around the text you add. This creates an area on the active layer in which you can change the color, gradient, and pattern attributes of your text, or to copy, cut, or move it. In Figure 13.2, for example, the background of the text "Cactus" is cut out using the Horizontal Type Mask tool, and then the text is placed in another file.

To create a cutout of a background using text as shown in Figure 13.2, start by opening a photo that contains a background you'd like to use for text. Next, select one of the Type Mask tools, choose a font, type in the text, and then select the Move tool. The text you just added will be

In Focus

Unlike the Horizontal and Vertical Type tools, which create a text layer, the two Type Mask tools do not create an additional layer when you use them. The item created is a "selection" that can be saved, dragged, changed, or otherwise manipulated from the active layer. If you want the selection to be a layer, you'll have to do that manually using the Layer menu.

selected. Resize or rotate the selection as necessary, so that the desired background is chosen, and then drag the selection to a new document. (You can also use the Select → Save Selection tool and related commands to save the selection for use later in different images. If a selection isn't saved [or placed in a new file] before closing Photoshop Elements, the selection is lost.)

Figure 13.2

Use the Type Mask tool to create special effects.

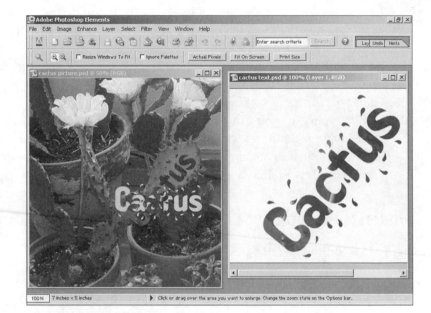

One more thing before we move on. An easy way to get a really cool effect using text is to mask background with text, and then move it just slightly away from its original location. Add a drop shadow and it'll look like it jumps right off the page!

Tweaking Type Attributes

After you've added text, you may want to format it, or change its font, size, or color attributes. In this section, you'll learn about all of these tasks. Before you get started though, take a moment to learn about the Photoshop Elements default settings.

When the program is first installed, Photoshop Elements has some default Type settings. These defaults are changed each time you use the Type tools. This means that the look of the toolbars is changing constantly. To see the default text settings for the Type tools, open a document, choose any Type tool, and click the capital T icon available on the options bar. You have two options: Reset Tool or Reset All Tools.

Choosing Reset Tool changes the Type tools in the options bar back to its defaults; choosing Reset All Tools changes all of the tools back to their defaults.

It would be wise the first few months you use Photoshop Elements to always begin with the default settings. This way, you can learn the ins and outs of the program by learning the defaults first, which are generally best for beginners.

In Focus

Use the Window menu and the Reset Palette Locations to put all palettes, toolbars, and default settings for the program back in place. It will look and feel new again!

Working with Fonts

Fonts are styles that are applied to text. Photoshop Elements, word-processing programs, printing software, and even the operating system itself come with their own set of fonts. The two types of fonts you'll work with are TrueType and PostScript fonts. TrueType fonts are an onscreen font. When printing, the output might look different than what's on the screen, because the printer must have the font to be able to print it.

In contrast, PostScript fonts are printer fonts. PostScript fonts must be printed on PostScript printers, are quite flexible, and allow you to print more accurately what you see on your screen.

There are two ways to use fonts. If you use a font in an image and don't embed the text into the image, and then you send it to someone who doesn't have that particular font on their system, their computer will substitute a font. However, if you embed the font in the final graphic making it a GIF or TIFF file say, the viewer sees the font as part of the image, and does not need to have that font installed.

Locating, Installing, and Using Fonts

With the different types and styles of fonts, how can you go about finding and installing fonts you lack? Better yet, how do you go about deciding which font to use?

Locating new fonts is as easy as visiting your local computer store and purchasing a font program. There are several available and they come with their own installation program. If you're not into spending money on fonts, you can usually get

Shop Talk

When downloading a new font, make sure you choose Mac or PC depending on your system. TrueType fonts for Macs are not compatible with PCs, and vice versa. (There are conversion tools, but it's easier just to download the correct one the first time!)

them for free on the Internet. Just search for "Free Fonts" or "Download Free Fonts" using any Web browser and you'll see how many options you have. After download-ing, use your computer's Help files for assistance in adding them.

Changing fonts is easy. Knowing which font to choose sometimes isn't so straightforward. To change the font and size of the text in a document, choose the Type tool, highlight the text, select the new font, font size, and any other option, and apply the changes. You can choose any font size you want from the list, and the choices range from 6 to 72 pt. But that doesn't mean you only have those choices!

In Focus

If you want to add vertical text to a file, use the Horizontal Text tool when typing so you can better see what you're typing when you type it. Once it's in and it looks okay, switch to the Vertical Type tool.

You can type in any font size you want in the box on the Type toolbar, and it can be really, really small, or really, really big. Photoshop Elements will help you along by resizing the text box as needed.

To decide on a font, consider the nature of the text you're adding. If it's a legal document, consider Arial or Courier, if it's a birthday card for a toddler, con-sider a font such as First Grader, Comic Sans, or Crayon. The first are considered more "formal," the latter more "casual."

Changing Colors

You'll also want to change the color of the text so that it can be clearly seen above the photo's background. The default text color is blue, and if you aren't feeling blue right now, you should choose another color!

To change the color of the text you've added, follow these steps:

1. Use the mouse to highlight the text.

2. From the Type toolbar, locate the Color Picker. It is a large square box with the color's text in it.

3. Click once on the Color Picker to open it.

4. Click and select a color, and/or use the slider bars to see and select other colors.

5. With the color selected, click OK. Figure 13.3 shows text that has been added and manipulated in both color and font.

Figure 13.3

Choose a new color to complete the image.

Adjusting the Size and Location of the Text Box

You can adjust the size of the text box if you like, and change the location of the text on the page. Changing the size of the text box by pulling or pushing in on the edges and corners has the same effect that selecting a new font size does—it simply changes the font's size. If you've already selected the correct size from the font size box, this might not be necessary.

What is most likely is that you will need to move the text to another area of the page. The following example walks you through creating a For Sale flyer like the one shown in Figure 13.3, moving text on the page, and resizing the text box itself. Try the process yourself by following these steps:

1. Open the file *house.psd* in the Chapter 13 folder that is included on this CD-ROM (or, open a picture of a house you have taken previously).

2. Add the text "For Sale By Owner" using the Arial font size at 72 pt. Type it in black. Select Layer → New Layer, and then add the text "Great Buy - Will Go Fast" on a second line. Select Layer → New Layer, and then add the text "Only $110,000" on a third line. Each text entry will now be a separate layer. See Figure 13.4.

3. Open the Layers palette and choose the text layer "For Sale By Owner," as Figure 13.4 shows.

4. Select the Move tool (it is selected in Figure 13.4). The pointer changes to the Move icon's cursor. Use this cursor to click anywhere on the text. When you do, a box appears around the text.

Figure 13.4

Use the Layer → New Layer option to create a new layer for each line of type.

In Focus

When resizing, the Move tool is unselected and the options bar becomes a toolbar that contains transformation options such as Reference Point Location, a place to type in a specific width and height, and options to rotate, scale, and skew. You'll learn how to use rotate, scale, and skew in Chapter 20, for now you should know that you can access them here.

5. Click a corner of the text and push in to make the text box smaller, or pull out to make the text box larger. The cursor appears at this time as a diagonal line with an arrow on each end. Once you position the first line correctly, perform these steps again with the other two text lines. (While resizing text using the text box and the Move tool, the text might look distorted. Don't worry though; it will turn out okay in the end!)

5. Click the Commit button on the Move toolbar to apply the changes. Then click anywhere on the screen to return to the default cursor.

Using Anti-Aliasing

A criminal uses an alias to cover up his true identity. When text is placed on the screen, it covers up things too—the pixels on the computer screen. These pixels are square, and sometimes, curved letters (or other objects) don't look quite right because of it. The edges can look jagged, especially when enlarged. Photoshop Elements offers *anti-aliasing* to take care of this.

Anti-aliasing, is a technique for smoothing out the edges of fonts that you use when creating text. By turning on anti-aliasing you can add some meat to the edges of the letters in your printed text so they appear more even. Anti-aliasing keeps the edges from appearing jagged and messy.

For most of your work, you'll probably want to leave anti-aliasing on. Although you usually won't be able to see the difference without a microscope or a magnifying glass, even subtle differences in type can improve the look of your project. (Think of this like sweeping under the couch—you know you did it, and it is cleaner—you just can't see it!)

You might not have any specific uses for anti-aliasing or be able to see any differences, but when it's turned on or off, others will. For instance, professional print shops create designs, print them on film (special papers) using special printers, and then use this film to create the screens they use for printing. The screen is used as a template for the ink that goes on the shirts, hats, jackets, or other media they are printing. If the edges of the fonts are jagged or messy, so is the image on the printed item. Anti-aliasing solves this problem by smoothing out the edges of the fonts before they make it to the film.

Shop Talk

Anti-aliasing is a software technique for smoothening the edges of lines, fonts, images, and other objects by placing transitional colors between the outermost colored pixel and the pixel beside it. This hides the jagged edges of lines and other objects caused by the inherent nature of the pixel itself.

In Focus

There are two types of fonts, those with serifs and those without. Serif fonts have finishing strokes coming off the end of a letter. These additional strokes can be thin or thick, and extremely ornate. When printing serif fonts make sure anti-aliasing is on to achieve the best results.

The fonts you'll have to be most concerned with anti-aliasing are those with curly corners. These edges tend to fade out and get jagged around the edges and won't show well. Some of these types of fonts include Classic, Copper Plate, and Gentry. However, it's best to leave anti-aliasing checked all of the time, no matter what font you've chosen. It can't hurt!

To turn anti-aliasing on and off, simply select the text in an image using the Text tool and the Layers palette, right-click the selected text, and choose Anti-Aliasing On or Anti-Aliasing Off, or, choose the Layer menu, the Type submenu, and then choose Anti-Aliasing On or Anti-Aliasing Off.

Adding Special Effects

It's good to have an effect on people. Now, you can have an effect on your text too! Once you've added text to a document, you can apply special effects to it.

In this section you'll learn how to:

- ◆ Apply a filter to text.
- ◆ Warp text.
- ◆ Put an outline (or stroke) around the text.
- ◆ Use the Drop Shadow and Cast Shadow tools.
- ◆ Rotate text.

Applying a Filter to Text

If you're a photo buff, you're probably familiar with camera filters. These filters can make an object in a picture look foggy, they can be used to correct incorrect lighting, and they are often used to make a photo look old. You can also use filters to distort or correct the photo, as well as blur it, warp it, or mask specific attributes. You can apply filters to your text too.

In Focus

In Figure 13.5, the Layers palette is showing. It's been dragged from its tab in the Palette Well and placed there, but it can also be opened from the Window menu. If you drag it from the well, it stays open on the page and you'll see the More button; when opened from the Window menu, it won't be docked on the page and you won't see the More button (unless you've dragged it from the Palette Well and manually closed it earlier, in which case this default behavior changes).

Figure 13.5 shows a postcard for a beach resort. The text has been filtered using the Texture filter and Grain option to make the text look sandy and grainy.

What makes applying filters to text different from applying other attributes such as font and color is that, when a filter is applied to text, the text must be simplified, making it an object rather than a text layer. This is important to understand, because once the text layer has been simplified, any corrections to spelling or other attributes can't be changed without starting over. Therefore, when applying filters to text, make sure you save the image before applying the filter, just in case you need to go back and correct an error.

For more information on filters, skip over to Chapter 17. There, you can see different types of filters and how they are applied to both text images.

Figure 13.5

Applying the Texture/Grain filter gives the text a sandy look.

Warping Text

Are you warped? Well, you might be! The Warp tools make it easy to bend and distort your type in arcs, waves, and other curves and twists. Warping enables you to create text that more closely matches the image you've added the text to. For instance, you might choose to warp the text in the form of a wave when working with a photo of the beach, or an advertisement for an ocean resort.

To warp text that has already been added to your document, follow these steps:

1. Open the file *beach.psd*, located in the Chapter 13 folder on the CD-ROM. Click the Type tool in the toolbox.

2. Click the Type Layer you want to warp.

3. Click the Create Warped Text button located on the options bar. It is not located on the toolbox where the original Type tool is located.

4. Because the text you've chosen is Faux Bold, you'll be notified that you can't apply warp to this type of font. You'll need to agree to have that feature removed from this text to continue.

In Focus

When you move the Horizontal and Vertical slider bars, you are changing the bend and distortion values for that attribute. When these values are set at 0 percent, no warp is applied. Positive and negative percentages apply perspective to the warp based on the number settled on. You can choose to warp only vertically, only horizontally, or both.

5. In the Warp Text dialog box, select a warp choice from the choices available in the Style list. The Wave choice looks ideal for the beach photo. Figure 13.6 shows the options.

Figure 13.6

Many warp options are available from the Style menu.

6. Move the slider bars for the warp option you've chosen in order to obtain the ideal warp for your text. Click OK when finished.

7. Click the Commit button to accept the change and apply it.

Putting an Outline Around the Text

Outlining text gives it a bolder look and can add more "umph" to your text. Outlining is used quite often with company logos to make the text stand out. The next time you are out and about, notice how many logos used at gas stations, stores, and other establishments are outlined.

To outline text in an existing document, follow these steps:

1. Select the layer of type you want to outline. Do this from the Layers palette.

2. Right-click the layer in the Layers palette and choose Duplicate Layer. Press OK.

3. Select the duplicate layer if it isn't automatically chosen in the Layers palette.

4. From the Window menu, open the Effects palette or drag it from the Palette Well.

5. Choose Text Effects from the choices offered from the Effects palette (see Figure 13.7).

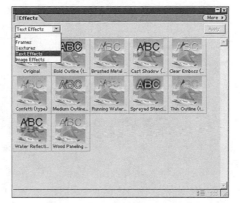

Figure 13.7

Choose Text Effect options from the Effects palette.

6. Click the foreground color in the toolbox (see Figure 13.8).

Foreground Color

Figure 13.8

Set the foreground color in the toolbox.

7. From the Color Picker dialog box, choose the color you want the outline to be. (The outline is always the foreground color.)

8. Choose a type of outline and click Apply. The changes are applied. The color of the outline is the same as the color of the foreground color in the toolbox. See Figure 13.9.

Figure 13.9

Apply text outline options.

In this example, the effects Bold Outline and Water Reflection were applied to the text "Florida Resorts." You can apply other effects, though, and not just from the Effects palette. For example, after applying a text effect, choose the Text layer from the Layers palette and choose Layer → Group With Previous to see the background through the lettering. Also try changing the opacity of the text layer for different effects by selecting the layer from the Layers palette and moving the Opacity slider. You can apply other types of filters too, by selecting the layer from the Layers palette, opening the Filters palette, and selecting a layer to apply. (There's an entire chapter on filters later—Chapter 17.)

Rotating Text

You have only two options for adding text: horizontal and vertical. What happens if you want the text to be something other than that, perhaps diagonal across the page or upside down? The answer to that lies in the Move tool.

The Move tool is available from the toolbox. This tool places a box around the text and enables you to move it as if it were any other object on the page. The cursor for the Move tool changes depending where you are in relation to the object. The four cursor options are as follows:

- Before you point the cursor at anything, it appears as a one-headed arrow.

- If you hover your mouse pointer on a corner of the text box, the cursor becomes a diagonal line with an arrow on both ends. You can then resize the object pro-portionally by clicking and pulling a corner of the text box. *Proportionally* means that the object's height and width will remain relative and the object will not be distorted.

♦ If you hover your mouse pointer on the center of a side, the cursor will become a straight line with an arrow on both ends. You can click and drag to resize the object, but the object will not remain proportional.

♦ *However*, if you rest your mouse pointer just outside of any corners or lines, the cursor changes from the default cursor to a curved line with an arrow on both ends. With this cursor you can click and drag to rotate the text.

You try it! Here's how to rotate text:

1. Open the file you've been working on in this chapter.

2. Click the Move tool from the toolbox and click the text to be rotated. A box appears around the text.

3. Position the cursor outside the text box until the cursor changes to the curved line with an arrow on each end.

4. Hold down the left mouse button and drag the box to the desired position. Let go of your mouse button when complete, and click the Commit button to accept the changes.

Notice that as you rotate the text the options bar changes. You can now use the options available to type in the height and width of the text box, the angle of rotation, and even scale and skew the selected text.

In this chapter, you learned how to work with text. You learned how to add text, how to change the attributes of the text including font, color, and size, and how to use anti-aliasing. In the "Adding Special Effects" section, you also learned how to warp, outline, apply a filter, and rotate text.

The Least You Need to Know

♦ You can use the Type tool, found in the toolbox, to add text to a document.

♦ Changing the font of text is as easy as selecting it with the mouse and choosing a new font name from the options bar.

♦ Changing the color of the text is easy, too—you just select it with the mouse and choose a new color from the options bar.

♦ Many special effects are available. To use them, you must add the Layer palette to the screen, choose the layer of text to modify, and then select the correct effect.

Getting Sketchy with Your Images

In This Chapter

- ◆ Using the Pencil tool
- ◆ Drawing lines and curves
- ◆ Understanding Opacity
- ◆ Using the Eraser tools
- ◆ Erasing with Auto Erase

The pencil's demise started when the personal computer was invented. We don't know the exact numbers, and we don't own stock in any pencil companies, but we'd be willing to bet that pencil sales have dropped sharply since computers became popular. Not only do we not write with pencils as much as we used to, Photoshop Elements has a Pencil tool just for drawing! You can use this tool to add hand-drawn items to a project or fix small errors in photos, and it's just like writing with a real pencil.

In this chapter you'll learn how to use the Pencil tool to draw lines and curves as well as how to erase mistakes. You have several options for erasing, including erasing backgrounds and using Auto Erase, and, of course, just simply erasing using a tool similar to a real pencil eraser.

Exploring the Paint Box

The Paint Box is an area of the toolbox that holds the drawing tools. We'll be focusing on the Pencil and Eraser tools, but other tools are also available. For instance, the Paintbrush tool enables you to add color to your image by painting it on with a brush-like tool. This tool is generally used to paint large bands of colors and is explained in detail in Chapter 15. You generally use the Pencil tool, on the other hand, to draw thin lines. This is our focus for this chapter, along with knowing how to erase mistakes.

Sharpening Your Pencil

You can finally throw out that noisy pencil sharpener that's taking up room on your desk. Why? Because the Pencil tool in Photoshop Elements is always sharpened and ready! In fact, it's like having all kinds of pencils at your disposal. You can configure how thick or thin you want the pencil line to be, and you can even choose the pencil color.

In Focus

The Pencil tool is generally used for small touch-ups on photos and can be used quite successfully this way. Creating artwork on a blank canvas, though, would take some practice!

The Pencil tool is located in the toolbox and is shown in Figure 14.1 (it's the sixth tool down on the right). When you choose the Pencil tool, the options bar changes to reflect the selection of the Pencil tool. Using the options bar, you can change how thick the line is, the opacity of the line, and more. To assist you in finding help, the Hints palette changes to reflect the selection of the Pencil tool as well.

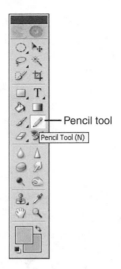

Figure 14.1

The Pencil tool is available from the toolbox.

Pencil tool

Drawing Lines

With the introductions (and our real pencils) out of the way, let's give drawing a shot. Start with something easy—a straight blue line. You can also experiment with drawing curves. Follow these steps:

1. Choose File → New to open a new document.

2. In the New dialog box that opens, choose the preset image size of 8 × 10 inches, 300 pixels per inch, RGB color, and make sure the Transparent option button is selected for the contents of the page. Click OK. See Figure 14.2.

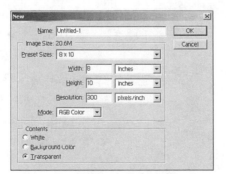

Figure 14.2

Configure the new document like this.

3. Click the foreground color in the toolbox (this is usually the first or top color shown). Move the slider in the Color Picker dialog box to blue and choose OK.

4. Click the Pencil tool.

5. In the Size window of the drawing toolbar, change the size of the pencil line from 1 px to 25 px. You can do this using the slider or by typing in the number 25. This makes the pencil easier to work with initially.

6. Hold down the left mouse button and drag the mouse over the area where you want the line to be drawn. Release the mouse button when you finish.

7. Try drawing some curves, and experiment with the different line widths, brushes, and modes. See the following tips for additional instruction also. Once you familiarize yourself with the tool, you'll be able to create something cool!

While you experiment and become familiar with the Pencil tool, try out these tips to get you started on the right track:

◆ Use the View → Grid menu option to show a grid on your page to assist you in drawing straight lines.

◆ To draw a line from one point to another, click once where you want the line to begin, hold down the Shift key, and click once again where you want the line to end. Photoshop Elements draws the line for you—as straight as an arrow. You can continue in this manner from endpoint to endpoint as long as you keep the Shift key pressed.

◆ Use the available rulers by selecting them from the View → Rulers menu option.

◆ Change brushes quickly by right-clicking the image.

◆ Use the two arrows next to the foreground and background colors to toggle between them.

◆ Switch to the Eyedropper tool by holding down the Alt key. The Eyedropper can then be used to take a sample of any color in the image and use this new color as the foreground or background color. Clicking using the Eyedropper changes the foreground color box automatically.

In Focus

Drawing with a mouse is one way to get lines on the page, but you have other ways, too. Drawing equipment such as drawing tablets, specialized mice, and digital pens are becoming popular and offer a little variety.

Now that you've had a chance to experiment a little with the Pencil tool, try to create something with it. Try the following exercise:

1. Open the *design1.psd* file from the Chapter 14 folder on the CD-ROM that comes with this book. It is located in the Chapter 14 folder. Maximize the file, then save it to your hard drive using a different file name.

2. From the View menu, choose Grid.

3. From the View menu, choose Rulers. Use the default ruler settings of inches.

4. Set the foreground color to bright blue.

5. Click the Pencil tool in the toolbox.

6. From the options bar, change the pencil size to 375 pixels.

7. Line up the circle that the Pencil tool now displays and click once in between the lines and squares to create the circles in the image shown in Figure 14.3. (You can find this image also in the Chapter 14 folder on this book's CD-ROM; it's called *design2.psd*.) You can make this a separate layer (or make each circle or row of circles a separate layer) by selecting Layer → New Layer before clicking with the Pencil tool.

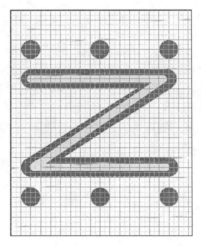

Figure 14.3

Use the Pencil tool to create a logo.

8. When you move your mouse pointer over the image, you can see a notation on the top and left rulers, showing what coordinates you are accessing. Click once with the Pencil tool to denote the start of the Z. If you have your rulers set to measure in inches (which is the default), the top left start of the Z is right around the (4,1) square; hold down the Shift key and click again around (4,10) to create the top-right part of the Z. The line is created automatically. You can make this a separate layer (or make each line segment a separate layer) by selecting Layer → New Layer before performing this step.

9. Holding down the Shift key, click again around the coordinates (10,1) to create the diagonal line, and again around (10,10) to create the bottom of the Z. Remember, you can make each of these segments a separate layer if you'd like by selecting Layer→New Layer before using the Pencil tool.

10. Change the size of the Pencil tool to 150, and draw a line through the Z using a light blue color and the same technique. This is shown in the file *design3.psd* (refer to Figure 14.3). You can make this a separate layer if you want to by selecting Layer → New Layer before performing this step.

11. From the View menu, remove the check from the Grid option.

By replacing the Z with the first letter of your business, and then adding a little imagination, you can create a logo to use on web pages, stationery, or business cards. You can also add a shape, textures, filters, patterns, and more. In later chapters, you can pull this file up again and add some more to it!

Don't Get Opacity with Me!

You have another option available when using the Pencil tool and that's Opacity. You use Opacity to define how "strong" the line or stroke is. For pencil drawing, this setting relates to how hard you'd actually be pressing the pencil to the page. If you set the opacity at 100%, the line is drawn as a single hard complete stroke. However, when the *opacity* is changed to 75%, the stroke is much less heavy. At 50% it's somewhat light, and at 25%, it barely shows on the page. At each setting, the pencil mark becomes more and more transparent and becomes see-through at its lowest settings.

You can see how opacity is used and how it affects an image by performing the following steps:

1. Open the *design3.psd* file and select the Pencil tool. Click the Pencil icon in the options bar and choose Reset Tool from the two choices.

> **Shop Talk**
>
> **Opacity** determines to what degree a drawn line, background, or other object reveals the layer underneath it. At 100%, nothing shows through from the layer underneath. At 10%, the entire background shows, and the object is almost transparent.

2. Change the foreground color to a dark purple by clicking the foreground color icon and choosing the new color from the Color Picker.

3. Set the Pencil size to 100 px.

4. Using the pencil and the tips presented in the previous section, add lines to the graphic so that it looks like Figure 14.4. Make the layers separate layers by selecting Layer → New Layer before using the Pencil tool for each of the lines.

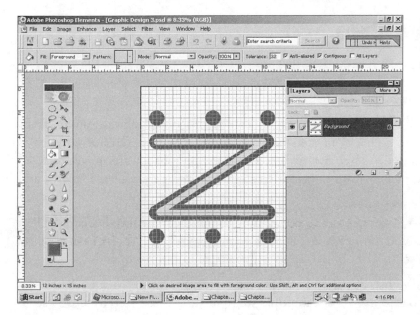

Figure 14.4

*Use the Pencil tool to apply
different opacities.*

5. For the first (and topmost) line created, leave the opacity at 100%.

6. Create the second and third line (moving down across the Z) with the opacity of 50% and then 20%. Refer to Figure 14.4.

7. Change the foreground color to light blue, and use the Paint Bucket tool to fill in the background. The Paint Bucket tool is located in the toolbox and is the fifth one down on the left side. The Paint Bucket tool fills a selection or layer with the foreground color. Again, refer to Figure 14.4. (You might also consider using different sizes, opacities, and styles for adding color to the six dots on the logo, too.)

Notice that we frequently instructed you to start a new layer because the Pencil tool doesn't create another layer automatically each time you use it, as does the Text tool.

Before we move on, a word should be said about the Mode options when the Pencil tool is selected. There are almost 30, and are detailed throughout this book in different contexts (painting, for instance). To apply a specific mode, simply select it from the list and apply it. You can apply some neat effects with these, as described in later chapters.

In Focus

After messing around in these toolbars and settings for a while, you've probably all but forgotten what the default settings were. You can revert back to the default settings for any toolbar by clicking the icon on the far left and choosing Reset Tools or Reset All Tools.

Erasing Your Boo-Boos

You can erase mistakes in several ways. Perhaps the easiest way is to use the Edit menu's Undo command. You have several other ways to undo mistakes, though, including the following:

◆ Use the Step Backward button on the toolbar or the Step Backward option from the Edit menu to go back one step (one operation). Use the Step Forward button to undo an undo (or go forward). Because stepping backward moves back one operation, pick up your pencil often so that more operations are created and saved.

◆ Use the File → Revert option to revert back to the file's last saved version. This option enables you to open a file, make several changes, and revert back quickly to its original state, without having to use multiple Undo commands.

◆ Open the Undo History palette, and choose any step to move back to. You can use the slider bar to move back multiple steps, or just click a step to move back. Figure 14.5 shows the steps used when working on the logo for the previous exercise.

Figure 14.5

Use the Undo History palette to choose a level of correction.

◆ For complex drawings, create separate layers for your pencil operations. (Just select Layer → New Layer before using the Pencil.) This way, you can use the Layers palette to simply delete a layer if you don't like it. This is much more effective than using the File → Revert or the Undo History Palette, because it lets you remove a portion of the drawing without losing any other data. (You'll find an example of this in the *design5.psd* file on the CD-ROM that comes with this book.)

The preceding Undo tools erase what you've added to an image. They may be ideal for some of your needs. But what if you want to erase other things such as a part of a background, the edges of a photo, or part of a layer? These items can't be erased using the Undo tool. Consequently, in addition to the Undo tools, you can use several specific tools to erase parts of the image that are messed up or you no longer want. While you can also use these tools to undo operations, they were created for more complex tasks.

This section covers the following tools:

- The Eraser tool
- The Background Eraser tool
- The Magic Eraser tool
- The Auto Erase option

Just Erasing

It is possible to just simply erase stuff. Just erasing using the Eraser tool is a little different from erasing with a pencil eraser; whatever is underneath the erased image is what you'll see when you've finished erasing. If you erase the lowest layer of an image, you'll see the "paper" underneath (the checkered layer).

The Eraser tool changes the colors and graphics in the image as you move your mouse pointer over them. If you're working (erasing) on top of a Background layer, these erasures do not leave a white or black space on the image; instead they change the erased area to the background. If you are erasing on a layer with locked transparency, the same is true as well. If you are erasing in neither of these scenarios, the erased area become transparent (see-through).

To use the Eraser tool to erase a part of an image (other reasons to erase are detailed later), perform the following steps:

1. Open the *design5.psd* file located in the Chapter 14 folder on the CD-ROM, which contains an image and multiple layers, and select the Eraser tool from the toolbox (it's the seventh tool down on the left).

2. Click the down arrow that contains the brush samples from the toolbar and choose Default Brush that is 100 pixels wide. (Even though these are called Brushes, it is just a standard term. It is used here to define the width and shape of the tool, in this case, the Eraser.)

3. From the Size drop-down list, notice that the value is 100 px. If you need to, you can change this number by moving the slider or typing in a new number. For now, though, leave it as is.

4. In the Mode drop-down list, choose Brush, Block, or Pencil. Brush erases using a circular eraser, Block erases using a square eraser, and Pencil erases using a fine line. Choose Pencil for the eraser.

5. When choosing Brush or Pencil, you can also set Opacity. At 100%, the erasure is complete; no signs of the object remain. At less that 100%, the object is lightened. Erasing takes place, but only lightly. Leave the opacity at 100% for this exercise.

6. Select the Purple Circles layer from the Layers palette. While holding down the left mouse button, move the mouse back and forth over the two middle purple circles in both the top and bottom layers to erase only those purple circles from the image. The objects are erased.

While this is a simple exercise in erasing, it introduces you to the most basic erasing option, the Eraser tool. You could not have deleted the layer to erase only the middle two purple dots, nor could you have used the Undo commands in this instance. You use the Eraser tool to erase objects in an image that has multiple layers. The underlying layer color shows underneath when the top object is erased. This is an important concept to understand because the underlying layer will show through when erasing with the Eraser tool.

One last point before moving on. Don't just think of erasing just as a way of getting rid of mistakes. You can use the Eraser tool and combine it with a fancy brush to erase the edges of a photo for a cool "aging" effect. You can use the eraser too in other ways, too, including removing parts of layers, parts of a photo, or applying a light-colored texture to a photo's background layer.

In Focus

If you download a single image from a camera, import a JPEG image from a floppy disk, or acquire an image from a scanner, you won't be able to use these tools to erase a tree, say, and have the sky portion of the picture show behind it after it's erased. Pictures that are acquired in this manner only have one layer—the picture itself.

The Background Eraser Tool

Erasing parts of your background—wouldn't that be nice? Wouldn't you like to erase that last fight you had with your spouse, or maybe that last stock purchase, while leaving the rest of your life history intact? Well, erasing undesirable episodes in your personal history might be impossible, but erasing parts of an image and leaving only the background showing behind it isn't!

The Background Eraser tool enables you to erase parts of an image, including parts of a background or a part of any other layer. In fact, it does the exact opposite of a paintbrush. Instead of putting color onto the image, it removes color from the image. It lets you choose a color to erase, and it only erases that color from the picture.

The Background Eraser samples the color in the center of the Eraser brush you're applying, and deletes that color wherever you drag the brush. This enables you to delete colors in an image while leaving the other layers above and below the active layer undisturbed. This tool only works when more than one layer exists, because one layer will have to be the foreground and the other the background. Therefore, when you work with this section, choose your file appropriately.

See if you can erase some background colors:

1. Open the *doll.psd* file in the sample folder. This file contains multiple layers, as shown in Figure 14.6.

Figure 14.6

Open the doll.psd *file that comes with this book's CD-ROM in Photoshop Elements.*

2. Using the Layers palette, select the layer that contains the areas you want to erase. In this example, choose the Shirt layer.

3. Select the Background Eraser tool by clicking the Eraser tool in the toolbox and holding down the mouse button to reveal the options.

4. Choose a brush size of 13 px (this is really an eraser size).

5. Select the Contiguous limit option. The Contiguous setting erases all of the areas of the layer that match the selected color and are connected to one another via pixels. The Discontiguous setting erases the color wherever it occurs as the brush is passed over it.

6. Set the Tolerance level. Low Tolerance levels erase only areas that are an extremely close match to the selected color, whereas a high Tolerance erases a broader range of colors. Set the Tolerance level to 50%.

7. Drag the mouse only over the red sleeves of the T-shirt underneath the vest. You'll notice the red sleeves disappear and the arms and the background show. Note that the first color you click becomes the selected color when you use the Background Eraser tool. Notice as you release your mouse button and click again, the background color changes to reflect the location of the click.

For a more challenging exercise, see if you can erase only the blanket from the picnic basket, leaving the basket itself untouched. Because these two items are on the same layer, you'll need to choose a smaller eraser size, and be a bit more careful where you click and what color you choose to erase. In fact, if you'll click on the blanket multiple times instead of dragging the mouse over it, you can undo only a little bit if you need to. (You'll find out how to do this more easily in the next section.)

> **It's Element-ary**
>
> You can create copies of layers using the Layers menu, or create Fill Layers of a solid color. When working with a single-layer image, such as a photograph, consider creating one of these additional layers so you can use the Background Eraser tool for editing. For more information about layers, see Chapters 7 and 8.

Erasing Magically

Erasing has always been somewhat magical, don't you think? The idea of removing something you no longer want is quite a luxury. Stain removers are great; they magically remove stains from clothing and carpet, and no one ever has to know they were there. It would be nice to have a magic eraser tool for all areas of life (such as erasing that cigarette burn you created in your dad's car in high school), but that will never be.

For erasing unwanted items in an image, Photoshop Elements offers the Magic Eraser tool, which is similar to the other erase tools that are available. However, this tool works by clicking, not dragging, and it erases entire areas. Its erasing technique is similar to using the Paint Bucket to fill an image with color, except that this tool erases the color. If you use this tool on a background or single-layer image, it erases to transparency, to the checkered layer. For an image with multiple layers, it erases the selected layer's colors, and leaves the background intact.

Try this procedure yourself by following these steps:

1. Open the *doll.psd* file again.

2. Using the Layers palette, select the Hat layer.

3. Select the Magic Eraser tool by clicking the Eraser tool in the toolbox and holding down the mouse button to reveal the options.

4. Accept the default Tolerance level. Remember that low Tolerance levels erase only areas that are an extremely close match to the selected color, whereas a high Tolerance erases a broader range of colors.

5. Select the Contiguous limit. The Contiguous setting erases all of the areas of the background that match the selected color and are connected to one another via pixels. The Discontiguous setting erases the color wherever it occurs in the selected area.

6. Click Anti-Aliasing to smooth the edges of the areas you erase.

7. Select Use All Layers to sample the erased color using combined colors from all layers in the image.

8. Specify an opacity level of 100%.

9. Click the hat once. The pixel you click determines the colors erased in the area. If the entire hat isn't erased, continue clicking the remainder of the hat until it's gone.

In Focus

It takes a bit of practice to learn how to apply all of the techniques in this book. However, once you become familiar with the program, you can combine the techniques (fill, erase, layers, and so on) to create incredible images!

You can use the same techniques here to erase items from layers in your own pictures. When erasing on the background layer, remember that you'll erase to the checkered background, so make sure you erase with something underneath. Refer to Chapters 7 and 8 for more information about creating, duplicating, and grouping layers, and assembling images in layers. Understanding layers fully will enable you, for example, to recreate a family photo and use the Eraser tools to finally eradicate your ex-husband or ex-wife!

Using the Auto Erase Option

The Auto Erase option is available when you use the Pencil tool. Before using this option, you'll need to choose a foreground and background color. Once you do that, this option enables you to draw using the Pencil tool with either of the colors you specify, depending on where in the image you start drawing.

For instance, if the foreground color is blue, the background color is yellow, and you draw something with the Pencil tool as shown in Figure 14.7, then, when you begin drawing again starting from a yellow part of the figure, the cursor actually seems to go *behind* the yellow part of the drawing, and anything you draw from that point is blue. This actually erases what is in yellow by drawing blue over it. On the other hand, if you draw using the Pencil tool on a blue area of the screen, the pencil writes in yellow. By keeping this box checked, you can automatically erase anything you've drawn using the Pencil tool by overwriting it with the background color. You can do this without having to select an eraser. If you do not choose the Auto Erase option, the Pencil tool does not take on this characteristic, and instead simply works as detailed earlier.

Figure 14.7

Familiarize yourself with the Auto Erase option.

Figure 14.7 is just a fun little image to get you started using the Auto Erase option. You can try to recreate it in this exercise. Try Auto Erase yourself by following these steps:

1. Decide on a foreground and background color before using the Pencil tool. For optimum effect, use the Paint Bucket to fill the page with the foreground color, as described earlier.

2. Select the Pencil tool and draw on the page.

3. To erase what you've drawn when you start drawing again, place a check in the Auto Erase check box in the options bar.

4. Make sure the Opacity is set to 100%, and then draw over the area to erase.

This chapter has shown you how to use the Pencil tool and draw lines freehand, using a grid, and using the mouse and Shift key. You've learned how to use the Pencil tool to create a logo to use on a business card or Web site. You've also learned how to use Auto Erase to draw using foreground and background colors. Because erasing is a big part of drawing and painting, you also learned about the four erasing options—the Magic Eraser, the Background Eraser, the Eraser, and Auto Erase.

> **It's Element-ary**
>
> When you draw over a part of the image with the foreground color, you draw with the background color. When you draw over a part of the image with the background color or any area that is not the foreground color, you draw with the foreground color.

The Least You Need to Know

- You use the Pencil tool to draw freehand. Pick foreground and background colors before using the pencil.

- The Opacity tool determines how "hard" you are pressing on the pencil or the eraser. The higher the number, the stronger the drawn line or erasure.

- The Undo command enables you to undo the last operation.

- The Undo History palette lets you choose a place to return to, which can cover multiple operations.

- The File → Revert command enables you to revert the file back to the last time you saved it.

- You can use the Eraser tool to erase the edges of photos, parts of a layer, or even certain people from images!

- The Magic Eraser works like the Paint Bucket feature—it erases entire sections.

Brushing Up Your Images

In This Chapter

- ◆ Understanding the Brushes palette
- ◆ Using the Brush, Impressionist, and Airbrush tools
- ◆ Understanding brush dynamics
- ◆ Creating a personalized brush

Even if you've never imagined yourself an artist, the Brush tools in Photoshop Elements will enable you to create, hide, emphasize, or change items in your artwork. As with the Pencil tool, you'll be painting with the mouse (unless you buy a digital tablet or some other drawing tool), so we'll start off with some simple painting exercises, and you can use your imagination to go from there.

This chapter introduces you to the brushing tools, including the Brush tool, the Impressionist Brush tool, the Airbrush, and specialty brushes. These brushes enable you to apply paint to a canvas or photo in the same manner as the Pencil tool in the previous chapter. The tools that go along with these brushes enable you to change the thickness of the brush, the size of the stroke, and the opacity of the stroke application, among other characteristics. You can also create a personalized brush or try different brush modes.

Exploring Elementary Brushes

Photoshop Elements offers many different ways to paint, including multiple types of brushes and tools, and each one has its specific options and characteristics. You have so many tools and options to choose from, there's most likely an exact match for your needs. In this section you'll learn about three options for painting:

- The Brush tool
- The Impressionist Brush tool
- The Airbrush option

In this section you'll also learn how to set the Brushes palette to meet your specifications and preferences.

> **It's Element-ary**
>
> When you select a Brush tool, the options bar changes to reflect your choice. There, you can select the Airbrush option. The Airbrush is simply a brush attribute, and is not a separate tool.

Working with the Brushes Palette

Clicking and holding down the Brush tool in the toolbox brings up two brush choices: the Brush tool and the Impressionist Brush. The Brush tool paints like a regular paintbrush; the Impressionist Brush paints strokes that look like impressionist artwork (artwork that looks like Impressionist painters' works, such as Monet's). For now, choose the regular Brush tool. You're not ready to style; you have to get the tangles out first!

Figure 15.1 shows the brush options after the Brush tool has been chosen. Notice that the options bar changes to reflect this choice. From this bar, the Brush window has been expanded using the down arrow beside it. Clicking this arrow brings up the view choices, which are shown here, too. We've set ours to Small Thumbnail, but you have other options as well (and if you didn't know already, you can apply these options to other palettes as well):

> **It's Element-ary**
>
> Remember, if there's an arrow on a tool in the toolbox, it means that more than one tool is available. You can click the tool once to choose the default tool (or the one used last), or click and hold to see all available tools.

- **Text Only**   Describes the brush stroke without graphics.
- **Large Thumbnail**   Displays a graphic of the brush stroke in large thumbnails.
- **Small List**   Includes text and a small graphic of each stroke type.
- **Large List**   Includes text and a large graphic of each stroke type.

◆ **Stroke Thumbnail**   Is the default type, showing the stroke itself and a small graphic that includes the size of the stroke.

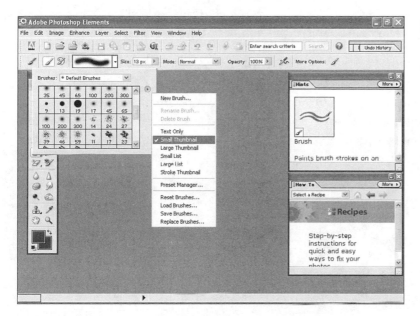

Figure 15.1
Click the down arrow to locate the Brush options.

Notice that other options here include creating a new brush, saving a brush, loading a brush, renaming a brush and more. We'll talk about these options later in this chapter.

The Brush Tool

Tom Sawyer would have loved this! A paintbrush that doesn't need any paint, and, no mess! Just choose the brush, make a few choices, and you're ready to go! Painting is as simple as moving the mouse around.

Let's paint!

1. Open the *fence.tif* image located in the Chapter 15 folder on this book's CD-ROM.

2. Choose a foreground color that matches as closely as possible to the blue fence in the picture. This will be the color you'll be painting with. (You'll learn about easier ways to match colors later.)

3. Select the Brush tool by clicking the paintbrush in the toolbox, holding down the mouse button, and choosing the Brush tool. Choose Reset Tool from the options bar.

4. Choose brush type number 9 from the Default Brushes option as shown in Figure 15.1 (for experimental purposes a larger brush is easier to see in action).

5. Change the brush size to 50 in the Size window of the options bar. You can do this using the slider or by typing in the number **50**.

6. Choose the Normal blending mode. Other modes will be discussed in subsequent chapters.

7. Choose the opacity from the Opacity window. An opacity of 100 percent covers completely; anything less covers more lightly. Because we're painting a wooden fence, choose an opacity of 50 percent. This way, the lines that define the fence posts will show through.

8. Left-click and drag the mouse over the image to apply the paint. Figure 15.2 shows this process in action.

Figure 15.2

Oh, if painting were only this easy!

As with the Pencil tool, you can use the Shift key and the mouse to paint a straight line from one point to another, which is helpful when painting on fence pickets such as this. You can also use the grid and rulers to assist you in lining up your paint strokes.

Now try painting the part of the fence that's closer to the ground next to the grass. This is best done by choosing a much smaller brush and a lighter opacity when painting near the edges. Carefully move the mouse around the areas of the grass and other parts of the fence. You can also paint over the grass if you want, and thereby weed-eat while painting! In addition, by letting go of the mouse while painting, the Undo commands will only undo a small amount of your work, enabling you to finish the job a little faster.

As promised, matching the colors of specific objects needs to be detailed. Lots of tools are available to help you match colors and patterns of objects while painting. The Pattern Stamp tool lets you paint with a pattern; the Clone Stamp tool lets you take a sample of an image. You use both the same way, and they let you click and choose a specific color (or pattern) in your picture, which you can then apply to other parts of the image.

Open the fence file again, and this time use the Clone Stamp tool (it's the eleventh one down the left side of the toolbox) to exactly match not only the original color of the fence in the sun, but the color of the fence in the shade too. To use the Clone tool, select it from the toolbox by holding down the mouse on the Stamp icon and choosing the Clone Stamp tool. Then, hold down the Alt key (Windows) or the Opt key (Mac) while clicking with the mouse on the object or area to clone. Now, choose your Paint tool and paint as usual. When you paint, you'll apply the color that you chose when you used Alt+click (Windows) or Opt+click (Mac). For best results, try different brush sizes for sampling, so you pick up only the exact color you want.

> **It's Element-ary**
>
> As with the Pencil tool, Paint tools do not automatically create additional layers when you apply them. By selecting Layer → New Layer before applying a Paint tool, you can manually create new layers while painting, making it easier to edit painted images by enabling specific layers to be edited instead of the entire image.

The Impressionist Tool

The Impressionist tool differs from the Brush tool in that it doesn't *create* color the way painting does; it *modifies* the colors and attributes of the image itself. You also don't choose the foreground and background colors like you can with the Brush tool; instead the colors chosen are modifications of the original color in the image. Basically, the Impressionist brush blends the colors together, creating a watercolor effect.

The Impressionist tool, then, is best applied to completed images, ones that you want to change to look like an impressionist painting. If you aren't sure what an impressionist painting looks like, see Figure 15.3 or use the Impressionist tool as demonstrated here to find out:

1. Open the *flowers.psd* file located in the Chapter 15 folder on the CD-ROM that comes with this book.

2. Hold down the Brush icon in the toolbox and choose the Impressionist tool, or, if the Brush tool is chosen already, just click the Impressionist Brush icon on the options bar.

3. Reset the tool in the options toolbar.

4. Accept the default settings on the options toolbar, and then hold down the mouse and run it across the yellow flowers in the image, being careful to stay within the limits of the flowers. The effect will extend outside of the flower and blend it with the adjacent colors.

5. Change the size of the brush to 35, and go over the cactus in the picture.

6. Change the brush size to 50, and go over the background, the pots, and any remaining parts of the picture not covered yet. Your picture might look something like the one shown in Figure 15.3.

Figure 15.3

French impressionist painter Monet would be proud.

While simply using the defaults and changing brush size can render wonderful effects, you can do even more when using this tool. For example, you can decrease the opacity of the brush to retain more of the original image's attributes or use an opacity of 100 percent to totally distort it. Other options are also available from the More Options button in the toolbar.

You can see the More Options box in Figure 15.3. The default is Tight Short, but you can choose any of the other options also. Figure 15.3 used Tight Short; this describes how the impressionist stroke is applied—in tight short dabs. Variations of tight, loose, and curl will meet the needs of any artist.

The Airbrush Tool

Ah, the airbrush. The Airbrush tool is reminiscent of days long ago spent at the state fair, when buying a T-shirt and having your name airbrushed on it by some big, burly, bearded guy was the norm, followed by wearing (and subsequently ruining) it while eating cotton candy and enjoying the log ride. To describe the Airbrush tool in a category, it more resembles a paint *sprayer* or using a can of spray-paint, than using a paint*brush*.

When using the Airbrush tool, you'll discover that it is the only Photoshop Elements tool whose effect changes the longer you apply it in a single place. It works like a spray-paint can, so if you spray a can of paint in one place for a long time, the paint becomes thicker and darker; if you spray it quickly, its effect is much lighter. That's the way the Airbrush tool works.

Using the Airbrush tool is just like using the Brush tool, except for a single step—selecting the airbrush before painting.

1. Open the image showing the fence with a flower pot again, and choose a foreground color. This will be the color you'll be painting with.

2. Select the Brush tool by clicking and holding the mouse on the Brush tool in the toolbox, and then choose the Brush tool. (You can't use the Airbrush option when the Impressionist Brush is chosen.)

3. Reset the toolbar, and choose a brush type from the Default Brushes option, as was shown in Figure 15.1. Choose a good graffiti size—we're going to spray-paint this fence!

4. Choose a brush size from the Size window of the options bar.

5. Choose a blending mode (choose Normal for now).

6. Choose the opacity from the Opacity window. An opacity of 100 percent covers completely; anything less covers more lightly. Choose 75 percent.

7. Click the Airbrush tool (next to the Opacity window on the options bar) to enable the Airbrush.

8. Left-click and drag the mouse over the image to apply the paint in a line, or, click the mouse once to spray a dot of paint. Notice that when you hold down the mouse in one place for an extended period of time, more paint is sprayed, just like a spray-paint can. Notice when you move the mouse across the page quickly, the spray is lighter.

As with other tools, other options are available when you choose the Airbrush. On the options bar, locate the More Options icon and click it. Here, you'll see sliders for Spacing, Fade, Color Jitter, Hardness, and Scatter, and a place to set Angle and Roundness (you can view these later in Figure 15.5):

- ◆ **Spacing** Changes the painted line from a solid line to one with gaps or spaces in between. Changing this creates skips between the paint. The higher the slider setting, the wider the skips.

- ◆ **Fade** Lets the paint fade off into nothing as the brush is applied. This happens automatically when you move the mouse quickly across the page, but you can set it manually here, too.

- ◆ **Color Jitter** Switches the paint between the foreground and background colors and allows for multiple colors to be created.

- ◆ **Hardness** Determines how hard or soft the paint is applied. Hard strokes are solid and firm; soft strokes are fuzzy, and multiply the effect.

- ◆ **Scatter** Determines how brush strokes are distributed as you draw strokes. Higher numbers make the strokes seem scattered all about; lower numbers keep strokes closer together.

- ◆ **Angle** When using elliptical brushes, this setting determines how angled the stroke will be.

- ◆ **Roundness** This option sets how the brush will be applied—as a circular brush or a linear one. Settings in between create effects in the middle.

- ◆ **Tablet Support** When using a pressure-sensitive digitizing tablet for drawing, check this box to set the dynamic options automatically, depending on how hard or soft you apply the stylus to the tablet.

In this section you got a brief introduction to painting, including a little information on selecting a brush and setting its size. The next section goes into a bit more depth with these topics.

Selecting a Brush

To paint successfully, you need to know what kind of brush to use. You have plenty to choose from, as you saw earlier from the Brush options. In this section you'll learn how to pick the right brush for the job, change the brush size, and understand and apply brush dynamics.

From the Brush palette you can see what types of brushes are available, what their default sizes are, and select additional brush types. Figure 15.4 shows the drop-down list with the available brushes shown. Besides the default brushes detailed earlier, many other types await your experimentation. These include, but are not limited to, Calligraphic brushes, Faux Finish brushes, Natural brushes, Thick Heavy brushes, and Special Effect brushes.

It's Element-ary

If you've ever been to a paint store and tried to pick out a paintbrush, you know how many brushes there are to choose from. If you've ever tried to paint a bedroom with a regular paintbrush, you probably learned that it's better to use a roller. If you've ever tried to paint a fence with a roller, you learned that it's easier with a paint sprayer. And if you've ever used a sprayer, you learned what a mess it makes on everything it touches. The point is, choosing the correct tool for the job *usually* makes that job much easier.

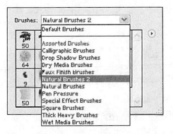

Figure 15.4

The variety of brushes you have available makes it easy to get the look you want.

Locate the additional brush options. To view the different brushes and get a feel for what type of effect they'll have on your artwork, browse through them:

1. Open a new document.

2. Choose a foreground color that will be the color you paint with.

3. Choose the Brush tool by clicking the Paintbrush icon in the toolbox, holding down, and selecting the tool.

4. Click the down arrow to show the selected brush presets.

5. Click the down arrow in the Brushes menu.

6. Choose a new brush category, such as Drop Shadow Brushes.

7. Click the right arrow in the Brush dialog box and choose Stroke Thumbnail. Refer back to Figure 15.1 if you are not sure where this is located.

Changing Brush Size

You wouldn't use a doll's hairbrush on a ten-year old girl with curly hair who's been in the wind all day, and you wouldn't buy a dog brush meant for a St. Bernard to comb your spouse's hair either (well, you might if he or she is in the doghouse!). What you really need is the right size brush for the job at hand. In Photoshop Elements, you can use the Size window after choosing a brush to change a selected brush's size.

Changing the size is as simple as sliding the sizing bar. Of course, you can always type in the width too, if you'd rather. To see what size the paint stroke will be after you make that selection, just move the mouse over the open document. You'll see a circle or square depending on the brush chosen, and the size will indicate the new stroke's width.

In Focus

You can try out a new brush size by painting a single strip with it. If you don't like that size, just choose Edit > Undo Brush Tool to remove the results, and then choose another size.

What Are Brush Dynamics?

How do you brush? Hard, soft, in choppy jumps, with a fading effect, from front to back? Even if you don't have a specialty stylus or graphic tablet for painting, you can still apply painting effects by choosing the correct dynamic for your brush. You can apply several dynamic effects, as shown in Figure 15.5.

Figure 15.5

Configure Dynamic settings from the More Options icon.

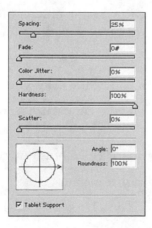

You set these effects from the More Options button in the options bar. Your options are the same as with the Airbrush tool (see "The Airbrush Tool" section previously for details).

Experiment with these options while painting on the *fence.tif* picture. Open the file, choose the Brush tool, and see what happens when you change these settings.

Applying Brush Dynamics

Applying Brush Dynamics is as easy as painting except there's one extra step. It's sort of like adding a detangler after trying to brush your kid's hair and not getting the desired results! Adding a little extra is sometimes all you need to get it just right. In the following example, we'll open up the *fence.tif* image and paint over the apples on the grass below the fence. You can use this same technique to get rid of similar unwanted items in your photos.

To use the Brush tool and apply the dynamic options, follow these steps:

1. Open the *fence.tif* image again.

2. Choose a foreground color by clicking the foreground color icon to bring up the Color Picker. The cursor changes to the Eyedropper. Click once on the grass underneath the fence. This will be the color you'll be painting with.

3. Select the Brush tool by clicking and holding down the mouse on the Paintbrush icon in the toolbox and choosing the Brush tool.

4. Click the arrow next to the brush type, and choose Wet Media Brushes, brush 17.

5. Choose a blending mode (choose Normal for now).

6. Choose the opacity from the Opacity window. An opacity of 100 percent covers completely; anything less covers more lightly. Choose 75 percent.

7. Click the More Options button (next to the Opacity window) and position the sliders for the Scatter option at 25 percent. (You can choose more than one option if you want.)

8. Click once on each apple that you see. The apples will be painted over, and because you've chosen to scatter the color, it will not be noticeable and will fade into the rest of the grass. Continue in this manner until all of the flaws in the grass are covered. You'll want to change the scatter back to zero to cover the apples directly next to the sidewalk, though, or it will look like the grass is growing there!

In Focus

Try out all of the brushes when attempting a job like the previous one. It might take some time, but the perfect brush is out there if you look hard enough!

Creating Your Own Brush

If the two hundred or so predefined brushes just won't do for your artwork, you'll just have to create your own brush. Once created, you can add the new brush to the Brush Library and/or delete any other brushes you've created. In this section you'll learn the following:

- How to create a temporary personalized brush.
- How to create a permanent personalized brush.
- How to save, delete, and rename a brush.

Let's start with creating a temporary brush.

Create a Temporary Brush

Sometimes you'll need to customize a brush for a one-time paint application. Chances are, you've probably already done this and not even known it! To create a temporary brush for one-time use, here are the steps:

1. Select a brush from the Brush options that most closely resembles the brush you need.

2. Set the size, brush dynamics, opacity, and other attributes you need the brush to have.

3. Paint or erase in the image. You've created a temporary customized brush! If you want to save this brush so you can use it again, perform the steps in the next section before doing anything else. Otherwise, the brush is only temporary and will not be available again.

It's Element-ary
One of this book's authors runs a graphics company that has more than 500 clients. Sometimes, a client's logo uses a specific type of paint, which consists of special attributes regarding texture, size, and dynamic options. When we create a new logo for a client and use a new brush, we save the brush and name it after the client account. This way, it's always available and gives the same result each time we use it.

Create and Save a Permanent Brush

If you like the brush you've created, you can save it in the Brush Library for future use. It's easy!

1. Create a temporary brush as detailed in the previous steps.

2. Click the down arrow next to the preset brushes, and then click the right arrow there to see more options. Choose New Brush.

3. Enter a name for the Brush and choose OK.

In Focus

We don't suggest going about changing the names of the default brushes, nor do we recommend deleting them. Some tutorials call for specific brushes by name, and if you've renamed or deleted them, you won't know what brush to use! Use the Rename and Delete tools for client brushes and brushes you have created yourself. If you do delete or rename preset brushes and you want to revert back, one way to do it is to reinstall the program in Custom mode. When you get to the Components page, uncheck everything except for Preset Libraries. As a result, only the libraries, including the Brush Library, will be installed. See Figure 15.6. (You won't lose any files or data if you do this, except for any brushes you've created.)

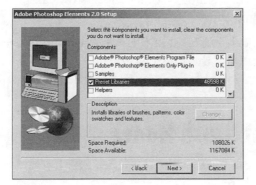

Figure 15.6

When reinstalling the libraries only, deselect everything except Preset Libraries.

Rename and Delete Brushes

After creating a brush and using it for a while, you might decide to rename the brush or even delete it. You can rename and delete preset brushes too, although I wouldn't do that just yet. You can achieve all of these tasks and more through additional brush options.

To rename or delete a brush, perform the following steps:

1. Click the Brush tool, hold it down, and select the Brush tool, so you can access the Paint options from the options bar.

2. Click the Brushes window to open the Brushes options.

3. Click the right arrow to view the additional options drop-down list.

4. To rename a brush (although we don't recommend renaming a program brush), select the brush to rename from the Brush options and choose Rename Brush from the choices. See Figure 15.7.

Figure 15.7

Click the right arrow to see the additional brush options.

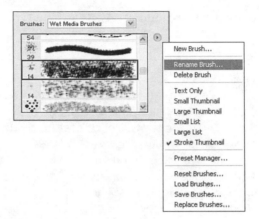

5. In the Brush Name dialog box that appears (not shown), type in a new name for the brush and click OK.

6. If you want to delete a brush, which we also wouldn't recommend, select the brush to delete from the Brush palette and choose Delete Brush from the choices.

Trying Different Brush Modes

Finally! Are you sick of hearing about brushes yet? Lucky for us all, we'll only discuss one more item here: brush modes.

Twenty-four modes are available. While it is beyond the scope of this book to list all of them and detail what they do, you can certainly experiment with them and find out for yourself. Figure 15.8 shows some of the available modes, and they've all been applied to the same white brush stroke on a light blue background. The modes can not only change the color of the brush stroke, they can also change the texture.

To apply modes, simply choose the mode to use from the list of choices in the Mode window before painting. They are applied in the same manner Dynamic options are.

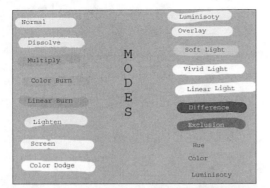

Figure 15.8

Start with a clean slate to experiment with the additional brush mode options.

It's Element-ary

Some of the modes are described pretty well by their names. For example, Normal is just that: normal. It's what the brush stroke looks like with no mode applied. Dissolve makes the brush look kind of melted or broken up. Soft Light, Vivid Light, and Overlay change the stroke color using the background as a part of the equation. The same is true for Difference and Exclusion; these tools use the background to create an opposite color. You get the idea. The best way to learn about modes is to apply them to objects and see what happens.

In this chapter, you have seen how to use the Brush tool, the Airbrush tool, and the Impressionist Brush tool, as well as how to resize a brush stroke, choose the opacity, select a dynamic option, and use predefined modes. You learned you could create your own brushes by modifying existing ones and saving your inventions in the Brush Library. Beyond that, you learned how to configure the Brush options to your specifications, including what type of thumbnail or list you want to see.

The Least You Need to Know

- The Brush tool offers two choices—the Brush tool and the Impressionist Brush tool.

- You can modify brushes to meet any specifications by changing the size, width, scatter settings, fade, spacing, hardness, and other options.

- Brush modes enable you to apply additional attributes to the brush such as texture and color.

- Creating your own brush enables you to personalize a brush and then save it to the Brush Library.

Chapter 16

Drawing Shapes

In This Chapter

◆ Getting a handle on drawing shapes

◆ Creating custom shapes

◆ Exploring the options bar

◆ Understanding the Shape tool options

This chapter introduces you to shapes and, specifically, how to draw them. The Shape tools enable you to add preset rectangles, ellipses, polygons, and other figures to your images easily. After adding the shapes, you can resize them, color them, and even place other shapes on top of them. In addition to shapes, drawing lines is included, as is setting options for using the Shape tools. So, let's get into shape! One, two, three, four! Again, two, three, four!

Getting Into Shapes

As you've learned in Chapter 4, you'll use two types of graphics in Photoshop Elements: Raster images (also known as *bitmaps*) and *vector graphics*.

Raster images are defined by a map of the specific pixels to be colored to create what you see. If a shape is a raster, then to resize, transform or recolor it, you have to remap the pixels. This generally requires the image program to resample the existing pixels and estimate the new shape, rounding here and tucking there to get a close approximation of the original shape. This results in a loss of quality for raster images as you work with them.

Shop Talk

Photoshop Elements automatically renders shapes and text as **vector graphics** which are defined by mathematical formulas. A significant advantage to you is that you can then transform these vector graphics, resize them and recolor them with no loss of quality. Other graphics such as Pencil or Paint tool additions are **rasters** in Photoshop Elements, so while you can draw a straight line with Pencil, Paint, or Shape tools, if you need to resize it for any reason, your product will be cleaner with the Shape tool because it is a vector graphic element.

Photoshop Elements automatically draws shapes as vector images in an effort to avoid this loss of quality as you work with shapes. A vector is a formula that describes the shape. A simple example is a circle which consists of a center point and radius. If you decide to make the circle smaller, the center point is unchanged and the radius can simply be changed. The program redraws the shape with no loss of quality.

You really don't need to concern yourself with the distinction as you begin to draw shapes. They will be vectors and you can work with them without losing any quality. There will come a time when Photoshop Elements may have to commit a vector shape in your image to a raster image in order to perform some action on the shape. This act of converting from a vector to a raster image is called simplification by the program. You will be prompted with a warning box before this occurs. You may be wise to always save an intermediate copy of an image in Photoshop Elements PSD format before simplifying so you can recopy the original vector layer if you need to later.

It's Element-ary

If you are in the business of creating logos or artwork for signs, banners, coffee mugs, T-shirts, or other promotional materials, it is best to create these logos and artwork using vector images. Vector images can be resized (think business card and then shopping center sign) without losing resolution or clarity. These images are also less expensive to print (when compared to bitmaps), and can be printed using a PostScript printer. PostScript printers can be used to produce the color-separated artwork necessary to create the items needed.

Figure 16.1 shows some artwork created for an actual client using only vector images. It also shows the available Shape tools from the toolbox. The vector images used to create this logo include rectangles, a scalable font, and some custom shapes. Opacity was even set for the larger rectangle around the logo, so it could be used to encompass it.

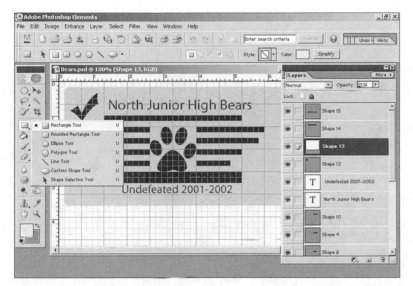

Figure 16.1

You can create cool logos in Photoshop Elements.

Later in this chapter, we'll create a logo like this one that you can use for your business or for a client of your own!

Working with the Shape Tools

Getting "into" shape is difficult; getting "a" shape is quite easy! Lots of Shape tools are available including rectangles, ellipses, polygons, and lines. You can even create custom logos, as shown in the previous figure, by laying one shape on top of another.

In this section you'll learn how to choose a shape and add that shape to an image, how to manipulate it, and how to add color to it. You'll also choose some shapes from the Custom Shapes option. After that, you'll learn about styles too.

Locating and Selecting the Shape Tools

Let's just dive right in. The first thing you need to do is locate the Shape tools and see what's available. Here's how:

1. Choose File → New to open a blank image to test this tool; set the size sufficient to allow some play space.

2. Find the Shape tool icon (fourth tool down on the left in the toolbox). Click the Shape tool icon and hold down the mouse button briefly to see all seven of the tools, which are the Rectangle and Rounded Rectangle, Ellipse, Polygon, Line, Custom Shape, and Shape Selection tools. Figure 16.1 shows these tools.

3. Select the Rectangle tool by doing any of the following: Hold down the mouse briefly and click a tool from the list, click the icon quickly and accept the last tool selected, click the tool once and choose a shape from the options bar, or right-click and choose from the list. Choose Rectangle.

   Notice that to the right of the Shape tools on the options bar are five choices for shapes being drawn. You can toggle between the shapes by selecting other choices here. As different shapes are chosen either here or in the toolbox, the available options change.

4. The cursor changes to a cross. Click once on your image canvas to start drawing the rectangle, and then, hold down the mouse and drag. When the rectangle is the size you want, let go of the mouse. This is how you draw other shapes, too. In Figure 16.1, you can see the multiple layers added to the image to create it.

Next, we'll introduce the options for each tool. The options bar changes each time a new Shape tool is selected.

In Focus

You can draw a square or a rectangle using the same techniques described here, except when drawing, hold down the Shift key. Instead of having to guess if the object is a perfect square or a perfect circle, or to use the rulers to measure, this option guarantees you a perfect shape each time.

Working with the Options Bar

When you choose a tool, the options bar changes to show the options available for the tool. Most tools have options for color, style, and how the shape is added to the image. You can also define the number of corners on the shape, the width of a line, and more. The following list explains the common options (see Figure 16.2), along with what they do. Once you have an understanding of this, you'll create a logo for yourself or a client using these tools, based on the Bears logo shown in Figure 16.1.

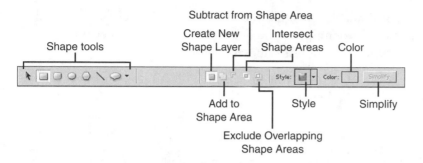

Figure 16.2

You can use the options bar to configure the options for the shapes chosen.

- The Color option in the options bar enables you to change the color of the shape you are adding.

- The Create New Shape Layer option is the default, which causes a new layer to be added each time you add a new shape. This is a good default, because shapes can be deleted or edited easily, simply by selecting the appropriate layer and tool.

- The Add To Shape Area option enables you to add a shape to an existing shape, thus to the same layer. (A new layer won't be created and you will in essence create a vector shape that is the sum of the two shapes you drew.)

- The Subtract From Shape Area option is basically an erase tool. It will subtract the new shape drawn from the existing shape on a layer, and wherever the two shapes overlap. It does not add the shape drawn, even where it doesn't overlap.

- The Intersect Shape Areas option is used to add a shape to an existing layer, and render a shape defined as the area where the two shapes overlap. Any area which doesn't overlap is empty when you are done.

- The Exclude Overlapping Shape Areas option enables you to add a shape to an existing layer, and to remove the overlapping areas in the shapes, leaving the non-overlapping area of both shapes.

- The Style option enables you to add a style to a layer or shape. The Styles available are various edge modifications used for effect such as a drop shadow or neon edge. If you try a Style option from the drop-down box and want to go back to no style, click on the Style down arrow, and click on the small round arrow button and select the Remove Style option.

- The Simplify button on the options bar helps you to transform a layer (or layers) into a raster image. This may be necessary for certain functions, but generally you can wait until the program prompts you to simplify. You may also wish to simplify if you need to do pixel editing.

◆ The Radius option is available when the Rounded Rectangle is chosen; it enables you to set the amount of rounding applied to the corners of the rectangle; 1 is very rounded, 13.89 (the highest value) is slightly rounded.

◆ The Sides option is available when you choose the Polygon tool; it defines how many sides the *polygon* should have.

Shop Talk _____

Polygons are shapes that have line segments that make up its sides, and there must be least three sides by definition. Rectangles, squares, and triangles are polygons, and so are pentagons, but circles and ellipses are not. Polygons must be "closed," too, meaning that all of the corners meet (like a rectangle or square).

Many different types of polygons have already been defined by really smart math guys—a three-sided polygon is a triangle, a four-sided one is often either a square or rectangle, a five-sided polygon is a pentagon, and lots more exist. You can use the Shape tool to create these polygons easily.

◆ The Weight option is available when you choose the Line tool; it defines how wide (or high if you prefer) the line should be. Lines are actually rectangles here with the height equal the Weight you set and the length defined by your mouse movements.

◆ The Shape option is available when you choose the Custom Shape tool; it offers custom, preset shapes.

◆ When choosing the Shape Selection tool, click anywhere on the image to select a shape or layer for editing. There's also an option to Show Bounding Box when this tool is selected.

Now, armed with knowledge of shapes and their options, let's recreate the Bears logo. While we're doing that, feel free to switch out the paw print for a different custom shape, change the text, or personalize the logo in any other way to suit your needs. As we move through the chapter, we'll add a style, color, and other options.

Creating a Logo

In this section, you can apply what you've learned so far, and create a logo. You can customize it for any business, reader, or client. Follow these steps:

1. Open the *bears.psd* file from the CD-ROM. It's located in the Chapter 16 folder.

2. From the View menu, choose to show the grid and rulers. Use this as a guide for your creation.

3. Open the Layers palette by dragging the tab from the Palette Well or from the Menu bar with Window → Layers to see the layers. It might help to expand the Layers palette using the resize tab in the lower left corner of the Layers palette window.

4. Choose File → New to open a new document. Choose a white background, RGB color, and the Default Photoshop Size from the size drop-down menu. Position the two files on the page so that you can see them both. You'll use the original as a guide, and you'll create your new logo in the new file.

5. Use either the Line tool or the Rectangle tool to draw in the lines for the logo, as shown in Figure 16.1. You can open the *bears_lines.psd* file from the Chapter 16 folder of this book's CD-ROM if you are having problems.

6. Select the Rounded Rectangle tool. Change the Radius if desired. Place a rectangle around the lines. You can also select the Ellipse tool if you want. It would be good practice to try both.

7. From the Layers palette, change the opacity of the new rounded rectangle so that the lines show through.

8. Save this new file to your hard drive. In the next section, you'll learn how to add the custom shape.

Shop Talk

An **ellipse** is like a circle that's been stretched. While a circle has only one center (focal) point, an ellipse has two. The outer points on the ellipse, which make up the line around the outside, are determined by the sum of the distances to these two focal points, and the distance is a constant. For you brainy types, the formula for an ellipse is $C = pi \times (R1 + R2)$.

In Focus

You can use shapes to "hide" other things. For instance, if you need to cut a person from a photo (say an ex-husband), and the background is a solid color, perhaps blue, you can create a polygon that is blue, and place it over the person you want out of the picture. The rectangle becomes just another layer, and you can edit the layer to match the background perfectly using tools such as Clone Stamp and Pattern Stamp. No one will ever know he was ever in the photo!

Drawing Custom Shapes

You can select custom shapes from a list of shapes for use in logos, images, and other artwork, and the custom shapes available in Photoshop Elements are vector images. Choosing a vector image of an apple (for use in a logo) is better than choosing an apple from clip art because of this distinction. Many clip art images are bitmaps, so consider looking for a vector image first in the Custom Shape tool.

When you choose the Custom Shape tool from the toolbox, the options bar changes to include a Shape window. Clicking the down arrow in this window brings up the Custom Shape choices, as shown in Figure 16.3.

Figure 16.3

Select a custom image from the Shape options.

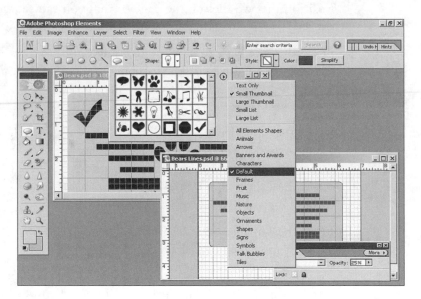

Notice in Figure 16.3 that Small Thumbnail and All Elements Shapes are selected. This is the default. This way, a thumbnail of each option is available, and, each of the available custom images is shown. If you want a specific type of image, say music only, place a checkmark next to the Music selection.

Here's how to draw a custom shape in your image:

1. Use the image you created from the last previous exercise, or open the *bears_lines.psd* file from the Chapter 16 folder on the CD-ROM. Select the Custom Shapes tool from either the toolbox or by clicking the talking bubble icon on the options toolbar.

2. Locate the Shape option on the options bar. You can see it in Figure 16.3. Click the down arrow to see the default shapes.

3. Click the right arrow button in the Shape dialog box to see the categories for shapes. Choose All Elements Shapes to see every shape available, or, choose a category. It will help if you drag the lower right corner of the dialog box to make it bigger.

4. Double-click the shape you want to add to your document. The Bears logo has a paw print, but you can choose any other custom shape to personalize your logo.

5. Make sure that the Create New Shape Layer option is selected, and then place the mouse on the document and drag as if you were drawing a rectangle.

6. Select a color for the artwork, if you desire. Just click the square in the options bar, and select a color. The layer should be selected for the new custom artwork. See the result in Figure 16.4. (Repeat these steps to add the checkmark, if desired.)

CAUTION

Swatch Out!

The options that were set when the last shape was drawn (Opacity, Exclude, Intersect, and so on) will still be selected when you draw another shape. Make sure to double-check all options each time, so that you know exactly what's being drawn. It helps to always have the Layer palette open so you can see layers as they are added, too. To reset the tools, right-click on the icon to the far left of the options bar and choose Reset tool.

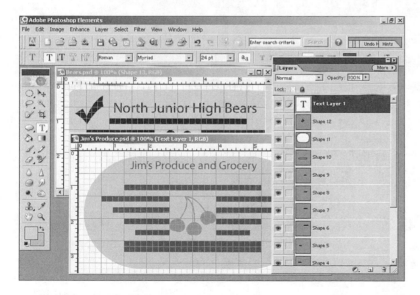

Figure 16.4

Add a custom shape to your image.

7. Finally, add the text using the Text tool. Choose text that personalizes the logo for your needs.

Now we've got the beginnings of a logo! Just a little text and a few extras, and we'll be ready to go!

Drawing Lines

Lines drawn using the Shape tool are initially drawn as vectors, and remain that way until they are simplified and transformed into raster images. Drawing a line using the Shape tool differs from drawing a line with the Pencil tool for this reason. When drawing with the Pencil tool, lines you draw are rasters from the beginning. Lines drawn using the Shape tool are really rectangles. Lines drawn here can be rescaled, resized, and otherwise changed, without distortion because of this.

In Focus

As detailed throughout this chapter, you can combine custom images, layers of shapes, and lines to an image. Don't forget, though, that you can add frames, text, and even filters and effects to create the perfect image. The only requirement is a little knowledge and a lot of imagination!

Add some lines to your working logo if you think that's necessary, or just draw a few lines for practice. Drawing lines is like drawing rectangles, only with a constrained height, so we'll move ahead to styles.

Applying Styles

For those of you with plenty of style, study this section, just for a while! Style shouldn't be an afterthought, though, so try to be stylish wherever you go!

After creating an image, you can apply styles to that image, too. Styles are cumulative, so if more than one style is applied, they'll accumulate on top of one another to form additional styles. You can also add a style at any time during the creative process. To add a style, click the down arrow on the options bar. If only it were that simple to have style in real life!

Figure 16.5 shows the Style options and how to access them.

We don't have room here to delve into a description of all of the available styles (about 150+), but you can browse through and apply them to see what they do. As you can see from Figure 16.5, the styles shown are classified as Glass Buttons. You can see that several other types of styles are also available.

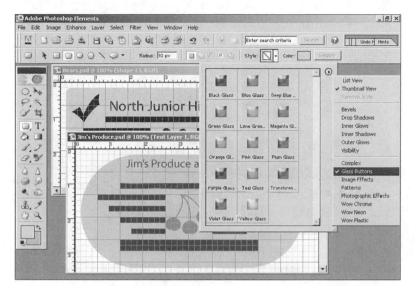

Figure 16.5

The Style options are located on the options bar.

To browse through these styles and apply them, follow these steps:

1. Use the same file you've been working on for this chapter, and choose the layer that contains the rounded rectangle shape or the ellipse you added. If you got lost along the way, open the *joes_produce.psd* file from the Chapter 16 folder on this book's CD-ROM, and choose the Shape 11 layer.

2. Select the Shape tool, so the Shape options bar is available.

3. Click the down arrow next to the Styles window and then the right arrow in the resulting Style dialog box.

4. Choose Glass Buttons. Choose a button from the choices available.

5. To apply a style, drag it to the image.

Swatch Out!

If you are specifically using vector images and predefined shapes to create a logo for a client with the idea of keeping printing costs down and promotional items affordable, don't apply a pattern style or any other multicolor style. This would require that the client use process printing (versus spot color) for all of their printing needs, and will cost them quite a bit more for everything (including business cards)! However, if you save a copy before applying the style, you can use that one for print and then create a stylized one for the web.

6. From the Layer menu, choose Arrange and then Send To Back (see Figure 16.6).

Figure 16.6

Apply a style option by dragging it to the desired layer.

7. If you have time, or don't like that particular button, choose Edit → Undo and change it! Experiment with as many styles as time allows. You'll be glad you did!

Once you've applied a style, you should reset the Style bar or remove the style, so that the same style won't be applied the next time you add a shape. To reset the toolbar, click the first icon and choose Reset Tool. To reset only the Style button, click the down arrow, then the right arrow in the Style options box, and then choose Remove Style.

Now, you not only have a logo, but you have a button for ordering on your website, too!

Manipulating the Shapes

You know how to resize an object, color an object, and apply styles to objects. Applying those changes to shapes is similar. However, because the Shape options bar looks a little different from the other options bars, and, for the sake of continuity, we'll review these techniques so that you can apply them to your shapes right now!

In this section you'll review the following as they apply to shapes:

- ◆ Resizing and moving
- ◆ Rotating
- ◆ Applying color
- ◆ Using Add, Subtract, Intersect, and Extrude

Resizing and Moving

When you think about resizing or moving a shape, just think of the shape as any other object in an image. The technique for moving or resizing is exactly the same.

◆ To *resize a shape* that's already been added to a document, select the Shape Selection tool from the Shape tool in the toolbox. Select the shape by clicking the layer in the Layers palette, and then click the picture. Once selected, you can move the item by pushing or pulling its outside handles.

◆ To *rotate a shape*, select the Shape Selection tool from the toolbox. Select the shape by clicking the layer in the Layers palette, then click the picture. You can now move the item by clicking outside a corner of the box where the cursor is a two-headed curved arrow.

◆ To *move a shape* that's already been added to a document, select the Shape Selection tool from Shape icon in the toolbox. Select the shape by clicking the layer in the Layers palette, and then click the picture. Once selected, you can move the item by dragging from the center handle.

Also notice the height/width link buttons. The Link button is visible and looks like a regular icon when unselected, but turns white when selected. When selected, the width and height remain proportional; when deselected, they do not.

Changing the Color

You can change the color of a shape when you add it or after it's been added and edited. However, after adding a style, this is sometimes impossible. Styles come with their own colors and can't be changed without removing the style first.

To change the color of a shape you've just added, click the Color box in the options bar and choose a new color. If you've already added the shape and performed other tasks, the process is a bit more complicated.

To apply a color to a shape that's already been added and edited and is the only shape in the layer, follow these steps:

1. Choose the Shape Selection tool.

2. Double-click the thumbnail of the layer to change the color from the Layers palette. The Color Picker opens automatically. This will not work if you double-click anywhere except the thumbnail.

3. Choose a new color from the Color Picker and click OK.

Using Add, Subtract, Intersect, and Extrude

As mentioned briefly in the earlier section "Working with the Options Bar," you can use five tools when adding shapes. The Create New Shape Layer option is the default, which causes a new layer to be added each time you add a new shape. The Add To Shape Area option is used to add a shape to an existing shape, thus to the same layer. (A new layer won't be created.) The Subtract From Shape Area option is used to add a shape to an existing layer, and then remove the area where the two shapes overlap. The Intersect option is used to add a shape to an existing layer, and show only where the two shapes intersect. The Exclude option is used to add a shape to an existing layer, and to remove the overlapping areas.

To try out these tools, work through the following exercise:

1. Open a new document with plenty of space for experimenting.

2. Add a rectangle to the page.

3. Click the New Shape Layer option and add another rectangle. Notice that a new layer is created by opening the Layers palette from the Palette Well.

4. Click the Add To Shape Area option and add another rectangle. Let it overlap the original one. Notice that the two shapes overlap and are on the same layer.

5. Click the Subtract From Shape Area option and add another rectangle. Let it overlap the first. Notice that this takes away from the original rectangle.

6. Continue in this manner to try all five options.

Think of the possibilities here! You can create your own custom shapes, logos, designs, and all kinds of neat things. Combine your creation with filters, effects, styles, and text, and you've got yourself a pretty nifty piece of work!

Setting Shape Tool Options

Last, but hardly least, are the Shape tool options. Each of the shapes available from the Shape tool in the toolbox has options that you can set. The default settings are "Unrestrained." This means that when you click a Shape tool, you can do just about anything you want to with it, including making it any size you want. However, you can limit what each tool does and change how the tools perform by default by setting additional options and limitations.

Types of Options

The options that you can set for shapes include procedures such as making all rectangles into squares, making any shape a fixed size, making all ellipses circles, smoothing the corners of polygons, and adding arrowheads to lines. You can also set terms for how shapes should keep their proportion. A good option is From Center. This enables you to draw the shape from the center of the object instead of the top-left corner.

Here's a list of the Shape options and how you can use them. You can access these options by clicking the small arrow next to the available tools on the options bar. You'll have to have a Shape tool chosen for this to be available.

- ◆ **Arrowheads** enables you to add arrowheads automatically to either the start or end of a line or both. You can also define the size of the arrowhead.

- ◆ **Circle** makes all ellipses circles.

- ◆ **Defined Proportions** creates a custom shape based on the proportions it had when it was created.

- ◆ **Defined Size** creates a custom shape based on a size it had when it was created.

- ◆ **Fixed Size** creates a shape using a specific size defined by the user in the width and heights boxes.

- ◆ **From Center** enables you to draw the shape from the center instead of the top-left corner.

- ◆ **Indent Sides By** turns a polygon into a star using a percentage defined by the user. This option is only available if you first checked the Star box under the Polygon options. (These stars are really neat!)

- ◆ **Proportional** creates a shape whose proportion you define by inputting values for width and height.

- ◆ **Sides** specifies how many sides a polygon should have by default.

- ◆ **Smooth Corners** or **Smooth Indents** smoothes the corners of the shape.

- ◆ **Snap To Pixels** snaps rectangles to pixel boundaries. This means that when drawing a rectangle, the edges of the rectangle will be lined up with the boundaries of the pixels on the screen.

- ◆ **Square** makes all rectangles squares.

- ◆ **Unconstrained** enables you to move the shape as you see fit, with no predetermined constraints.

- ◆ **Weight** is used with lines to determine how thick the line will be by default.

Applying Options

Now that you have an idea of what types of options are available, let's apply some of these options. To view and change these default options, follow the steps here:

1. Click the Shape tool in the toolbox so that the Shape options bar appears, choose the Rectangle tool, and then click the down arrow next to the Shape options (see Figure 16.7).

Figure 16.7

Configure the default options for shapes here.

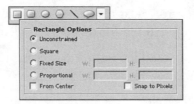

2. Notice that "Unconstrained" is selected by default. To change the tool's behavior, make the appropriate selections. Use your mouse to hover over each selection for a brief explanation of what each one does.

3. Make the appropriate choices for your needs, and then click outside the dialog box to apply them.

> **It's Element-ary**
>
> Remember, you can return all of the settings to their defaults using the far left corner of any options bar. Just click the first icon in the Shape options bar and choose Reset tool.

4. Repeat these steps for the other available shapes.

In this chapter, you learned how to draw shapes using the Shape tool, how to access custom shapes, and how to edit those shapes. Editing topics included changing a shape's size, color, and style. Finally, you learned about changing a Shape tool's options by resetting the tool's default behavior.

The Least You Need to Know

- Vector graphics enable images to be rendered in different sizes.
- The Shape icon in the toolbox offers seven options for drawing shapes.
- A shape's size, color, style, and other attributes can be changed using the Shape options bar.
- Styles enable you to apply special effects to shapes added to an image.
- You use the Shift key when drawing a rectangle or ellipse to draw a square or circle.

Part 5

Advanced Techniques and Special Effects

So many special effects; so little time. Blur filters, artistic filters, noise filters, lighting filters, image effects, textural effects—where does it end? With Photoshop Elements, the tools are at your disposal. Your job is to learn which effect or technique to use and when.

In this section, you'll learn all about the special effects and advanced techniques you need to get that image or photo just right. You can apply effects to layers and parts of layers, or even to multiple layers. Pay special attention to the big college words such as *opacity* and *pixellate*, and you'll have all the tools and skills you need.

Applying Filters

In This Chapter

◆ Choosing and applying filters

◆ Using the Filters and Effects palettes

◆ Understanding filter options

◆ Selecting the right filter

◆ Optimizing filter effects

Filtering the water we get from the tap takes out impurities in the water, thus making it safer and tastier to drink. Oil filters and air filters in cars remove harmful particles, making the engine run better and making it easier to maintain. Filtering photos works kind of the same way. By applying a filter (or any effect) to a digital image, we can make it cleaner, improve on it, or make it easier to look at.

Several types of filters exist, and while some "clean up" the photo, such as filters that improve lighting or that sharpen the photo, others can be used to distort, too. There are noise filters, artistic filters, and texturizing filters, which are all used to give a desired special effect to the photo.

In this chapter you'll learn all about these filters, including how to set the filter options, and later, how to choose and apply the various filters available. Of course, you have ways to optimize the effects of the filters you apply, and we'll introduce that, too.

The Filters Palette

Before we get too deep into *filters*, let's look at the Filters palette. You can open this palette from the Window menu by placing a check next to it, or by dragging it from the palettes bar. Figure 17.1 shows the Filters palette. In this screenshot, the palette has been enlarged by pulling from the lower left corner of it, so that most of the filters can be seen.

Shop Talk

A **filter** is a tool that lets you apply special effects to an image. Filters can be used to distort or clean up an image, make it look three-dimensional, enhance the lighting, or change the texture of the image. Filters are located in the Filters palette.

From inside this palette, you can choose a filter to apply to a photo, scanned image, imported image, or layer. Be careful though, it's easy to go overboard with filters the first time you discover them. Therefore, keep your audience in mind. If you are printing pictures of the grandkids for grandma, she'd probably be happier with a nice filter like diffuse (rather than a filter that distorts their faces).

Figure 17.1

Open the Filters palette using the Window menu options or by dragging from the palettes bar.

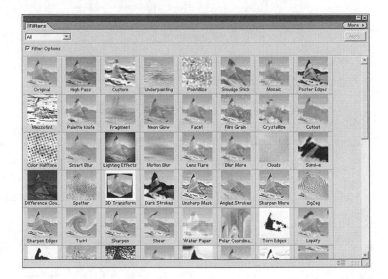

Changing Display Options

From the Filters palette you can view thumbnails or a list of the available options, depending on how the More options are set. (We prefer thumbnail view so we can see each one as we scroll through them.) In Figure 17.1, the thumbnails shown are for *all* of the available effects and filters. The word "All" appears in the window of both palettes to indicate what is displayed.

Several filter choices appear under the All choices. You can separate these filters and effects by category for viewing. For example, in the Filters palette, the filters appear in the following categories: Artistic, Blur, Brush Strokes, Distort, Noise, Pixelate, Render, Sharpen, Sketch, Stylize, Texture, Video, and Other. This chapter focuses on the Filters palette.

To choose a different category for viewing:

1. Open the Filters palette.

2. Click the down arrow underneath the tab in the Filters palette window. By default, the window has All showing.

3. Scroll down through the choices until you locate the category you want. Click it.

CAUTION

Swatch Out!

You only get the More option on the palettes if you either open them from the Window menu, or drag the Palette Well tab to open it. If you just click the tab in the Palette Well, the More button doesn't appear.

In Focus

As you browse through the Filters options, notice that the thumbnails change. Each one gives an example of the filter that a particular choice would have on your photo. You can always apply one and choose Edit → Undo, too, if you just want to experiment.

Applying Filters

After deciding on a filter to apply, the process is pretty easy from there. The hard part is deciding which one to apply! In any case, it's sure easier than changing an oil filter!

Choose and apply a filter by following these steps:

1. Open a photo from your camera, one you've scanned in, or any other image you have that you want to test filters on. If you don't have one in mind, choose the *Car Show.psd* file from the Samples folder in Photoshop Elements.

2. Open the Layers palette to see the layers available and choose a layer if appropriate.

3. Open the Filters palette, click the down arrow to select a category, and choose All to see all of the options. If a check doesn't appear in the Filter Options check box, place one there now. This enables you to set advanced filter options if you desire.

4. Choose a filter to apply. You have three ways to apply a filter to the image once you choose it: Drag it to your image, double-click the filter or click once to

select it, and click the Apply button. Apply the filter. If you are working with the *Car Show.psd* file, choose the High Pass filter to make the image look like it was taken in foggy conditions.

5. An option dialog box now appears, which contains sliders and buttons to control the specific filter you selected. Make sure to check the Preview check box, and then position the sliders until you get the optimum effect. Click OK when finished.

6. Wait patiently while the filter is added. A status bar at the bottom of the Photoshop Elements window shows the filter application's progress. The application of the filter can take only a few seconds or several minutes depending on your computer and the filter you choose.

7. You can now apply additional filters if necessary, add effects, or use any other option to finalize your photo. For the *Car Show.psd* file, try some Stylize filters such as Glowing Edges and Trace Contour. For family photos, try Artistic filters such as Sponge and Colored Pencil. By experimenting with the filters, you'll discover what you like and what you don't!

8. If you don't like any change, click Edit > Undo *<filter name>*, or press Ctrl+Z.

Keep in mind that you can add multiple filters (and/or effects) to a photo or image. Combining filters *and* effects can produce some really nice results. Chapter 18 is all about the Effects palette and using effects, so we won't go into it here, but keep in mind that both can be used together.

You can also apply a filter to only part of an image. This is useful if you want to view the effect quickly and don't want to have to wait for it to apply itself to an entire image, or if you just want to apply the effect to a specific part of an image, such as text, a person's face, a building in the background, a bird, or some other object in the picture. All you have to do is select the part of the image first, using any selection tool.

Choosing the Right Filter

So how do you ever decide which filter to apply? Who decides what is right and what is wrong? As far as filters go, that's a tough question. As we mentioned earlier, Grandma would probably think a distortion filter was the "wrong" one for a photo of the grandkids, while you might think that distorting their little faces seems perfectly acceptable. You'll just have to experiment with the available options to know which filter is best applied where and when. In this section, you'll begin that journey. We detail all of the Artistic and Blur filters here, including how to configure their settings.

Artistic Filters

Artists have all kinds of tools at their disposal. Most of these tools are paints stored in closets, and brushes scattered across rooms, placed upside down in paint jars, or lying in the kitchen sink hoping to be cleaned.

The artistic tools available to you in Photoshop Elements are similar to an artist's tools and include the Palette Knife, Colored Pencil, Watercolor, Rough Pastels, Dry Brush, Sponge, and more—and they can't fall into the kitchen sink garbage disposal! You can see the available tools in Figure 17.2. Each one applies a specific artistic look to the picture or image.

Figure 17.2

The Artistic filters are located in the Filters palette.

Notice in Figure 17.2 that the box Filter Options is checked. Most of the filters available have additional options that you can set after the tool is chosen, and checking this box gives you the opportunity to change those settings. For example, applying the Watercolor filter brings up the dialog box shown in Figure 17.3. Notice that the Brush Detail, Shadow Intensity, and Texture can be set. Each setting has a default. It is usually best to try the default first, and if that doesn't give you good results, use Edit → Undo and try changing it again. Think of it as rinse and repeat. While experimenting with these, use the + and − buttons to zoom in or out in the preview area.

In Focus

Although the filters do the best job they can at applying an artistic technique, an attempt at watercoloring a house (or any other image with limited contrasting colors) may look more like a photo negative than a watercolor! The watercolor technique may do better with pictures of higher contrast and well-defined lines. With high contrast images, increase the Brush Detail to get finer lines and strokes, lessen it for more brush lines.

Figure 17.3

Specify additional options when applying a filter.

You can probably guess what some of the artistic options do. The Watercolor option makes the picture look like it was drawn using watercolors instead of being a photo. The Colored Pencil option redraws the image using pencil strokes. Use the thumbnails in the Filters Artistic palette to get a feel for the other techniques.

Some tips for Artistic filters include the following:

- Don't use more than one Artistic filter on the same photograph. Applying more than one usually results in an unwanted effect.

- Touch up the photo after applying the filter using the Brush tools detailed in Chapter 14, if parts of the photo seem incorrect or unmatched.

- If you don't get the effect you want after applying a filter, choose Undo and try again. The next time, move the sliders left and right to improve the effect.

- Don't forget about logos, signs, hand-drawn artwork, and other files. You can apply filters to them, too! (You'll have to simplify the type first, but you'll be prompted to do that.)

Blur Filters

The six blur filters are Smart Blur, Motion Blur, Blur More, Gaussian Blur, Blur, and Radial Blur. You can see samples of each of these by choosing the Blur filter from the

Filters palette. Each of these filters softens the image (or selection) in a different way by reducing the amount of detail in the image.

The name of the filter gives insight into what the filter does to an image. The Blur and Blur More filters soften the image (or the selected part of the image), by smoothing the transitions between the colors in the image. Using either of these tools gives the image a watercolor-like effect.

The Motion Blur makes the image seem like it's moving, and is good when editing photos or images of cars, ships, animals, or other moving objects. Use the Motion Blur only on a specific selection in the image, such as a surfer or airplane, to get really neat effects.

The Radial Blur applies the blur in a circular fashion, not unlike how you'd take a photo using a digital camera while rotating the camera. Smart Blur lets you specify how blurred you want the image to be and how the edges of color transitions should be handled. The neatest Blur option, though, is Gaussian Blur. This blur lets you control precisely how much effect you want to add.

You apply each of the blur filters the same way, and each one has options you can set. Use the following example as a guide to applying any Blur filter:

1. Open any photo you'd like to apply a blur to, such as a picture of a person golfing, a moving car, or a bird in flight. A sample photo appears in Figure 17.4.

2. From the Filters palette, choose Blur, and then the type of blur to apply. For the picture in Figure 17.4, we chose the Radial Blur filter.

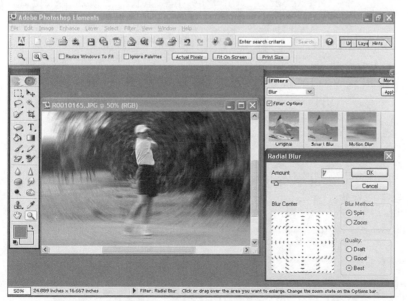

Figure 17.4

Saving a practice swing using Radial Blur.

3. Make sure a check appears in the Filter Options check box, and then click Apply. (You can also drag the choice over to the image.)

4. When the Blur dialog box appears, as shown in Figure 17.4, use the sliders to control the amount of blur you desire. This figure shows the dialog box for a Radial Blur. Be patient after choosing OK!

You have several options for the different blur options dialog boxes. While it's too much to describe each one of them here, several terms are common to each:

◆ **Radius** specifies how far from the center of the image the blur will be applied.

◆ **Threshold** specifies at what point pixels in the image are eradicated, based on the difference between them.

◆ **Angle** is a number ranging from –360 to +360 that specifies the blur angle in a Motion Blur.

◆ **Distance** defines how far the blur will extend in the image.

In Focus

The best way to get to know the Distort filters is to spend some time looking at the thumbnails for each one and applying them to images. You can set lots of different options, and experimentation is the best way to learn these options. Keep in mind, though, that distortion filters are memory-intensive. This means that it might take a while to apply one to the image, so choose carefully!

It's Element-ary

The Liquify filter is a beast all unto itself. The Liquify effect makes things look like they are fluid. When you choose this filter, a new window appears and you'll be asked to choose a brush size and brush pressure. You'll then use the brush to change the image inside this new window. Choosing OK applies the filter to the actual image.

Distort Filters

Lots of Distort filters are available. You'll find ZigZag, Twirl, Shear, Polar Coordinates, Liquefy, Glass, Wave, Ripple, Ocean Ripple, Pinch, Diffuse Glow, and Spherize. Applying these filters is just like applying any other filter described in this chapter. Take a look at the different types of Distort filters available. As with the other filters, the Distort filters have options that you can set.

As you apply these filters, you'll run across terms in the filter options dialog boxes that you might not understand. Some of the more common terms you'll see in these dialog boxes include the following:

◆ **Angle** specifies how the angle of the distortion should be applied. A higher number generally intensifies the effect; a lower number lessens it.

◆ **Amount** and **Ridges** in the Zigzag filter specify how many ridges (in percent) and what type should be applied to the image. More ridges and amounts equal more distortion.

- **Distortion** and **Smoothness** define how distorted an image should be. Higher numbers distort and smooth more; lower numbers distort and smooth less.

- **Wavelength**, **Amplitude**, and **Scale** in the Wave filter determine how the waves should look based on their length, the number of repetitions, and how large or small the wave is.

- **Graininess** determines how "grainy" or sandy-looking the Diffuse Glow filter should be when applied.

Pixelate Filters

What the heck is a *pixelate*? Sometimes we think software engineers just make up words! Another funny one is *pointillize*. Even if these words aren't in the dictionary, they do mean something to us.

Pixelate is a filter that gathers pixels together that are similar in color, and then replaces them with something new. For instance, choosing the Pixelate filter Mosaic recreates the image so that it is a montage of the colors in the image. This medley of colors is created out of square blocks (like pixels), and the image is transformed to look like a mosaic painting.

Of the other Pixelate filters, Pointillize changes the image to dots of colors instead of squares, and thus creates artwork that resembles pointillist paintings.

If you want to make an image look like it is hand-painted, try the Facet option. If you want the image to look like it is made of hundreds of broken pieces of glass, try the Crystallize option. Other options exist, too. As usual, viewing the thumbnails and experimenting is the best way to learn.

Render Filters

Render filters can make an ordinary photo speak out and have character. These filters are really something special, and there aren't so many that it is difficult to choose one. You have several Render filters to choose from: Lighting Effects, Lens Flare, Clouds, Difference Clouds, and 3-D Transform.

You can apply these types of effects easily to express heat (Lens Flare), closeness (Lighting Effect), to set a background of clouds (Clouds), to make the image look like it was taken at night (Difference Clouds), and to apply special effects using the 3-D Transform option.

Applying this filter is just like applying any other. Here's how:

1. Select the image, a part of the image, or the layer to which you want to apply the filter.

2. From the Filters palette, choose Render, and then the type of filter to apply.

3. Make sure a check appears in the Filter Options check box, and then click Apply. (You can also drag the choice over to the image.)

4. When the filter's dialog box appears, use the sliders (if available) to control the amount of filter applied.

Texturizing Filters

Like the Pixelate filters, Texturizing filters can make the image look like it is created from pieces of glass (like a mosaic or a stained-glass window), it can be made to look grainy, it can be made to look like the image has been drawn on canvas or burlap, and it can be made to look like it was created from a patchwork quilt. These texturizing effects make the image appear as if it was created on these surfaces. You can also apply a cracked look using Craquelure.

By using the Texturizer filter and selecting Burlap from the Texture options, we've made the picture in Figure 17.5 look like the image has been transferred to a burlap sack!

Figure 17.5

Use the Texturizing filters to make a photo appear to have been transferred to other materials.

Other Filters

Way too many filters are available to list them all in this chapter, and that would just bore you anyway! However, some really cool filters are available. To help you decide which filters are best and for what applications, here are a few suggestions:

- Use the Artistic filter Smudge Stick to make something look dirty.

- Use the Sketch filter Chalk and Charcoal to make the image look like it was drawn in the chalk and charcoal style.

- Use the Distort filter Pinch to make an image seem "squeezed," like in a carnival mirror.

- Use the Blur filter Motion Blur to make an image seem like it's moving.

- Use the Other filter Offset to make the image look like a horizontal or vertical TV picture gone bad (one part above and one part below, or one part to the left and one to the right).

- Use the Other filter High Pass to make the image look foggy, or the day look stormy.

There's actually a category called "Other" filters. Using this category, you can create and apply custom filters. With all of the predefined filters available, though, you probably won't need custom filters for everyday tasks!

Specifying Distorted Areas

Sometimes you'll want to distort a small piece of an image or photo without distorting the entire image, or better than that, without anyone knowing any part of it has been distorted. For example, applying a Motion Blur filter to a coyote in an image, so that it looks like the camera caught it in motion, certainly adds to the image but might go undetected as a manual addition.

You can use the Lasso tool, the Marquee tool, or Selection Brush tool to specify a specific part of the image to filter or distort. The rest of the image won't be affected. You have several ways to specify distorted and nondistorted parts of an image.

Do one of the following to define what parts of an image to filter:

- To apply a filter to an entire layer, deselect everything, and then select the layer to apply the filter to in the Layers palette.

Swatch Out!

When applying filters to specific parts of an image rather than the entire image, don't overdo the distortion and filter techniques. Too much distortion causes the selected area to stand out and look mismatched.

◆ To apply a filter to only part of a layer, select the layer in the Layers palette, and then use any selection tool to select an area in the layer.

◆ To apply a filter to multiple layers at the same time, link the layers together in the Layers palette.

◆ Select what you don't want to apply the filter to, and then choose the Select > Invert tool to select the rest of the image.

◆ To apply a filter to a shape, use the Shape Selection tool to select the shape.

Optimizing Filter Effects

A friend of ours used to say, "You just never know when to stop, do you?" It sounds like a bad thing, but because it had to do with persistence, we're really not sure it was that bad. However, too much of *anything* can ruin a perfectly *good* thing.

The best lesson we can teach you about how to optimize filter effects is to tell you not to overdo it. While these effects are cool, they don't apply to everyone or every picture. While we have some personal preferences, it's good to follow a few good rules:

1. Don't distort pictures of your family; use the filters that offer lighting enhancements and artistic looks.

2. Unless necessary, don't choose a filter that "darkens" a photo; these tend to make them gloomy looking. If you must, though, you can always color-correct after the fact.

3. Unless you are going for a specific look, don't distort a picture beyond recognition; you'll be the only one who appreciates it!

4. Use Charcoal or Colored Pencil filters to create a nice outline of images; they'll look hand-drawn.

5. Use the Brush Stroke filter Ink Outlines for caricatures and comics.

6. We can't think of any reason to add "Noise" to an image. This doesn't mean there aren't times, but…

7. Use the Stylize options to enhance signs in an image (you can make them look neon), or to trace the contours of an image.

In addition, optimizing a photo or image can be left to the options in the Enhance menu and the Image menu, using both automatic enhancements and manual ones. You can apply these enhancements after adding filters and effects, and you can combine both filters and effects for more emphasis. Whatever you do, experiment and have fun—the Undo command is there for a reason!

This chapter introduced you to both the Filters and Effects palettes, and you learned how to use and apply filters. While applying a filter was easy, selecting one wasn't. We introduced you to lots of types of filters, including Noise, Pixelate, Lighting Effects, Texturizing, Artistic, Blur, and more. You have so many filters to choose from, knowing which one to apply and when can be challenging. In the end, you learned how to specify specific areas for filtering and distortion instead of applying it to the entire image, and also learned how to optimize the filters you apply.

The Least You Need to Know

- The Filters palette enables you to view thumbnails of each filter before applying it.

- A check in the Filter Options check box enables you to see the advanced options and change them if necessary.

- You can use Render, Sharpen, Blur, and other filters to enhance an image without distorting it.

- Distort, Noise, and Pixelate filters enable you to severely distort an image.

- You can use filters such as Watercolor, Ink Outlines, Charcoal, Dry Brush, and Water Paper to render the image in another format.

Adding Special Effects

In This Chapter

- Understanding the Effects palette
- Choosing and applying effects
- Understanding the difference between Frames, Textures, Text, and Image Effects
- Analyzing effects using the History palette

So you want to have an effect on people? Choose the right effect for your images!

Effects are similar to the filters you studied in the previous chapter; not only do you choose and apply them in the same manner, but some of the effects available are also modified filters! In this chapter you'll learn how to use the Effects palette to view, choose, and apply effects, as well as to understand the differences between the four effects categories. You'll also learn how to track effects using the History palette, and how to optimize the effects you choose.

Using the Effects Palette

Using the Effects palette is easy. Just open it from the Windows menu, and you're ready to go! You can view all of the effects in a single window, as shown in Figure 18.1, or you can view only a single category of effects: Frames, Textures, Text, or Image effects. (The window is stretched to show you all of the available effects.)

Figure 18.1

The Photoshop Elements Effects palette—at your service.

It's Element-ary

There are special effects and just effects. Special effects are like the stuff in the movies and are mostly located in the Image category. You can use them to distort images, redraw them using neon colors, or make the image look like it's made from tiny pieces of other material (such as glass). Frames are just plain old effects; choose one to frame a picture—oh the excitement! Text effects are pretty straightforward too—they just spice up your type. Textual effects can be considered special effects, and you use them to add texture to an object, layer, or part of an image. If you want to add a "special" effect, look in the Image category!

Choosing the Effect You Want

To be effectual is to be powerful, capable, and influential. That's what your effects should be too. They should grab the viewer's attention, and should have an impact on the picture. Keep in mind when choosing an effect, that the effect you choose should enhance your work, not take away from it—don't just apply an effect because you can.

Besides choosing an effect that adds something to your work, you'll also have to choose an effect that your work can be added to! Some effects can only be used for specific items or selections. Look closely at Figure 18.1 or open the Effects palette yourself, and you can see that a few of the effects have something written after their name. Some have words in parentheses such as "Type," "Layer," or "Selection." (Thumbnails are showing in Figure 18.1, but you can click the toggle button at the bottom of the palette to go back and forth between the list view and the thumbnail view. List view enables you to see the entire name of the effect, including the type of object you can apply it to.) This means that those specific effects can only be used for certain types of data. For example, an effect that has the word "Layer" after it can only be used with a single selected layer. An effect with the word "Type" after it can only be used with text. And an effect with the word "Selection" after it can only be applied to a selected piece of the image.

In Focus

Open up the Effects menu and choose All from the selection window. Drag and resize the Effects palette until you can see all of the effects. Next, view the effects by their four types. Once you finish with this little tutorial, you should be pretty familiar with the types of effects available.

Framing Effects

Our construction friend who frames houses for a living wouldn't agree that framing is easy, but framing images in Photoshop Elements certainly is!

You have several styles of frames to choose from in the Effects palette. You can choose a frame to finalize your work, and give it that "something extra." Choose a Photo Corner frame to make the picture look like it has folded edges, use a Brushed Aluminum frame to give the image a "modern" feel, use a Waves frame around scenic ocean shots, use a Wood frame for a "classic" look, and try a Vignette frame to use around a selected piece of the image.

In Focus

Apply the frame last if you have multiple layers. Applying a frame "flattens" an image, so make sure you finish all editing on all of the layers before you apply the new frame. Better yet, save an intermediate copy of the file before applying the frame. The Undo History is only available until the file is saved, and if more than 20 subsequent steps are done, you won't be able to revert back anyway.

Take a look at Figure 18.2. It's a picture of some flowers that have been framed and had other attributes applied. Let's open that file and recreate it! Here's how:

1. Open the *frame.tif* file from the Chapter 18 folder on the CD-ROM. Use the Rectangular Marquee tool together with Image > Crop from the menu bar to crop the image so the yellow flowers are centered. For help using the selection tools, refer to Chapters 5 and 6. Save the new file to your hard drive. (You can also find a copy on the CD-ROM—it's *frame2.tif*.)

2. Use the Elliptical Marquee tool to encircle the flowers only.

3. Open the Effects palette from the Window menu or from the palette list in the toolbar, and click the drop-down window in the Effects palette and choose Frames.

4. Select the Vignette frame and click Apply. Because we're framing a selected part of an image, the frame chosen must have the word "Selection" after it. There are several types of frames that can be applied to selections: Vignette, Recessed, Cut Out, and Text Panel. You'll be prompted to "flatten" the layers, so click Yes.

5. The new frame is applied. You can find a saved copy of this intermediate step (*frame3.tif*) on the CD-ROM.

6. Select a new foreground color. Figure 18.2 uses a light blue.

7. Add a new layer from the Layer → New Fill Layer option. Choose Gradient from the three choices (Solid Color, Gradient, Pattern).

8. In the New Layer dialog box, name the new layer **Gradient Fill 1** and click OK.

9. After clicking OK in the New Layer dialog box, the Gradient Fill dialog box appears. Choose Radial from the Style choices, and set the angle at –180 degrees.

10. Click the arrow by the Gradient button and choose the gradient you desire. (Once applied, you can change the opacity if you want.) For Figure 18.2, the first gradient was chosen. Click OK. This final image is saved as *frame4.psd* on the CD-ROM.

Figure 18.2

This figure shows flowers with a Vignette frame and gradient fill foreground.

Take a look at the Layers palette now. You should see four layers. The Background layer is the picture itself, and Layer 2, which is the new layer, should be added. Layer 3 contains the gradient, and Layer 1 is the selection of the flowers.

You can do other neat stuff too. For example, you can use the Shape tool to draw a funky shape (even a star if you use the polygon options) and then simplify, select, and save the selection. This will give you the funky selection on the layer you want, and then you can apply a selection effect to frame the unique shape. You could easily put a star around your kid's face in a class picture, for example.

Framing is always a good addition to photos of flowers, family, and friends—or foes—and offers a quick and easy way to finish off a photo.

Image Effects

A second type of effect category is the Image effect. Image effects apply to layers only, not to selections or text. Choosing and applying an Image effect is similar to choosing and applying a Frame effect, except you must choose the layer from the Layers palette instead of selecting the area with a selection tool.

To choose and apply an Image effect, use the Effects palette to view the Image category separately. Then, use the Layers palette to select the layer to apply the effect to, and select the effect. You don't have any options to specify here; just choose the effect you want and click Apply.

How do you know which effect to apply? First, take a look at the thumbnails, and try to visualize what would look best with your particular image. Besides that, consider the following tips:

- To make it look like it's snowing in your picture, try the Blizzard effect.

- To make the image look like it's been drawn on the neighbor's sidewalk with chalk, try the Florescent Chalk effect.

- To make the image look like it was drawn on alligator skin, try the Lizard Skin effect.

- To make a layer look like nighttime in Las Vegas, use the Neon Nights effect.

- To make the layer look like it's an oil painting, try the Oil Painting effect.

> **It's Element-ary**
>
> When you use the Blizzard effect, the image is pointillized, which is actually a filter. When you apply the Lizard Skin effect, the filters Gaussian and Stained glass are applied, among others. The point is, many effects are combinations of existing filters. So you might try playing with a series of filters to see what kinds of self-created effects you can produce.

In Focus

Before applying an effect, make an intermediate copy or save the work done so far just in case you want to revert back to it, the way we did in the first example when applying the Frame effect. With many of the effects, once you apply the effect, characteristics that otherwise could have been modified become unmodifiable.

♦ To make an image appear foggy or blurred, try the Soft Flat Color or Soft Focus effect.

Figure 18.3 shows the Frame effect enhanced with both Blizzard and Lizard Skin (making it look like needlepoint). The layer containing the flowers is enhanced with the Oil Painting effect.

Although some combinations of Image effects can be used to create textural effects as shown in Figure 18.3, there are specific effects already configured just for that. In the next section, you'll explore the textural effects available from Photoshop Elements.

Figure 18.3

Use the Effects palette to locate, choose, and apply Image effects.

Textural Effects

Using an existing Textural effects is usually easier than applying several other effects to create a textured effect of your own. However, there aren't that many predefined textured effects to choose from, so if you don't see exactly what you want, you might have to create one yourself anyway. You'll have to experiment by combining several other effects to find the one you want if that's the case.

If you can use one of the available textured effects, you can apply them in a variety of ways. Most of the time, they're used for background layers with images placed on top of them. However, many of these effects can be applied to existing layers. Open the Effects palette to view the available textured effects.

One of the ways to apply a textured effect is to select a layer from the Layers palette to apply the effect to. You can also add a new layer to add the effect to before applying it. You can do this to enhance the image or give it a different look and feel. Figure 18.4 shows a before and after example.

Here's a neat little trick for creating an image that combines an image we've been working on and a newly created textured layer:

1. Open the image *frame4.tif* from the Chapter 18 folder of the CD-ROM, or any image you have to which you'd like to add an effect.

2. Use the Layer → New Layer command to create an additional layer.

3. Open the Effects palette and choose Textures from the drop-down list.

4. From the Layers palette click the new layer (it should be chosen already). Then choose the effect Wood—Pine (layer) and select Apply.

5. Notice how the frame changes to reflect the new texture; *frame5.tif* shows this.

6. Try other textures too, such as Marbled Glass, shown in *frame6.tif*, Bricks, shown in *frame7.psd*, and others. All are shown in the before and after shots in Figure 18.4.

Of course, you can apply textures to other layers too. With multiple layers already in an image, it's quite a bit easier. Just select the layer you want to apply the texture to and choose Apply. Keep in mind that you might have to use the Layer commands to bring the correct layer to the front of the image, and/or change the opacity of the textured layer to let it show through.

In Focus

After applying a textured effect, choose the textured layer from the Layers palette and apply less than 100 percent opacity for some really neat results. In the previous example (use *frame.tif* from the CD-ROM), add the textured effect Psychedelic Strings, and then, from the Layers palette, change the opacity to 40 percent to enhance the photo. This makes the frame look like it's made of cloth.

Figure 18.4

You can use a textured background to enhance an image.

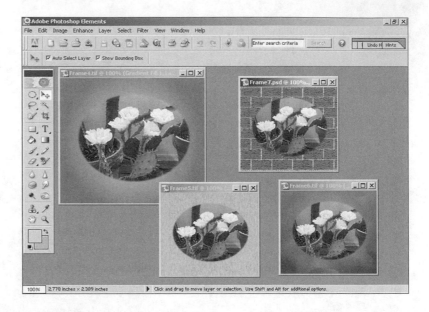

Textual Effects

Text, type, it's all the same! You can spice up the text you've added to your image using the Text tools available from the Effects menu. It's pretty easy; just select the text, select the effect, and choose Apply.

To see, choose, and apply textual effects, perform the following steps:

1. Open the Effects palette and choose Text Effects. There are 11 of them.

2. Add the text to the image (as detailed in Chapter 13).

3. Select the text, and then double-click the effect to apply it.

4. Once you apply the effect, the text layer changes to a regular layer and the text cannot be edited. In addition, no other text effects can be applied because the text isn't considered text anymore; it's a layer. Click the checkmark to save the changes, or choose to reject.

Analyzing Effects with the History Palette

Although you've probably gotten to know the Edit → Undo command pretty well, let's revisit the History palette for a minute. No, it isn't some long, horrible history lesson you'll have to sit through; it's just a fancy way to undo what you've already done.

The History commands let you correct mistakes you've made and revert back to happier times—moments when the image looked kind of like what you wanted. It enables you to undo that distort command or remove textures you've added. You can even erase erasures! However, there's no redo command when you use Undo History to erase stuff. Make sure you mean to do what you mean to do, and consider saving an intermediate copy before you do it!

To see how the Undo History commands work, you'll have to open a document and make some changes to it. The Undo History commands show what's been done to an image, and if you haven't done anything to it, there won't be anything to see! You can open the Undo History palette from the Undo History tab located with the other palettes, or from the Window menu. Figure 18.5 shows a sample Undo History window. (If you use the Help files with Photoshop Elements, the Undo History palette might sometimes be referred to simply as History; don't let this confuse you.)

Once open, move the slider to the command to undo. Photoshop Elements will undo all of the previous commands. Remember, though, that there's no undo for erasing from the Undo History palette, so make sure you're sure!

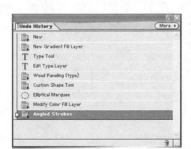

Figure 18.5

Use the Undo History palette to see what steps have been taken so far.

Sorting Through the History Palette Settings

Because the History palette settings haven't been introduced yet, we'd better introduce them now. You should consider configuring a few item, such as how much information you'll store in the History list. Save too much, and you could slow down the application; don't save enough and you might regret it later!

To view the History settings, choose Edit → Preferences → General. (If this is grayed out, save your work and try again.) Located in the Preferences dialog box is a number in the History States window. The default is 20, meaning that Photoshop Elements will save your past 20 commands. To reduce memory usage (if your computer seems to respond slowly, try this), reduce this number. If you think you might need more than 20 undo options, raise the number. Make sure you have plenty of memory if you raise the number though—we suggest at least 192MB of *RAM*.

Shop Talk

RAM stands for Random Access Memory, and your computer uses it to remember temporary data such as History, to calculate and apply changes to an image, to hold program instructions, to hold information to print, and lots more. RAM plays an important role in how fast your computer responds. The more RAM, the better!

Under Edit → Preferences you can also find the Memory and Image Cache options. Here, you can also tell Photoshop Elements how to use what memory you do have. By default, it uses 50 percent of the available memory for running the application, and leaves the other 50 percent for other applications. If you are running several applications at once, you might want to consider lowering this number so that the other applications will get their fair share of the available RAM. If you usually only run Photoshop Elements and you have lots of RAM (more than 128MB), leave it at 50 percent for the best performance.

In this chapter, you learned how to apply effects using the Effects palette. The four types of effects are Frame, Image, Text, and Texture. You can use these effects to enhance an image by placing a frame around it, by distorting or lightening an image, by spicing up text, and by adding a textured background. We also introduced the History palette, which offers a way to easily undo mistakes and past commands.

The Least You Need to Know

- The four types of effects are Text, Texture, Image, and Frame, which enable you to add effects to images.

- Use the Effects palette to choose and apply the effects.

- You can undo effects with the Edit → Undo command or with the History palette.

- Some effects can only be used for layers, some only for text, and some only for a selection. For example, you can apply a text effect only to a text layer.

- The History palette remembers your past 20 steps by default; the Edit → Preferences General menu enables you to change this.

Working with Layer Styles

In This Chapter

- ◆ Understanding the Layer Styles palette
- ◆ Changing default style settings
- ◆ Adding a shadow or glow to a layer
- ◆ Setting a layer's opacity
- ◆ Blending layers

In the last few chapters, we focused mainly on applying a change (filter or effect) to an entire image, a background layer, or just to the text in that image, because these are the most basic ways to apply a change. This chapter focuses on images that have multiple layers, and on manipulating more than a single layer in an image to obtain a desired effect.

The best way to apply an effect to a layer is to use the Layer Styles palette. In this chapter, you'll learn how to use this palette, what layer styles are available, and how layer styles are best applied. You'll also learn about Style settings, what they are used for, and how to change them.

Working with the Layer Styles Palette

The Layer Styles palette is available from both the Photoshop Elements Window menu and the Palette Well. Lots of styles are available. These styles enable you to create visual effects when you apply one or more of the available styles to a single layer or to multiple layers.

It's Element-ary

While images can be single-layered images from say, a digital camera, images can also be manually created using multiple layers. For example, you can create a background layer (perhaps just a solid color or even a transparent base layer), copy and paste an image from another file to create an Image layer, add some text to create a Type layer, and change the hue, saturation, and similar attributes to create an Adjustment layer. You can edit each of these layers to obtain the final image you are looking for. In this chapter, I'll assume you know how to create layers, and have read Chapters 7 and 8. If you aren't quite sure about layers, look back to those chapters.

Optimizing the Workspace for the Styles Palette

If your workspace is anything like ours, you barely have room for your mouse to move around on your desk. (If you're really messy, maybe you have real mice under your desk, too!) While keeping your desk worker-friendly and in order might be difficult, keeping your Photoshop Elements desktop organized is easy. Figure 19.1 shows the Layers Styles palette (on top) along with the Layers palette (on bottom). When working with styles and layers, it's best and easiest to have these open and resized large so they are readily available.

To refresh your memory about palettes to make working even more productive, remember that you have two places to drop one palette over the other. The first puts them in one tabbed window (drag and release one palette over the other almost anywhere when the originally open palette window shows a change) and the other puts them in one window stacked one on top of the other (drag and release the second palette all the way to the bottom of the originally open palette window so a dark line appears at the bottom of the originally open window). You can always revert back to the default palettes by using Window → Reset Palette Locations.

As far as styles go, the image in Figure 19.1 contains a modern-looking Neon Layer style applied to the background layer, a combination of several layer styles applied to the layer named Layer 1, and a Wow Chrome Layer Style applied to the outside of the picture of the flowers. You'll learn how to apply layer styles like this to your images in this chapter. Well, what are we waiting for?

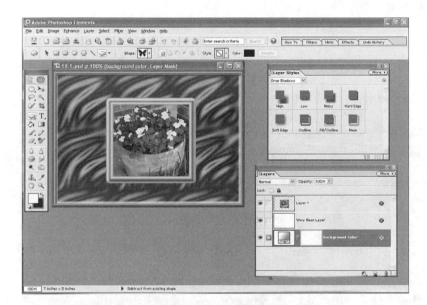

Figure 19.1

Use the Layers palette and the Layer Styles palette to apply layer styles.

Adding Special Effects Using the Layer Style Palette

Special effects enhance your work and your photos. In fact, special effects can actually sell an idea! For example, a Realtor can use Photoshop Elements styles to enhance a picture of a house he or she wants to sell by applying a frame around the photo and applying a style to text, or a new dad can apply a glow to the picture of his newborn. The possibilities are endless.

Go ahead and browse through the various layer styles so you are familiar with what is available. Follow these steps to add special effects:

1. Open an image or a file that has several layers. If you don't have a file available, open the file *carp.psd* located in the Photoshop Elements Samples folder. You can locate the Sample folder by using File → Open, and browsing to the Program Files folder, then the Adobe folder, the Photoshop Elements folder, then the Samples folder.

2. Open the Layer Styles palette from the Palette Well.

3. Click the down arrow to view the 14 categories of styles in the Layer Styles palette. Browse through each.

4. Now, open the Layers palette, and click on the layer named Shape 1, and choose the Layer Style Outer Glows Fire from the Layers Styles palette. Double-click the Fire style to apply it.

> ### Swatch Out!
>
> It is best to double-click the layer style to apply it, versus dragging it to the image. Double-clicking ensures that the layer style is applied to the layer you want. Sometimes dragging over the layer style applies it to the wrong layer!
>
> To see this phenomenon, select the Shape 1 layer in the Layers palette. Select the Outer Glows Fire style from the Layer Styles palette as shown in the last step previously. Now, drag the Fire style over to the image instead of double-clicking. Let go of the mouse at the top-left corner. Instead of having the style applied to the layer selected in the Layer palette, the style is applied to the text in the top-left corner of the image! Just remember to double-click and not drag in this situation.

The way the style is applied to a chosen layer is its default. Although no options come up when you apply the style as with other effects, options are available after it is applied. These style settings are covered in the last section of this chapter.

Adding a Drop Shadow

Drop shadows don't have anything to do with raindrops, tear drops, or eye drops, but it does have to do with shadows that drop. A drop shadow effect makes the image look like it stands up off the page. This works especially well for text (see Figure 19.2), especially if the style is combined with a Text Effect such as Brush Metal or Cast Shadow. The image in Figure 19.2, for example, uses the style Drop Shadow Soft Edge, as well as a frame, and the picture itself has been doctored using the Photoshop Elements QuickFix features. You can add drop shadows to images or entire layers; they are available from the Styles palette. (If you are a little rusty with doctoring the images, refer back to Chapters 9 and 11.)

It's easy to apply a drop shadow to text: Just select the text layer, choose the style to apply, and double-click it to apply it to the image. It works the same way with a layer or an image. Just select the layer from the Layers palette, choose the effect, and apply it.

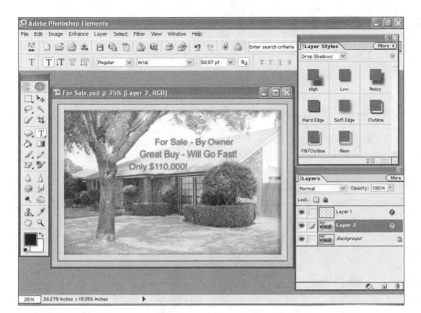

Creating a Glow Effect

The Outer Glow style and the Inner Glow style add a light coloring to the outside or inside edge of a layer, which you can use to draw attention to a layer or object.

Adding one of these glows is the same as adding any other Layer Styles effect. Just choose the layer you want to apply the glow to, and choose the glow you want from the Layer Styles palette tab. Photoshop Elements applies the Outer Glow to the layer.

Try adding a glow to the outside of a family photo, a picture of the moon or stars, or to add special effects to a photo. The Outer Glows Fire style offers a nice special effect that can make the object or text look like it's surrounded by fire. Any Inner Glow makes the object look like it has dropped behind the image.

Fiddling with Opacity

What if you could see just how transparent a person was? That would be useful, although currently impossible. You can set and see the transparency of your layers in Photoshop Elements, though, by setting the opacity of a layer.

You've already been introduced to opacity in previous chapters, but for your review, *opacity* is how transparent the layer or selection is. If the opacity is set at 100 percent, the layer is completely filled and nothing shows through where there is content in a layer. Setting the opacity at 50 percent makes it somewhat see-through, and at

25 percent, really thin. You can set opacity for brush and pencil strokes too, enabling you to set "how hard" it seems you are painting or writing.

To change the opacity of a layer (any layer which is not a background layer), follow these steps:

1. Use the Layers palette to select the layer you want to change the opacity of.

2. Notice that the default opacity is at 100 percent. The layer is completely opaque (exactly opposite of transparent).

3. Move the slider bar under the opacity window to a number from 1 to 100, with 1 being the most transparent, and 100 being the least. (Use the Opacity window that's available from the Layers palette.)

4. Change the opacity of any other layers.

When you compare the images in Figure 19.3, you'll notice that the opacity has been changed in the gradient layer from 100 to 50 percent, thus changing the entire look of the image.

Figure 19.3

Top: Leave the opacity at 100 percent for one effect. Bottom: Change the opacity for another effect.

Beveling a Layer

What is a bevel? Sounds like a gavel to us, or at least some kind of tool you use to beat stuff up with! It isn't, though. It's a kind of outline, and it seems to work best with text and creating buttons for Web pages. Bevel options work well for both buttons and for links to e-mail, because beveling a layer makes it look like it's in 3-D.

You have lots of options for beveling, and they are available from the Layer Styles palette. Figure 19.4 shows an example of both beveled text and beveled buttons. The photo is a bit exaggerated to show you the intricacies of beveling, and you can tell that the text looks like it's coming off of the page! In real life, just a little bevel will be fine for a professional look.

To create a beveled image, add some text to an image, and choose the correct bevel from the Layer Styles palette. In Figure 19.4, a glass button from the Styles menu was added, too, so you can see the effect of that too.

In Focus

You can change how deep the bevel is from the style settings. These settings are detailed later in the chapter.

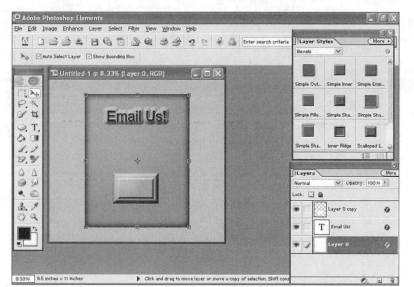

Figure 19.4

Use the Bevel options to make the image seem to jump off of the page.

Having Fun with Blends

A "blended" family is created when two families become one. The recipe is simple: Take two families, put them in the same house, and watch them interact! Perfect sitcom material.

Photoshop Elements lets you blend two pictures, or two layers, to create special effects, too. You have lots of options for blending these layers (17 in fact), and they are available in the Layers palette. Most of the time we keep that blend setting in Normal mode; however, you can do quite a bit of manipulation by choosing the others. These blend settings define how two modes interact with each other.

The problem with using blends is knowing what blend to use and when to apply it. Although too many blend options exist for us to go through them one by one, several are pretty neat and worth a closer look. When you first work with blends, follow these tips to get the best results:

- If you want the blend to darken everything, try the Multiply or Darken options.

- If you want to lighten everything, try the Screen or Lighten option.

- If you want to remove color, try the Color Dodge and Color Burn options. Refer to Chapter 11 for more information about using these tools.

- To add light or a photographic effect to a photo, try the Soft Light, Hard Light, Linear Light, or similar options. You can also use these options to make it seem like a light is shining on an object from a specific angle.

- Try Difference and Exclusion to blend the layers based on their base color, how much they contrast, and their brightness.

It's Element-ary

Understanding what each of the 17 blend options do can be quite difficult. Basically, Photoshop Elements looks at the "base" color of the image (which is the original color of the first layer), the "blend" color (the color that's on the second layer), and then the "resulting" color—the combination of these. For each of the 17 options, there's a rule of some sort for figuring out the resulting color. For example, choosing Darken prompts Photoshop Elements to look at both the base color and the blend color, and then it chooses the darker one of the two to be the result color. Pixels lighter than the blend color are replaced, while pixels darker do not change. Fortunately for you, you don't have to care how it's done. Just try the blend option and if it suits you continue on, but if not, undo and try the next option.

Blends are easy to apply, but the image has to have at least two layers. (Of course, you can apply other tricks, too. You can duplicate the background layer if you want, or select part of the image, apply the blend filter, choose invert selection, and then delete to allow the unblended background to come through.) First, choose the layer that isn't the background layer. Next, open the Layers palette and choose a blend. The blend is applied automatically! If you don't like it, just click Undo. Remember to click Undo if you don't like a particular blend; otherwise, the blends will just accumulate.

Changing Style Settings

Now that you know how to apply styles to layers, how do you go about changing how they look? As we mentioned earlier in the "Beveling a Layer" section, you can change how deep the bevel is by changing its style settings. You can change attributes for the other styles too. Double-clicking the cursive *f* in the Layers palette is what you'll use to change a style's settings.

As the previous sentence implies, you have to apply a style to a layer before you can edit its settings. With other tools (such as Effects and Filters), the settings options come up *before* you apply them. With styles, those options are editable only *after* you apply them.

Refer back to Figure 19.4. You'll see a small, cursive *f* beside each layer that has a style applied. In Figure 19.4, three layers are available with this option.

Changing Settings

Before we can talk about what settings can be changed and for what style, you'll have to know how to get to the options. Follow these steps:

1. Open an image you've recently applied a style to using the Layer Styles palette. If you don't have one, open the *cactusJ.tif* file located in the Chapter 19 folder of this book's CD-ROM.

2. Open the Layers palette by dragging it from the Palette Well.

> ### It's Element-ary
>
> If your Style Settings dialog box doesn't look like the one shown in Figure 19.5, don't fret. You won't be able to access certain options like Bevel Size unless you've chosen something that has a Bevel Style applied. You also can't change the Outer Glow of something if that style hasn't been chosen!

3. In the Layers palette, select a layer that has a style applied to it, denoted by the small, cursive *f* on the right side of the layer name. For the *cactusJ.tif* file, that's the layer named Cactus, or the Text layer, Jacks.

4. Double-click the cursive *f*. (You can also use the Layer menu and choose Layer Style → Style Settings.)

5. The Style Settings dialog box opens as shown in Figure 19.5. Depending on what layer style has been applied to the layer chosen, the dialog box will have various options available.

Figure 19.5

Change the layer's styles by clicking the small f in the Layers palette.

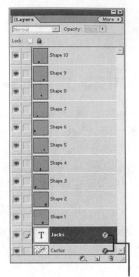

The Cursive F

From here, you can use the sliders or the text boxes to make changes to the style you've applied. As you can see from the figure, the options match the styles you've seen before: Outer Glow, Inner Glow, Bevel Size, and more.

If you can see those style settings, so what? That doesn't do you any good if you don't know what each setting means and is used for. This is precisely why we waited so long to bring this part up! We hope you can now distinguish between the items here. For example, you know what bevels are, and you know a little about lighting. Let's expand on these options.

Lighting and Glow Settings

Lighting Angle is used mainly with styles such as Inner Glow and Outer Glow that apply light onto the subject. Moving the slider can make it seem like a light is being shone onto the selection from a specific angle. Lighting Angle is always available no matter what style is applied. In contrast, you can place a checkmark in the Use Global Light box to give the appearance of a consistent light source being applied to the image equally and from no angle.

A couple of other options need mentioning:

◆ Use Shadow Distance to specify how large the shadow should be when applied to an image.

◆ Use Outer Glow Size and Inner Glow Size to specify how far the glow should stem from the original item.

Try changing these lighting settings to add emphasis to family photos, pictures of outdoor activities, or to make an image look cloudy or foggy. Increasing these settings adds more of an effect or makes the effect larger, and can be used with any style that uses shadows or glows.

Bevel Settings

You have two options for editing beveled items: Bevel Size and Bevel Direction. These are pretty obvious settings and enable you to specify how large the bevel on the object should be as well as what direction the bevel should start with.

Special Effects

You can create some pretty fancy effects by combining several types of layer styles and then setting options for them. Don't think for a minute that the Style Glass buttons can only be used to create buttons! You can apply the button's style to text, to a background layer, or to an object!

The same is true of other styles, too. Try applying a Drop Shadow to text or another object to make it look like it's dropping back into the page itself. Try the Complex styles to create awesome backgrounds for any photo or object. Try an Image Effect such as Rain, Snow, or Water Reflection to add texture to your image. Or try Patterns to get 3-D effects, and the WOW options for psychedelic effects.

Figure 19.6 shows an example of a combination of effects applied to an image you've seen earlier. You can also see the Layers palette.

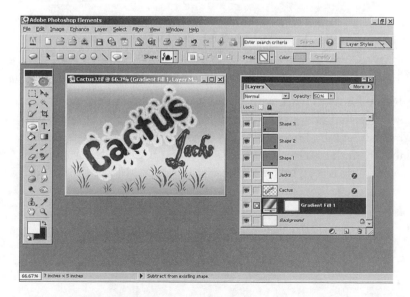

Figure 19.6

Here are the effects of applying a style to a layer such as text or graphics.

Copy or Remove a Layer Style

Whew! After applying all of those experimental (and sometimes ugly) effects to an image, you might just be ready to remove the layer entirely! However, you might like a specific layer so much, you want to copy the effect and apply it to another layer!

For example, consider the For Sale flyer created earlier in Figure 19.2. If you spent a lot of time creating the style for the first text layer, "For Sale—By Owner," and you wanted to apply that style to the other two text layers, you could do so by copying the style and applying it to the other layers.

To copy a layer style and apply it to another layer, follow these steps:

1. Open the *ideas.tif* file from the Chapter 19 folder on this book's CD-ROM.

2. Select the text layer Ideas from the Layers palette. (Open the Layers palette by dragging it from the Palette Well.) This layer has the Wow Plastic Red, the Bevels Inner Ridge, and the Complex Sunset Sky effects applied.

3. From the Layer → Layer Style menu, choose Copy Layer Style.

4. In the Layers palette, click on the .inc layer.

5. From the Layer → Layer Style menu, choose Paste Layer Style. The style applied to the Ideas text layer has now been applied to the inc. text layer. You can use the same technique to apply styles to other layer types. For example, choose the Shape 1 layer and apply the style to it. (At this point, the two layers are independent. Making a change to the first layer won't change anything about the second.)

You can delete a layer style also, as well as deleting an entire layer. To delete an entire layer, simply choose it from the Layers palette and tap the Delete key. To delete a layer style, select the layer from the Layers palette, choose Layer → Layer Style → Clear Layer Style. In this case, the layer is not deleted, but all styles applied to it are.

In this chapter, you learned how to work with layer styles and the Layer Styles palette. Specifically, you learned how to add effects to layers such as shadows, bevels, and image effects. You also learned how to blend two layers into one using special blending tools available from the Layers palette. Finally, you learned how to change the style settings for your new layers, including how to change lighting, the size of the bevels, and how to set the Glow options.

The Least You Need to Know

- You use the Layer Styles palette to apply styles to layers.

- Clicking the small, cursive *f* in the Layers palette enables you to edit the default settings for any effect applied to a layer.

- Beveling makes the image look like it's sitting in a frame or is a button that can be pressed, and is best used for text and web buttons.

- Glows enable you to add light from the inside or the outside of an object, and this light can be edited using the style settings.

- You can use the effects available in the Layers Style palette on any layer; a Style Glass button effect can work on objects other than buttons.

- Don't be afraid to experiment with these styles—that's what the Undo command is for!

Transforming Layers and Shapes

In This Chapter

◆ Understanding the Transform tools

◆ Transforming layers, backgrounds, selections, and multiple layers

◆ Rotating layers and shapes

◆ Understanding scaling and distorting

◆ Transforming a 2-D object into a 3-D object

When we think of transformations, we tend to think of *Dr. Jekyll and Mr. Hyde*, or that guy in *The Fly*. Though transformations can be bad, they can be good too, like when a caterpillar becomes a butterfly or when your youngest son transforms himself into a successful college student! That's the type of transformation we're going to shoot for here: transforming images so that they are improved upon, thus making a better photo or image.

In this chapter, you'll learn how to transform entire layers, parts of layers, and multiple layers. You'll also learn how to rotate layers and shapes, scale selections and effects, distort, and use the Free Transform tools. Finally, you'll learn a little about transforming a 2-D object into a 3-D one.

What to Transform

Using the Transform tools gives you the freedom to transform several different types of items. As mentioned in the introduction, you can *transform* entire layers, a part of a layer, or multiple layers.

The Transform Tools

Four tools are available from the Transform menu: Free Transform, Skew, Distort, and Perspective. Before you haphazardly start changing your layers using these tools, you need to understand what they do and what they are used for.

We'll start with the easiest tool and work our way through the most complex. The Skew option lets you stretch an object or layer into a new shape. Pulling out or pushing in at the corners or sides applies this effect to the layer. It's a pretty basic transformation—nothing too fancy. The Distort option is like the Skew option and does basically the same thing, except where the Skew option works along a single axis, working either horizontally or vertically, the Distort command works independently of any axis and provides more distorted images, letting you distort diagonally as well. This is a great choice for really distorting something!

> **Shop Talk**
>
> **Transforming** an object means to change it, alter it, or convert it to something else. Photoshop Elements almost always uses the word to mean to change the *shape* of the object to make it fit better on the page, to distort it, or to give it perspective.

The Perspective command makes things look like they are moving toward or away from you, or makes things look like they're on a slant. The Free Transform tool enables you to both scale and rotate an object at the same time, and is the most flexible of all of the Transform tools.

When you select a transformation, the options bar changes to reflect the choice, and offers a place to type in the vertical and horizontal scale of the transformation. It lets you choose to maintain aspect ratio or not, set rotation angles, and set the reference point. You'll also have options to skew, rotate, and distort. You can see how the options bar changes in the figures in this chapter.

Choosing an Entire Layer

Transforming one entire layer is probably the easiest way to transform, so we'll start there. You'll need to know where the Transform tools are to get through this chapter, though, so play along at home so you'll know what we're doing later.

To transform a layer, open the *ideas.tif* file from the Chapter 20 folder on the CD-ROM that comes with this book. Then do the following:

1. Open the Layers palette from the Palette Well or the Window → Layers option on the menu bar and select a layer to transform by clicking it. Select the layer named Shape 2.

2. On the menu bar, choose Image → Transform and pick any one of the choices available. Some choices may be grayed out and unavailable depending on which layer you choose (see Figure 20.1).

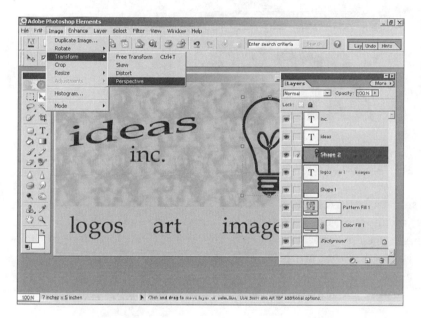

Figure 20.1

The Transform tools are located in the Image → Transform menu options.

3. From the resulting box that appears around the layer, push or pull on the handles (little boxes around the outside of the square) to skew, distort, or otherwise transform the layer. You can also configure these changes by using the tools in the options bar. Hover your mouse pointer over the options in the options bar to see what's available.

Unlike other tools that offer handle boxes, there is no rotate choice for any of these options except for Free Transform. If you want to rotate the object after transforming it, select it with the Move tool or use the Image → Rotate command. For more information on handles, refer back to Chapter 8.

Figure 20.1 shows the Transform tools and the *ideas.tif* image. The text layer with the word "Ideas" on it has had perspective applied to it, and the light bulb is selected and has handles around it. To apply a chosen transformation, you'll pull and push on these handles.

Choosing the Background Layer

You can transform the background layer or a single layered image if you want to, and sometimes this can produce some really nice effects, such as making the image seem like it's moving away from you, or extending outward or inward (see Figure 20.2).

Figure 20.2

Using a single layered image or distorting the background layer can produce nice effects.

To choose and transform a background layer, choose the layer from the Layers palette and, from the Select menu, choose All. (You can also press Ctrl+A (Windows) or Opt+A (Mac). With the background layer selected, choose the Transform tool from the Image menu and apply it. Now, just push and pull the handles, or use the options bar to apply the changes. Figure 20.2 shows what you can achieve by changing the background layer. Instead of the logo simply being square, it now looks tall as if it's moving away from you.

Although transforming the background layer sometimes works, it generally seems to work better if you change the background layer to a normal layer first, or if you only alter the top layers. In Figure 20.2, notice that white space surrounds the new image. In most cases, you'll want the background to be transparent, so the image you create can be added to other files or as another layer, or can be used effectively on a web page. To achieve this, make the background layer a normal layer before transforming it. To make the background layer a normal layer, double-click the layer in the Layers palette and click OK. Once you do this, it is no longer a background layer.

In Focus

If you must change a background layer, create a new layer to act as the background, and make the original background layer a regular layer by double-clicking it in the Layers palette.

Choosing Part of a Layer

If you only want to transform a specific part of a layer, you'll have to apply one of the selection tools. We prefer the Rectangular or Elliptical Marquee tool in most cases, but occasionally We'll use the Lasso tool, too.

In the following example, you'll select part of a layer using a selection tool. With a part of the layer selected, it can then be transformed independently from the other items in the layer. After selecting the object, you'll transform it, and then copy that transformation to a new document. This new piece of the layer that's been transformed will now be able to act as a small image on a business card, flyer, invitation, or other image.

You try it! Open the *flowers.tif* file from the Chapter 20 folder on this book's CD-ROM, or open a picture you have of someone water skiing, snow boarding, or any other photo at all. Then follow these steps:

1. Open the Layers palette and select the layer to transform by clicking it.

2. Choose the Elliptical Marquee tool from the toolbox (it's the tool on the top-left corner of the toolbox). Hold the mouse down on the tool to select it from the list of available Marquee tools.

3. Use this selection tool to encircle the yellow flowers or the object or person in your picture.

4. From the Image menu, choose Transform, and then choose Distort.

5. From the square that surrounds the selection, adjust the item using the square handles around the perimeter until it's the way you want it, or make these changes from the options bar. To create a nice effect for the image, and make it look like it's being viewed through one of those mirrors at the fair, push in from the top-left corner, and then pull out from the bottom right. You can see that the selection seems to jump off the page.

6. Click the checkmark to the right on the options bar to apply the changes, or click the slashed circle to trash the change. Note that you cannot undo intermediate dragging steps using the Undo option, which is usually available.

In Focus

Photoshop Elements will prompt you if you need to do something like simplify a layer before transforming it, or will tell you if you can't perform a specific task on a specific layer and for what reason. Don't get bogged down with remembering facts such as these; you'll be reminded!

7. From the Edit menu, choose Copy.

8. From the File menu, choose New From Clipboard. You can now use this cropped and distorted image in a logo or other creation.

Choosing Multiple Layers

If you bake a cake that contains multiple layers and go to slice a piece, you cut through all of the layers, not just one or two. Basically, you are transforming the cake, and you are selecting all of the layers at once. Okay, maybe this is stretching things a bit, but you can do the same thing with a multiple-layer image. You can transform it by selecting all of the layers, and thus transform the entire image at the same time. If you want to transform multiple layers at once, you can link the layers before transforming them.

In Focus

Depending on what types of layers you have and if those layers are locked, the steps to link and transform will differ from one instance to the next. The following instructions are general in nature; however, if you are prompted to perform any simplifying or copying of layers, do so as prompted after first saving an intermediate copy in PSD format if you think you may want to revert back to it at a later time.

To understand how to link layers and transform the finished product:

1. Open the *doll.psd* file from the Photoshop Elements sample folder.

2. Open the Layers palette by dragging it from the Palette Well and pull the edges of the palette so you can see all of the layers.

3. From the Layers palette, select the Hat layer. Link the Hat, Shirt, Pants, and Vest layers now. Click in the square located to the right of the eye in the layer you want to link, as shown in Figure 20.3. A lock appears in the middle box. (Because the Hat layer is selected, it is also linked.)

4. From the Image → Transform menu, choose a transformation to apply. For this exercise, choose Skew.

5. Pull or push the handles at the edges of the image to transform it. By pulling out on the bottom-right handle and pushing in on the bottom left, you can make the doll's clothes seem to blow right off him, hat and all! Remember, you can also use the options bar for precise movements.

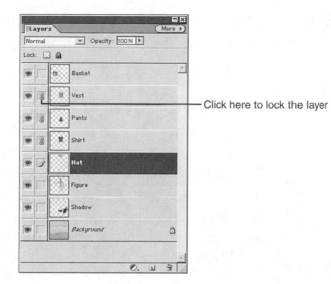

Click here to lock the layer

Figure 20.3

Click to the right of the eye in the Layers palette to link an image's layer.

In some cases, the layers will still not move together. If this happens, start again, and choose Select → All before transforming.

When working with images of your own, you might be prompted to unlock or lock layers, or, to simplify a layer before proceeding. If this happens, you'll need to agree to do this by clicking Yes or OK in the dialog boxes offered. If you don't want to simplify, lock, or unlock layers, you'll either have to choose another transformation or create a layer copy from the Layers menu.

Rotating Layers and Shapes

Although you've seen the choice Free Transform in the Transform menu, we haven't yet detailed it, but we'll do so now. You can use the Free Transform tool to select a layer or a shape, and rotate it to any position—even upside down or backwards! You can use a separate tool, Rotate, to rotate an entire image or selection, too, which is perfect for changing the view of an image produced by a digital camera or scanner, or for precisely rotating a selected image or layer.

Rotating a Layer or a Selection

The best tool award for rotating a layer or a selection goes to the Image → Transform → Free Transform tool!

Using the Free Transform tool is easy, and it's pretty much like using the Move tool. Just select the image with the selection tool or choose the layer from the Layers palette, choose the Free Transform tool, and move the object as you wish. While moving, you can push or pull from the handles, or hover just outside the box near a corner handle to rotate the image.

When the Free Transform transformation tool is selected, the options bar changes to reflect the choice. There, you can skew, scale, and rotate the image, and type in numbers for the horizontal and vertical scale. With the object selected, you can also right-click it to see many of these options.

Besides just rotating an image, you can turn the image upside down or backwards by clicking and dragging a handle and pulling the image across itself. For example, clicking and dragging the top middle square in an image down across the image will turn the image upside down. Clicking and dragging the middle square on the right side of an image over to the far left across the image will flip it so it's backward.

> **In Focus**
>
> Try rotating an image and turning it upside down, and then changing the opacity of the new image to create an effect like something reflecting on water. You can also combine this trick with the Distort/Ripple Filter, the Distort/Ocean Ripple Filter, or even the Distort/Glass Filter.

Rotating a Shape

Shapes are rotated using the Free Transform tool, too, or you can rotate them using the Move tool. Either way, it's as easy as selecting the shape with a selection tool, and then choosing Free Transform from the Image → Transform choices. Of course, as with any selected object, you can apply other Transform tools, too, such as Skew, Perspective, or Distort.

> **In Focus**
>
> The Image → Rotate menu has three distinct sections separated by lines. To apply a rotation to an entire image, choose a rotation choice from the first section. To apply a rotation to a selected piece of an image or to a single layer only, choose a rotate choice from the second section.

Rotating the Entire Image

A Rotate tool is also available. It's located from the Image → Rotate menu choices. This tool enables you to rotate entire images (among other things). For example, when a photograph from a digital camera is opened that was taken in landscape view, it's sideways to the person viewing it. Use the Rotate tool to rotate it 90 degrees right or left so you don't get kinks in your neck.

From the Transform → Rotate options, you can rotate an image 90 degrees either left or right, 180 degrees, or to any custom angle. While this is good for changing the view when working with the photo, a couple of other surprises are in store. Two other options, Flip Horizontal and Flip Vertical, are great for screen printers and embroiderers, and others in similar fields. This is because they enable you to take a logo and flip it horizontally to help a client visualize how its logo might look on a storefront, from the inside of the store! You can use this same technique to show reflections on water, or if you want an object coming toward the center of the page instead of going away from it.

The Rotate Tool Choices

You can use the other Rotate tool choices when you're rotating using either Free Transform, the Move tool, or the Rotate tool. When something is selected, such as a layer, part of a layer, or the entire image, more options in the Rotate menu become available.

Instead of trying to manipulate a selection using the mouse, you can choose one of the more precise options from the Rotate menu. For example, if you know the image needs to be rotated 90 degrees, just select the object, choose Rotate from the Image menu, and choose 90 degrees. This tool is better than rotating using the Free Transform tool when you want one of these specific rotations. Remember, though, that the Rotate menu is broken into three distinct sections separated by lines. To apply a rotation to a selected piece of an image (such as an object or color) or to a layer only, choose from the second section in the Rotate menu, as shown in Figure 20.4.

That's a lot of going in circles! Let's move on to something else!

In Focus

Remember, you have two ways to rotate: You can use the Image → Rotate command or you can use the Image → Transform → Free Transform tool. When you choose Free Transform, you'll get a text box where you can type in how to rotate the angles in the options bar, which might make using the tool more effective.

Figure 20.4

Use the Rotate tool to rotate the image a predetermined amount, or specify an angle of rotation.

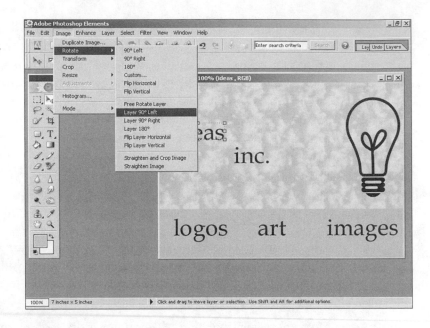

Scaling

Architects draw blueprints "to scale." When drawing to scale, every foot, yard, or other predetermined distance equals one inch on the drawing (or some other specific measurement). The blueprint and the actual object are proportional. Photoshop Elements has a scaling feature that's similar to this. Scaling in Photoshop Elements means that you can enlarge or reduce an object relative to its center point. So what the heck does that mean? Basically it means that you make the object larger or smaller.

In Focus

When using the Free Transform tool to resize an object, you are actually scaling the object. You can scale the object by dragging from the corners, or by using the tools in the options bar.

To understand scaling and what it can do to an image or selection, you should apply it a few times. Just open a file that contains a few layers, select a layer or part of the layer you want to scale, and then choose Image → Resize → Scale.

Next, you'll notice that the options bar has changed to include several features for scaling. You don't have to use these features, though; you can simply drag from the corner handles to resize the object. While resizing, hold down the Shift key to maintain proportion or select the Maintain Aspect Ratio button from the options bar.

(Maintaining proportion means that the image won't become distorted as you re-size it.)

Try enlarging a person in a photo to make him or her look closer or bigger than he or she really is. Try *reducing* the person's size, too, to make him or her look skinnier, farther away, or smaller than he or she really is!

In Focus

Fool around with the options bar and the Scaling tools. You'll notice you can set angles and rotate objects, too. You can even change the reference point location from the center of the object to another part of it, like a corner.

Distorting

Back in high school one of this book's authors paid about $100.00 for a distortion box for a Stratocaster guitar so it would sound like a favorite rock band. The distortion box made that beautiful guitar sound twisted, angry, ugly, and warped. It was music to the ears of a certain wannabe rock star then, but now? To be honest, it's not such a big thrill anymore.

We all have our own views about what's nice and what isn't. As far as distorting images goes, you'll have to decide what you like and what you don't. The distort options in Photoshop Elements can certainly be used to produce a variety of distorted images, though, so you'll have lots of options to choose from!

The Distort tool is available from the Transform menu and works the same way the other tools do. Just select what to distort, choose the Distort tool, and move the corners of the image around until you get the desired effect.

Transforming 2-D Objects into 3-D Objects

You can transform two-dimensional objects into three-dimensional objects using the 3-D Transform Filter. For example, you can take a flat photo of a book, specify corners using a wire frame, and then make the book appear as if it's 3-D. You could also take a picture of a ball or a can and make it appear 3-D as well. Doing so enables you to "move" the 2-D object, too, showing it from different angles. You can create three types of 3-D images: boxes, spheres, and cylinders.

Creating these objects takes lots of practice and manipulation. The tools available once the 3-D Transform window is open can seem rather complicated. In this section, you'll learn to take a picture of a round object and transform it using the 3-D Transform tools, and as you learn the tools and how to use them, you can apply the techniques to other objects as you experiment.

To create a 3-D image from a 2-D photo, follow these steps:

1. Open a photo of someone or something you'd like to transform from 2-D to 3-D. For now, let's stick to one that is similar in shape to a cylinder, sphere, or cube. If you don't have a file to open, use the *ball.tif* file located in the Chapter 20 folder of this book's CD-ROM.

2. Use a selection tool to select the object to transform. If you are using the *ball.tif* file, use the Elliptical Marquee tool (the top-left tool in the toolbox; hold down the mouse over the icon to select it), hold down the Shift key, and select the ball.

3. Choose Edit → Copy, and then File → New From Clipboard to get the image ready for the 3-D transformation (see Figure 20.5). Doing so removes any background from the image, making it easier to work with while learning. (This is saved as *ball2.tif* on the CD-ROM that comes with this book.)

4. Choose Filter → Render → 3D Transform. Figure 20.5 shows a sample 3-D Transform dialog box.

Figure 20.5

Select the image using the Elliptical Marquee tool.

5. Select the Sphere tool from the 3-D Transform dialog box and click the mouse in the top-left corner of the picture in the 3-D Transform dialog box. Drag the cursor over the object to place a wire frame around it. If you mess up, choose Cancel, and from the Filters menu, choose 3-D Transform again. It will now be

located at the top of the list. Otherwise, try to move and reshape the tools as detailed in the next couple of steps.

6. Move the entire wire frame by clicking the Selection tool in the 3-D Transform dialog box and then clicking and dragging on a handle of the frame. It's the tool on the top-left corner.

7. Reshape the frame by clicking the Direct Selection tool and clicking and dragging a handle of the frame. It's the tool on the top-right corner.

8. Click the Trackball tool, the fifth one down on the right, and click once on the picture in the 3-D Transform dialog box. Pull the ball to the desired area, as shown in Figure 20.6. Notice that, while Photoshop Elements can guess what type of shape you have, it can't guess what's showing on the back or sides of it!

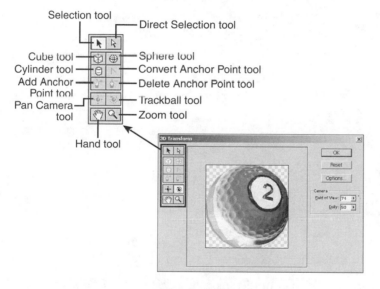

Selection tool — Direct Selection tool

Cube tool — Sphere tool
Cylinder tool — Convert Anchor Point tool
Add Anchor Point tool — Delete Anchor Point tool
Pan Camera tool — Trackball tool
Hand tool — Zoom tool

Figure 20.6

Use the 3-D Transform window to transform the object.

9. Click the arrow next to the Field of View option, and move the slider or type in a new number to change how the image is shown.

10. Change the settings for Dolly to make the object seem closer or farther away. Dolly, in Photoshop Elements, is short for a dolly camera support, which is a camera mount that allows a cameraman to move a camera easily and smoothly. The Dolly options allow you to simulate camera movement.

11. Click OK. Now, you can add an effect such as rotate, or a filter such as blur, to make the object look like it's in motion. You can now place this image in another image or leave it on its own to serve as part of a logo or other creation.

You can use these same techniques for working with cubes and cylinders. After choosing the Cube tool, and placing it on the image, you'll notice handles on the corners of the wire frame. When working with objects such as these, you can add or remove these handles, thus making the object easier to manipulate. You can also zoom in or use the Hand tool to view the object differently. Experiment with different types of objects to get a real feel for this tool's power.

> **CAUTION**
>
> **Swatch Out!**
>
> If you make a mistake inside the 3-D Transform dialog box, such as choosing the Pan tool to apply a new look or changing the shape, don't press the Cancel button to undo it. Doing so only closes out the 3-D Transform dialog box without applying any changes, and you'll have to start over!

In this chapter, you learned how to transform images of all types, including entire layers, background layers, parts of layers, and multiple layers. We discussed four transformations: Skew, Distort, Perspective, and Free Transform. Following that, we introduced rotation. You have several ways to rotate an image, including the Move, Rotate, and Free Transform tools. Each tool offers different capabilities. Finally, we offered an introduction to rendering 3-D images from 2-D ones.

The Least You Need to Know

- Layers, selections of layers, and multiple layers can all be transformed.

- The Transform options are Skew, Distort, Perspective, and Free Transform.

- Free Transform is the most flexible of the four tools, and you can use it to rotate, flip, and resize images.

- You can employ the Rotate tool to rotate images, selections, and layers; it's more precise (yet less flexible) than the Free Transform option.

- Changing 2-D images to 3-D ones is possible, and takes a little bit of extra effort to learn. The 3-D Transform tool is available from the Filter → Render options.

Chapter 21

Cool Things You Can Do

In This Chapter

- Creating a panoramic image from several individual images
- Creating an animation
- Using batch processing

You can do millions of really neat things with Photoshop Elements, including combining several individual photos into a single panoramic image, creating an animation, and using batch processing. In this chapter, you'll learn the basics and how to get started with these three operations.

Creating a Panorama

A panorama is an image that shows an entire landscape, such as a city or a mountain range, or perhaps players in a marching band line. These pictures can be quite beautiful, but regular cameras usually aren't capable of taking these photos. Most times, you have to purchase a special lens or camera just for this purpose. However, using Photoshop Elements, you can use any digital camera to take several pictures of a landscape (that overlap) from similar views, and then combine them into one using the Photomerge tools.

Taking the Photos

When creating a panoramic photo, you'll get the best results when using photos taken from similar angles of the same thing—for example, photos of a city skyline. Although you can Photomerge a dog and a cat, you won't get a real panoramic picture. So, to make the Photomerge tool work the way you want it to, you'll have to take your pictures carefully.

In Focus

Pretend you want to print the photos onto paper, and then overlap them, one on top of the other. You'd like the edges to match up, too. Don't zoom, distort, move the camera up or down, change the lighting or exposure, or change the focus of the lens. All of these will cause dissimilarities in the photos.

When taking the photos, make sure your images overlap some, because it's this overlap that Photoshop Elements uses to find similarities and then combine the photos. A good rule of thumb is to have the photos overlap about 25 percent.

You'll also want to keep the zoom lens still. If you zoom in on one photo and not on another, the images won't match up. The same is true of angling the camera. Keep the camera on a tripod or flat surface such as a car top or fence and just rotate it horizontally for each picture to get the most usable raw pictures.

Once you have the pictures taken, you're ready to try the Photomerge tool.

Beginning the Composition

You can create both vertical and horizontal panoramas. This section walks you through the easiest way to create your first panorama, a vertical one, and from there, you can get creative!

To create a panoramic image, you need to place all of the photos you want to use for it in a folder called Source. You can create this folder on your desktop, root drive, the My Pictures folder, or any other place on the hard drive. Once you do that, close any open images and then, in this folder, collect all of your raw photos to be used to build your panorama. Open the ones you want to use for your panorama in Photoshop Elements. From the File menu, choose Create Photomerge.

Once you do this, the Photomerge dialog box opens, and includes a list of the photos you have open. (If you haven't opened them, or want to add another picture, you can use the Browse button to locate the Source folder and open them from there.) See Figure 21.1.

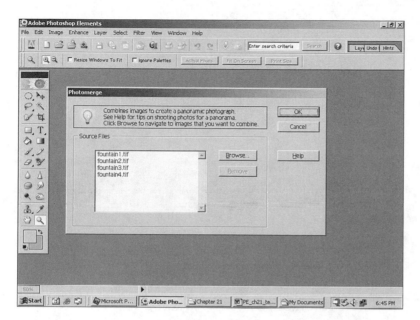

Figure 21.1

Collect the images in the Source folder and open them in Photoshop Elements to start.

All of the photographs in the Photomerge dialog box will be added to the panoramic image. In this example, four images will make up the panorama. Click OK if all are listed (or after you've added any ones that aren't open), and watch Photoshop Elements create the panorama! The images need not be in any particular order in the workspace.

You'll see a preview of the panorama once it's finished. Don't press OK, or you'll be accepting the image the way it is! You want to edit this panorama before you choose OK. If you accidentally press OK, and you need to edit the photos separately later, you'll have to start over. You have to do the editing in the editing window shown in Figure 21.2.

In Focus

Even if the panorama looks good, use the Zoom tool in the editing window to get a closer look. Doing so verifies that the images are aligned properly. You can also use the Magnifying Glass to enlarge your view, or press the Alt key while clicking the mouse to zoom out.

With the preview successfully created, you are now ready to perfect it, cancel it, or save it. If you are happy with it the way it is, press OK. If you want to start over, press Cancel. If you got an error that said the panorama couldn't be created, you'll need to work on creating it manually, or if you think it's necessary (because of the way the pictures were originally lined up or taken), you might want to take a new set of pictures and start over. If you think the preview will work, move on to the "Aligning Images" section, next.

Take a look at the example panorama in the color insert.

Figure 21.2

Use the editing window to perfect your panorama image.

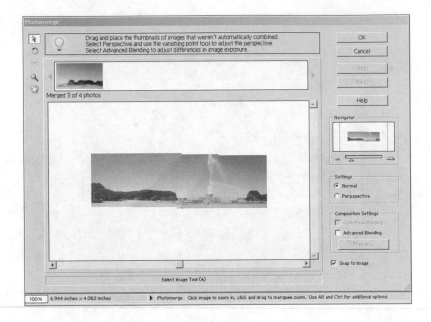

Aligning Images

Before you choose OK to accept the panorama as it is, you'll probably want to do a little editing. You have several things you can change, including the perspective, blending, and repositioning the individual sections of the panorama.

Some of the editing tasks you'll want to do include the following:

- Use one of the two Zoom tools to zoom in on various areas of the panorama. One Zoom tool is represented by a magnifier icon, and one by a slider bar underneath the Navigator.

- Use the Hand tool to change the view.

- Use the Selection tool followed by the Rotate tool to rotate any image.

- Use the Selection tool to select an area of the image to reposition.

- Place a check in the Advanced Blending check box and click Preview to see if this automatic feature enhances the picture.

- Place a check in the Perspective check box to see if this view is better than the Normal view for your work.

Once you finish, zoom in and out again to get a full view of the photo, making sure everything is in order. When it is ready, click OK!

The Finished Product

When you press OK, Photoshop Elements brings up the photo in the application itself (see Figure 21.3). From there, you can edit it as if it were like any other image, but you cannot edit it by the piece anymore.

As with other images, you can use the QuickFix tools, the Enhance tools, and the Selection tools. When you're ready, click File → Save and save the picture.

In Focus

If you encountered problems during this process, you can either start again by retaking the photos, or you can manually line them up after zooming out. If you can retake them, use a tripod, make sure that the photos overlap by about 25 percent, and don't use any zoom or distortion.

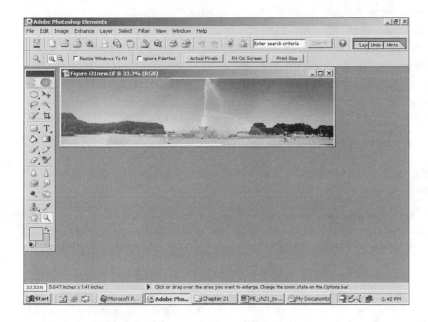

Figure 21.3

The panorama will appear in Photoshop Elements once the required calculations have been completed.

Creating an Animation

Animation on a computer is done the same way that animation was done in the old days and the way we did it as kids (remember flip-books?). Back then, artists drew images by hand, and made each image slightly different from the next. The images were then shown quickly, and it looked like the object was moving. When we were kids, we did it the same way, except we drew our figures on a notepad and then flipped through it.

It's Element-ary

There's a neat little tutorial in the Help files of Photoshop Elements called *Jumpman.psd*. This tutorial helps walk you through a more complicated animation creation.

In Photoshop Elements, it's pretty much the same. We create multiple "layers" that are like cells for artists or notepad pages for kids, and we play them (or show them) in a loop. The animation tools here are pretty basic, though, and the only thing you should consider creating are small, simple animations.

If you want to create a really cool animation, you're going to have to come up with (and create) the image or character first. You can create it in Photoshop Elements by combining shapes, lines, and/or by choosing a custom shape. Once the character is complete, you'll have to also create its movement.

Figure 21.4 shows what we're talking about. This image has several layers, and each layer has a butterfly on it. Notice how the butterfly is positioned in different places? This is the path the butterfly follows as these layers are shown. In addition, the butterfly is shown using different sizes, making it seem like it is nearer and then farther away, and it faces different directions to enhance the idea of movement. With the butterfly being different sizes, it also makes it look like its wings are actually moving. Pretty neat!

Once you've created the character, perform the following steps to prepare the animation:

1. Open a new file with a transparent or white background large enough on which to place several different forms of your character (see Figure 21.4).

2. Place the character on the image. A layer will be created.

Figure 21.4

Use a custom shape to create an animated character.

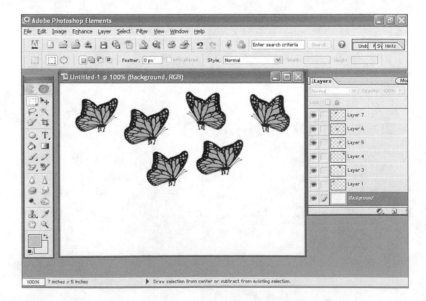

3. Place the same character on the image again. A new layer is created. When placing the character, keep the animated path you are creating in mind.

4. Continue to create layers and add the image until you have five or so layers. As you add the character to the layers, consider what path it will take as the layers are displayed in the animation.

5. For each layer and image, resize, rotate, and move the character so that it will look like it's moving.

With its "movements" created, you can create the animation in Photoshop Elements.

Creating the Animation

You'll need to create something like what Figure 21.4 shows before you can preview your animation. We created that particular image of the butterfly in another program, and then used the Copy and Paste commands to import it into Photoshop Elements. However, you can recreate it using the butterfly that's available from the custom shape tools and by adding a little bit of color.

Once you create the layers, you're ready to go! Choose File → Save for Web, choose GIF, check the Transparency and Animate check boxes, and click the Preview in Browser button at the bottom. You might also want to place a checkmark in the Loop check box, so you can watch it several times to see if you like it.

After you've seen your animation in action, consider changing the Frame Delay in the Save for Web dialog box to make the transitions move faster or slower, and use the arrows at the bottom of this dialog box to view the frames one at a time.

The Animation tool in Photoshop Elements won't do much more than this. But, while you won't win any award with these creations, it doesn't mean you won't have fun making them. They can also be adapted to the web and work quite well if they are small and simple.

> **In Focus**
>
> When creating animations, try various techniques to make the movement seem more real, such as bringing the object nearer and then farther away, moving limbs, applying shadow, flipping the object, and anything else you can think of.

Batch Processing Files

If you've ever done anything repeatedly and gotten sick of it, you'll appreciate the whole idea of a batch file. For those of you who aren't computer geeks, a *batch file* is a short set of instructions (a program, if you will) that remembers the steps involved in a repetitive task and then repeats them on command.

This means that if you have to do something 50 times, such as change all of your Photoshop Elements files to JPEGs, resize all of your photos, or rename all of those photos, you only have to train the computer to do it, and then sit back while it's done automatically! Oh if life were so easy—we'd have little batch files for changing diapers, going to traffic school, mowing the lawn, and stuffing envelopes!

So how do you go about training the computer to do these things? Let's find out!

Creating a Batch Process

We wish that Photoshop Elements could create a batch file to pay our bills or defragment our hard drives, but it can't. It can only do work in Photoshop Elements, and work on images in formats Photoshop Elements recognizes. Consequently, you'll have to decide what you want to do repeatedly to some images. Converting file types comes to mind—it's pretty easy, and a common-enough task, so we'll begin there. You can use these same steps to resize photos or rename them.

Let's pretend that you took a hundred or so photos while you were on vacation, and you need to convert them all to JPEG to get them ready to post on your website. Follow these steps to create a batch process that converts those images to JPEGs:

1. If you haven't already created the Source and Destination folders on your computer's hard drive, do so now.

2. Copy all of the images to convert into the Source folder.

3. From the Photoshop Elements file menu, choose Batch Processing.

4. In the Files To Convert section of this dialog box, shown in Figure 21.5, click the Source button to locate the Source folder where your files are stored and click OK.

5. In the Conversion Options section of this dialog box, choose the file type to convert to.

6. If you want to convert the image size as well, place a checkmark in the Convert Image Size check box and choose a size to convert to.

7. Click the Destination button to locate and select the Destination folder.

8. Rename the files, if you desire, by choosing a new naming scheme from the drop-down lists available in the File Naming section.

9. Click OK.

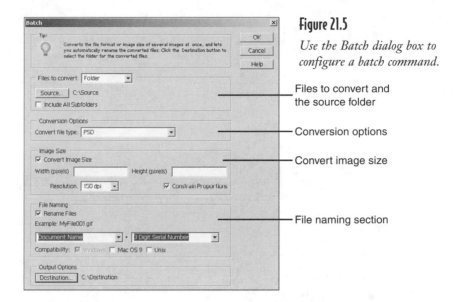

Figure 21.5

Use the Batch dialog box to configure a batch command.

Files to convert and the source folder

Conversion options

Convert image size

File naming section

As the batch file executes, each photo in the folder will appear in the work area of Photoshop Elements, and you can watch as the files are renamed, converted, and resized.

In this chapter, you learned how to combine several photos into a single panoramic image—including how to arrange and align the composition and images. You also learned how to create a basic animation, and to perform batch processes.

The Least You Need to Know

- A panoramic picture is a combination of several pictures and creates a landscape or scenic photograph.

- Using a tripod when taking panoramic pictures enables you to keep the camera steady, thus producing better raw photos.

- To create an animation, first create a character, and then the characters movements. Place each image on its own layer using the Paste command.

- A batch process is a set of instructions that is performed repeatedly.

- Batch processes enable resizing groups of images, renaming groups of images, or converting groups of images.

Part 6

Presenting Your Pictures

So, you've created some really cool photos, images, logos, and artwork, and you want to show them off. First, you've got to save your images. Then you can print them or publish them on the World Wide Web. You can even send your images to an online photo-processing service and get prints mailed to you in a matter of a few days.

Saving images for the web is a little different than saving images for personal use. You've got to choose the right file format so your viewers will be able to see them quickly once they've accessed your website.

It's time to go public: In this final section, you'll learn the best ways to print and save, and optimize your images for the web.

Putting Pictures on Paper

In This Chapter

- ◆ Sending your images to your desktop printer

- ◆ Previewing before you print

- ◆ Discovering how to print several images at once

- ◆ Creating a contact sheet showing all of your images

- ◆ Ordering prints from an online photo center

You've got that photo, drawing, or design looking just the way you want, thanks to the powerful set of image editing tools in Photoshop Elements. Simply pointing at a monitor and showing passersby what you've done isn't enough. Nor is e-mailing your images. You want to put your image in a permanent form that you can frame.

Photoshop Elements enables you to print your pictures in several ways— normally, in a group of multiple images on a sheet, on a contact sheet with other miniature versions of images in a folder, or even by sending them online to a digital photo service. In this chapter, you'll learn how to take advantage of these printing features and etch your images, if not in stone, at least on photographic paper.

Getting Started with Printing

Printing your photos or other images with Photoshop Elements is as simple as saving, selecting, or using one of the Brush tools. Unlike those other functions, printing leaves you with a real, tangible benefit: a print you can literally touch, admire, and carry around to show your friends.

Printing is so easy, in fact, that many users tend to overlook some of the options and enhancements that can help conserve expensive photo paper or make images turn out just the way you want. First, you'll learn the quick and easy way to print, and then you'll explore ways to preview and adjust your images so you can print "smart."

Just Print It!

Do you have an image you want to print? If so, open it in the Photoshop Elements window. If not, open the *reallybad-fixed.tif* file in the Chapter 22 folder on this book's CD-ROM. (This image went through some "quick fix" adjustments in Chapter 9 to bring it up to printable level.)

In Focus

The smaller the size of your file, the easier it will be to print. Some printers have lots of built-in memory, while others are memory-poor. Before you choose Print, consider reducing file size by choosing Layers → Flatten Image to flatten the file if it contains multiple layers. You can also choose Image → Resize Image to reduce the resolution or change the height or width.

Make sure the image is open in Photoshop Elements and located in the frontmost, active image window. Choose File > Save to save your latest changes if you haven't done so already. Before you print, check the image size; if the status bar doesn't display the size, click the arrow in the status bar and choose Document Sizes from the context menu. The image is more than a megabyte in size.

To reduce the size, choose Image → Resize → Image Size. In the Image Size dialog box, make sure the Constrain Size box is checked (see Figure 22.1). Change the width to 6 inches; the height immediately changes to 4.09 inches. Click OK, and the image size is reduced. The file shrinks, too, to a more manageable 372 kilobytes (372K).

Once the image is a manageable size, you can go ahead and print it. Here's how:

1. Choose File → Print from the Photoshop Elements menu bar or click the Print icon.

2. Wait for Windows or the Mac operating system to launch the printer dialog box for the active desktop or network printer.

3. If needed, enter the number of copies or otherwise set options within the dialog box. The details offered vary by printer and by the manufacturer's driver software you've installed.

4. After setting any options, click Print. Your computer sends a copy of your image to your printer.

Figure 22.1

Resizing images makes them easier to print.

The preceding steps show just the simplest—and least interactive—way to send an image to a printer. As you'll discover in the next section, Photoshop Elements also offers far more interactive and advanced print management tools.

Printing Hard with a Vengeance!

More power lies beyond the basic printout capabilities of File → Print. You'll find these exciting features in the interactive Print Preview dialog box, which displays your image in the Print Preview window.

The Print Preview window, shown in Figure 22.2, offers many ways to enhance the way your image prints. These options do not directly control your printer. Rather, they help configure the way Photoshop Elements structures your image before sending it to your printer.

Figure 22.2

The Print Preview window enables you to adjust the way your image appears on the page.

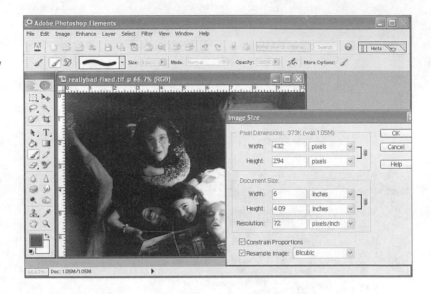

In Focus

Make sure the More Options box is checked if you want to access all of the Print Preview dialog box's options, such as adding crop marks or a caption to your image.

It's Element-ary

You can print a single layer of a multilayered image rather than all layers at once. Select the layer you want in the Layers palette, and click the Eye icon next to all other layers so the selected layer is the only one that is actually visible. Then choose File → Print to print that single layer.

To adjust the printing from the Print Preview window, open *reallybad-fixed.tif* from the Chapter 22 folder on this book's CD-ROM, and choose File → Print Preview or press Ctrl+P (Windows) or Cmd+P (Mac). The Page Preview area on the left side of the window shows what your printed page will look like. The Picture Preview appears in the relative size and positioning the image will occupy on the final printout.

To change the size of the printed page to a 4 × 6-inch sheet of photo paper (which corresponds to the 4 × 6-inch image you just resized), click Page Setup. In the Page Setup dialog box, choose 4 × 6 from the Size drop-down list, and then click OK. When you're ready to print, click Print to close the Print Preview window and print.

Photoshop Elements lets you control the size and position of your image. The Position controls and Scaled Print Size controls offer interactive adjustment for these features.

Changing the Print Location

You do not need to settle for the default centered print presentation. You might want to offset your picture to fit onto preprinted stationery. You might want to use the upper left corner of the page to allow space for a handwritten letter using the rest of the page. Or you may just like the off-centered look. For whatever reason, Photoshop Elements enables you to set image position before you print.

To reposition the image on the printed page, follow these steps:

1. Deselect the Center Image check box found in the Position section of the Print Preview window.

2. Do one of the following:

    ◆ Click and drag the Picture Preview and reposition it in the Page Preview area.

    ◆ Enter new values for the Top and Left position of your image in the available text boxes.

If you enter new top and left values, the Print Preview window immediately updates, reflecting the changes you have made. To return your picture back to its original centered position, simply reselect the Center Image check box.

Changing the Print Size

Your daughter made you a picture frame in her first-grade class, but it's a nonstandard size: 3.78 × 5.875 inches, for instance. Don't start trying to alter the frame—instead, you can adjust the print size of your image as easily as you can adjust the location. Choose one of the following options. For each of these choices, make sure that Scale to Fit Media remains deselected in the Scale Print Size section of the Print Preview window. (You'll learn more about this option in the following section.)

◆ **Scale to a particular value.** Enter a value in the scale box. Photoshop Elements uses this value as a percentage of the original (100 percent) scale and automatically resizes your image to match in the preview window. (Be sure not to scale the image so it's bigger than the page you want to print it on, or you simply won't print part of the image.)

◆ **Set the width or height**. To choose a particular value for either the width or height of your image, first select the units you wish to work in. Available choices include inches, cm, mm, points, and picas. Make your choice from the pull-down menu to the right of the width or height text entry fields. Next, enter a new value into either field. Upon entering a new value, the preview window automatically updates.

◆ **Set the size by hand.** You can interactively set the relative size of your image in the Print Preview window. To accomplish this, make sure that you've checked Show Bounding Box. In the Print Preview window, simply drag any corner.

No matter which method you choose, the Picture Preview area lets you see at a glance how your image will appear on the printed page.

Making the Most of the Page

The Scale to Fit Media check box is a particularly nice option that helps you make the most of your picture (not to mention that expensive photo paper). Try it now with *reallybad-fixed.tif* open in the Print Preview window. Your image automatically stretches to correspond to the width (if your image is primarily horizontal in orientation) or the height (if your image is vertical).

Of course, the efficiency of the Fit Media option depends on the orientation of your original image and that of the picture to be printed. As you can see in Figure 22.3, the choice of either portrait or landscape orientation for the printed page dramatically affects the results.

In this example, the horizontal orientation of the image better matches the landscape page layout shown on the left compared with the vertical page layout shown at right. When the orientations match, you can print more of the picture on your paper. You change orientation by clicking Page Setup and clicking either Portrait or Landscape in the Page Setup window.

Figure 22.3

Change page orientation to print a larger version of the image.

Swatch Out!

Even if you choose Scale to Fit Media, Photoshop Elements won't print exactly to the edge of a piece of paper. Every printer has a border area. For example, inkjet printers commonly have a $1/8$ to $1/4$-inch border around the perimeter of each printed page onto which they cannot print.

Viewing a Directory with Contact Sheets

Professional photographers commonly use a tool called a contact sheet when they want to quickly view the entire contents of a roll of film. Photoshop Elements lets you carry this concept into digital photography so you can print a contact sheet of the contents of directory full of photos. Another way to think of contact sheets is as small thumbnail images of many pictures you can see all at once.

Gather your images into a directory (the standard My Pictures directory in Windows is an obvious good location) and select File → Print Layouts → Contact Sheet. The Contact Sheet window shown in Figure 22.4 appears.

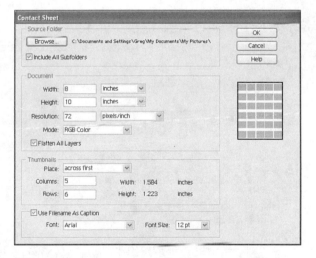

Figure 22.4

Create your own digital contact sheets with this window.

Follow these steps to create your own contact sheet:

1. Click the Browse button in the Source Folder area. The Browse for Folder dialog box appears.

2. Navigate to the directory you want to use for your contact sheet. Select the directory name and click OK. The Browse for Folder dialog box closes and you return to the Contact Sheet window.

3. If you want to include pictures in the subdirectories below this folder, click Include All Subfolders.

4. In the Document Size area, set the width, height, and resolution of the image you're about to build. Photoshop Elements is about to create a new picture consisting of thumbnails of the images in the directory you've specified. If you need higher-quality thumbnails and intend to print to a good printer with higher resolution, choose a better resolution than the default 72 dpi. In our own experience, 72 dpi produces fine contact sheets for nearly all cataloging needs.

5. In the Thumbnail Placement area, select the number of images that will appear across and down your contact sheet.

6. If you want to include captions, make sure Use File Name as Caption remains checked. You can set the font size and face as desired.

7. Click OK and wait for Photoshop Elements to build your contact sheet. This may take anywhere from several seconds to several minutes. During this time, expect the program to open a flurry of images, resize them, add each one to a core picture, and then close them.

8. When the final results appear, choose File → Print to print out your contact sheet.

The Photoshop Elements contact sheet provides a convenient way to view and catalog the contents of your directories and enables you to show a friend or client a number of available pictures to choose from for use in a project. Figure 22.5 shows a typical contact sheet.

Figure 22.5

This figure shows a typical Photoshop Elements contact sheet.

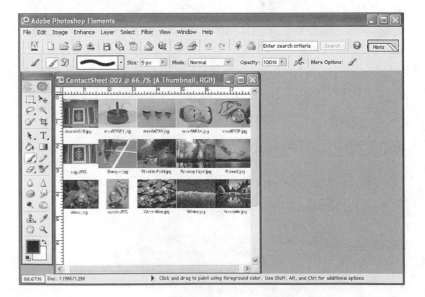

Swatch Out!

The process of assembling thumbnails can be disconcerting the first time you choose it because it takes a while and you might wonder whether the program is still working or if it has stopped for some reason. But do not interfere with Photoshop Elements while it builds your contact sheets. Doing so can crash the program or the contact sheet.

The Print Package

Good quality photo paper can be expensive. To make the most of paper, it's often a good idea to print more than one image at a time on a sheet. Accordingly, Photoshop Elements 2.0 offers a new print package feature that enables you to print several images on a single page.

To create your own print package, Choose File → Print Layouts → Picture Package. Wait for the Picture Package window to appear, as shown in Figure 22.6. If you've used this option before, it may take several seconds or a minute to load the choices you made in your previous session.

Click Browse to choose a file

Source area　　Document area

OK and Cancel buttons

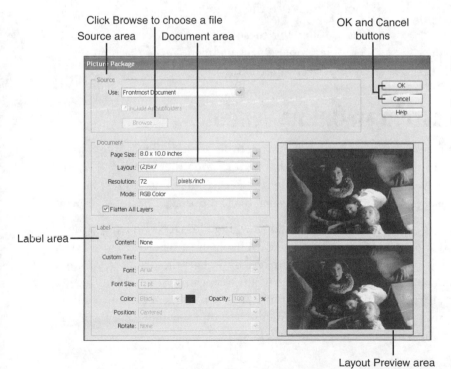

Label area

Figure 22.6

Picture Package enables you to print multiple images together.

Layout Preview area

In Focus

By default, each picture in your print package will be filled with repetitions of your original image. To replace any one of these pictures with a different image, click it. Then the Select an Image File dialog box appears. Navigate to a new file and click Open. Photoshop Elements opens this file, resizes it, and copies it into your layout.

In Focus

Because your picture package is displayed as an image in the Photoshop Elements window, you may, if you desire, save the image to disk for reprinting later on.

In the Document area, select the page size and layout you want to use. Choices include more than a dozen common layouts including two 5×7 images, four 3.5×5 images, and so forth. Set the resolution to match the output quality of your printer. If you're using expensive paper and own a printer that can output 300 dpi, choose 300 dpi.

In the Source area, choose Frontmost Document from the Use pull-down menu. "Frontmost" refers to the photo that's open in front of any others in the Photoshop Elements window. Your layout is filled with the contents of that image window.

When you're satisfied with your layout and have added all the pictures you desire, click OK. Sit back and wait as Photoshop Elements builds your image—which, when complete, is displayed in the Photoshop Elements window with the file name Picture Package. Insert your paper or other sheet into your printer. Choose File → Print and send your compound image to the printer.

After following these steps, you will have created a complete image package made up of the pictures you interactively specified.

Ordering Prints from an Online Vendor

Elements lets you focus on the most important functions associated with digital image editing: capturing the images, editing them, and saving them to disk. When it comes to printing, you may not want to handle the work yourself due to a substandard or nonfunctional printer or a special need such as an oversize, poster-size print.

Photoshop Elements gives you the ability to transmit digital image files from your hard disk to an online photo service. The service available as of this writing, Shutterfly (www.shutterfly.com), prints out your digital images and mails the prints to you. Shutterfly also gives you space on a web server where you can post your files so you or your friends and relatives can view them online. You can connect to Shutterfly and send your photos from within Photoshop Elements, without having to use a special file transfer application. To do so, just follow these steps:

1. Make sure you are connected to the Internet.

2. Choose File → Online Services from the Photoshop Elements menu bar.

3. The Online Services dialog box opens with a user agreement. Read the user agreement and then click Agree.

4. A Progress dialog box appears, indicating that Photoshop Elements is downloading a service list. Then an Online Services Wizard dialog box appears. Select the service you want and click Next. (You can choose to download any new Recipe how-to instructions that are available from Adobe, download a plug-in application that enables Photoshop Elements to open images in the new JPEG2000 file format (see Chapter 12), or send images to Shutterfly.)

5. In the next screen of the Online Services Wizard, click Upload Images to Shutterfly for printing or sharing, and then click Next.

6. Another Online Services Wizard dialog box appears, notifying you that "Adobe is not responsible for any part of any dealings between you and any third party." Click OK.

7. The next screen of the Wizard prompts you for a Shutterfly username and password if you are already a member. If not, click Sign Up. Your web browser opens and takes you to a sign-up page on the Shutterfly website where you can sign up. Once you have signed up you can return to this Wizard screen. Enter your username and password and click Next.

8. The Wizard's next screen prompts you to click Add to upload your pictures to your Shutterfly account. Click Add, locate photos in the Open dialog box, and click Upload (see Figure 22.7). A series of Progress dialog boxes appears as your files are transferred to Shutterfly.

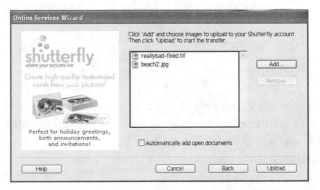

Figure 22.7

Upload your file to an online photo service from within Photoshop Elements.

Shop Talk

You're probably asking yourself what you may actually be doing when you "upload your pictures to your Shutterfly account." *Uploading* is the opposite of downloading; when you download a file from the Internet, you cause the file to move from a web server to your own hard disk. When you upload, you move a file from your hard disk to a remote server—in this case, one operated by Shutterfly.

9. Once you have uploaded your files to Shutterfly, you have to actually order prints. You begin that process in the Wizard's next screen. Click View at Shutterfly. Your web browser connects to the Shutterfly website and displays the photos you just uploaded in the form of an "album" (see Figure 22.8).

10. Click Order Prints, and then follow the steps illustrated in subsequent web pages to select the images you want to print, choose sizes, and provide your shipping information.

In a few days, an envelope should arrive containing your printed images.

Figure 22.8

Your photos are stored online so you can view them and order prints.

Shutterfly isn't the only service available to print your online photos; it's just the only one at the time this was written that had signed an agreement with Adobe to provide digital photo printing services through Photoshop Elements. You'll find a list of similar services on Yahoo!'s Web site at dir.yahoo.com/Business_and_Economy/ Shopping_and_Services/Photography/Digital/Labs/.

The Least You Need to Know

- Photoshop Elements makes printing as simple as File → Print.

- Choose File → Print Preview to adjust print output.

- Adjust page orientation and paper size to match your images.

- Create contact sheets to build a visual overview of directories that contain image files.

- Conserve paper—create a Print Package to print several images on a single sheet.

23

Creating Images for the Web

In This Chapter

- ◆ Understanding the Save For Web dialog box
- ◆ Optimizing images for the web
- ◆ Understanding file formats
- ◆ Creating animated web images
- ◆ Creating Web Photo Galleries

Ah, the World Wide Web. Some call it the "World Wide Wait"! Stop! Don't make it any slower than it already is—read this chapter first!

Here, you'll learn how to save images for the web, and how to optimize them too. "Optimizing" means that pictures will load faster and look better than they would without intervention. You'll learn about different types of file formats too, including GIF, JPEG, JPEG2000, and PNG, and what makes one better than the other and under what circumstances. You'll need to understand how to name images too; you'll discover some pretty specific rules about that! Finally, we'll introduce creating animated images and web photo galleries. Photo galleries are a fast and easy way to share your photos.

Saving for the Web

People access the web in all sorts of ways. Some have high-speed DSL and cable connections, but many more use lower-end 56K dialup modems. When saving your image for the web, you have to take into account this vast disparity of Internet bandwidth that makes downloading a big image file a time-consuming task for some.

Photoshop Elements enables you to save images in one of the three formats that Web browsers can display:

- **Graphics Interchange Format (GIF).** This is a good option for line art drawings rather than photos because GIF only uses a maximum of 256 colors. GIF also enables an image to have a transparent background, and for you to create animations.

- **Joint Photographic Experts Group (JPEG/ JPG).** This is a good option for photos; a new variety, JPEG2000, offers even better compression and image quality as well as the capability to make a color transparent. Support for JPEG2000 gives Photoshop Elements a big advantage over other graphics programs.

- **Portable Network Graphics (PNG).** PNG comes in two varieties, PNG-24 for 24-bit color images and PNG-8 for 8-bit color images. Not all browsers support PNG, though, so we'll save its discussion for later in this chapter. For now, it is important to know that it is quickly becoming an alternative to JPEG and GIF because it has no loss of either image quality or actual pixels within the image and offers more colors, and is thus gaining popularity.

> **CAUTION**
>
> **Swatch Out!**
>
> An image in indexed color (in which each color in the image is assigned a number and assigned a place in a color table) or bitmap mode cannot be saved in JPEG or JPEG2000 format, until you modify it to RGB color mode. If you want to use JPEG (an excellent option for photos), choose Image → Mode → RGB Color to convert the image to RGB mode. Consider saving this version of the file with a new name so you still have the previous version.

JPEG Versus JPEG2000

Adobe is introducing support for a new graphics format, JPEG2000, along with version 2.0 of Photoshop Elements. JPEG2000 compresses images even further than conventional JPEG and with even higher quality. In fact, while the old JPEG compression was lossy, the new JPEG2000 standard actually enables you to save your images with *lossless* compression.

Compression becomes important whenever digital images need to be transported from one computer or disk to another. But compression schemes differ in how they affect the digital information in an image.

A common side effect of file compression is loss of image fidelity: A **lossy** image compression scheme like the one used by Joint Photographic Experts Group (JPEG) will produce a picture that loses image fidelity. On the other hand, **lossless** compression like that used by Tagged Image File Format (TIFF), in contrast, retains full image fidelity when saved.

Other differences between JPEG and JPEG2000 include the following:

◆ **Transparency.** One color in a JPEG2000 image can be identified as transparent, so JPEG2000 images can have transparent backgrounds.

◆ **Layers.** JPEG2000 supports image layers (see Chapter 7 for more about layers).

◆ **Flexible Color Depth.** JPEG2000 facilitates variable color depth, to save space as needed. This enables Photoshop Elements to save less color information when possible and thus reduce file size. Ideally, files for the web should be 10K or 20K—or less than 50K in size if possible.

Transparency is the ability of some image formats (GIF, JPEG2000, and PNG) to designate one color as transparent; when you identify the color as transparent, you can use it as the background of the image. The image will then seem to have no visible background and appear to be floating on the background of the web page you are viewing.

Suppose, for example, you create an image that has a blue background, but the background of the web page is white. If you select the blue background color and name that color as the transparent one, the blue will disappear and the image will be floating on the web page's white background, which gives a more pleasing effect.

These are just a few highlights of the differences between the varieties of JPEG. You can read more about JPEG2000 by visiting www.jpeg.org/JPEG2000.htm.

Saving to JPEG2000 in Photoshop Elements proves to be slightly more complicated than saving to the traditional JPEG format. In the section "Using the Save For Web Dialog Box," you'll learn how to do both, and we'll take a look at the differences.

Naming Your Web Images

When naming a file for use on the web, you have to make sure it follows some specific rules. Make sure you do the following:

- Use underscores when you need to separate two words; do not use spaces. Spaces can cause problems with some browsers, so it's best to avoid them.

- Stay away from special characters such as &, *, $, %, ^, @, and others. Stick with letters and numbers.

- If you must use special characters, you can use the tilde (~), hyphens, and periods.

- Keep names short. Names of eight or fewer letters are desirable, though not required.

- To keep your web pages, images, and file names neat, use only lowercase letters. To work well with Unix servers, where capitalization matters, common practice is to use all lowercase for file names.

In Focus

It is important to understand the difference between image size and file size. *Image* size is the physical dimension of the image in terms of width and height, while *file* size is the amount of disk space the file consumes. Reducing the image size almost always reduces the file size, and is a good place to begin when saving a file.

Using the Save For Web Dialog Box

The Save For Web dialog box, shown in Figure 23.1, offers everything you'll need to get that photo saved in the best way possible. Don't panic, it's really easy to use once you understand all of the parts!

Use this dialog box to optimize the photo, choose a file format, compress the photo to make it load faster, choose color options, and preview the image. While these are all important tasks, most important is the ability to reduce the file size. File size is everything on a web page, and determines how fast the page loads once a user accesses it.

The Save For Web dialog box has several parts. The top-right side of the dialog box has the optimization settings, the large part in the middle is for previewing, testing, and comparing optimization settings, and the bottom-right side is for changing the image size. There's a Zoom tool too, and a display that appears beneath the preview image that tells you how fast the image would be downloaded in the current format (GIF, JPEG, or PNG).

Let's explore the different parts of the Save For Web dialog box. Open the *pelican.psd* file located in the Chapter 23 folder on this book's CD-ROM, and follow these steps to save the image in one of the World Wide Web formats:

1. Choose File → Save For Web *or* click the Save For Web icon in the shortcuts bar. The Save For Web dialog box appears as shown in Figure 23.1.

2. Select a file format from the Settings drop-down list. In Figure 23.1, JPEG Medium quality was selected, which is just one of many options.

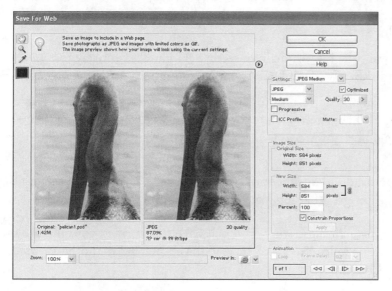

Figure 23.1

Learn to use the Save For Web dialog box if you want to optimize images for web display.

3. Set the options for your file format from the other drop-down lists in the Settings area. If you're not sure what to choose, check the preview image that appears to the right of your original.

4. If you want to resize your image, specify a new size in the New Size area. You can set an exact width or height, or you can choose to resize to a percentage of the original. To retain your original proportions, make sure to keep the Constrain Proportions box checked—a bracket and a lock symbol appears next to the Width and Height boxes when you do so. Remember that reducing the image size generally has a huge impact on reducing the file size.

5. Just beneath the preview image, inspect the time it will take a typical web user to download your image. In the example shown, it will take a person on a 28.8K modem five seconds to download this image with these settings. That's pretty good. (If you want to see how long the file will take to appear at a different modem rate, click the arrow to the left of the Help button and choose a speed from the popup menu that appears.)

6. Choose JPEG Maximum and choose a quality setting of 100 (or type a setting in the Quality text box, or move the slider after you click the down arrow); the download time increases to 79 seconds. Not so good.

7. Change the JPEG settings to Low next; the quality settings will be 10. Notice the difference in the quality of the picture when doing so. Also notice that the time to download the image is now only three seconds on a 28.8K modem! Fast, but is the quality sufficient?

8. Decide if you want the low or medium setting (High takes entirely too much time and bandwidth), and click OK. The Save Optimized As dialog box appears.

9. Click the arrow adjoining Save In to navigate to a directory where you want to save your image. Then, enter a name for your new web image in the File Name box. (Choose a different file name or file type if you want to preserve the original image.)

10. Click Save. Photoshop Elements optimizes your image according to the options you've picked. A progress bar lets you track the optimization and save process.

Once you've worked through these steps, you will have transformed your picture into a form that you can easily upload to a World Wide Web site and that others can download in a reasonable time.

CAUTION **Swatch Out!** _____

When you save files for the web, be careful with the file names you create. The file name appears at the end of the Uniform Resource Locator (URL) that describes the file's location on the web. For one thing, most web servers use the Unix operating system, where the common practice is to use lowercase for file names—capital letters can also confuse web surfers who might enter the file name incorrectly. Also be sure not to use blank spaces in file names; if you must, insert an underline symbol between words in the file name.

As mentioned previously, saving to JPEG2000 in Photoshop Elements proves to be slightly more complicated than saving to the traditional JPEG format. But let's try it.

Open the *pelican.psd* file located in the Chapter 23 folder on the CD-ROM that comes with this book, and try the steps out yourself:

1. Choose File → Save As.

2. Choose JPEG2000 from the Format drop-down list.

3. Click Save. The JPEG2000 Options window appears (see Figure 23.2).

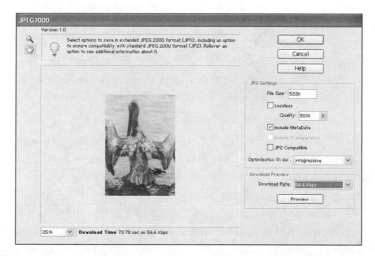

Figure 23.2

The JPEG2000 Options window.

4. Choose one of the following JPEG2000 compression options:

   ◆ If you want to save your work losslessly (without any loss of image fidelity), click the Lossless button. The file size information disappears, though the download time remains displayed.

   ◆ If you want to use normal image compression, leave the Lossless button unchecked. Adjust the Quality slider to the level of compression you want (or type a number in the Quality box). The File Size box updates to show the approximate size of the file you will create. Watch the preview window to see a preview of how your file will look. If you like, you can zoom in using the preview size adjustments.

5. When you're satisfied with the look and size of your image, click OK.

6. Wait as Photoshop Elements compresses your image. This may take several seconds or as long as a minute, depending on the degree of compression and the speed of your computer. While JPEG2000 produces far better compression, it usually takes longer to save to this format than to traditional JPEG. The results are worth it, though.

Figure 23.2 shows the JPEG2000 Options window that enables you to set your options before saving to a new file.

Saving images in GIF format is pretty much the same as saving JPEGs; you simply choose GIF instead of JPEG when optimizing in the Save For Web dialog box, and configure the settings as desired. In the next few sections, you'll learn how to optimize GIF files.

Optimizing Images

Now that you've played around a little with the Save For Web dialog box, and you've learned how to work with JPEGs and decrease file size, image size, and download times, you might be surprised to learn that you can and should still improve how you optimize your files.

For example, even if the file size isn't too big, say it's between 10K and 20K, and can be downloaded quickly, you should still try to optimize. Bandwidth is precious, especially if you pay for it. Many servers charge you for the amount of bandwidth you use with outgoing data, and in many parts of the world, such as much of Europe, people pay for incoming bandwidth too. Chances are, you don't just have one image on your website anyway, so optimizing all of the images to the smallest file size possible, while still maintaining good color resolution and quality, is important in all cases.

It's Element-ary

You can also reduce download times by reducing the number of colors you have in an image. One way to reduce colors and still produce quality images for the web is to use web-safe colors. Web-safe colors are the 216 colors that are used by browsers on both Windows PCs and Macs. When any user who has 256 colors configured for a monitor or computer accesses a site with web-safe color images, this ensures that the images will be properly displayed for them.

Consider the following tips for image optimization:

◆ Crop out any part of the image that isn't necessary.

◆ Keep all images under 50K. Try to stay between 10K and 25K or so.

◆ Assume that some quality will be lost, and use the preview options to see just how much loss you can put up with. Take advantage of the JPEG lossy compression schemes to reduce file size.

◆ Save in GIF format when you are publishing illustrations, logos with only a few colors, line art, and similar artwork. When using GIF files, try using only 8 or 16 colors, then increase the number of colors gradually to test the quality and the download time.

◆ Transparent pixels do not show up on web pages, so use transparency when creating logos and such for the web. You can include transparency in files saved in the GIF format. (When you know the background color of the web page where your image will be displayed, use the matte features to blend the transparent pixels with a color that matches the background.)

◆ Save GIF images using web-safe colors. Using web-safe colors ensure that the images you use will appear to others as you want them to, and will be viewed well on 256-color monitors.

◆ Save photos using JPEG instead of trying to save them using GIF and web-safe colors. GIF does a poor job of compressing photographs, and quality becomes an issue.

These are just a few of the optimization options available to you. The next few sections will offer more.

It's Element-ary

When optimizing an image, you have to compare file size, download time, and image resolution. For example, while a particular image might look good saved as a JPEG using maximum quality, it could take over a minute to load using a 56K modem. Not too many people are willing to wait that long these days. However, you can save the same image as a JPEG using a low quality setting, and the image can then be downloaded in as quickly as 20 seconds using the same modem speed. You get what you pay for, though, and color, resolution, and image clarity suffer with the lower settings.

Testing Images

You have several ways to test an image while optimizing and saving it using the Save For Web dialog box. You can see it in the Preview pane of course, and use the Zoom options to zoom in or out. One of the Zoom options is Fit to Page; that's usually the best for previewing.

There's also a Preview option at the bottom of the page so you can view the image using your favorite browser. In fact, you can install several browsers and view your image using all of them just to double-check. Doing this virtually guarantees that anyone can open and view your picture, and that it will look the way you want.

Finally, you can choose the advanced options when you preview an image using the Standard Windows or Standard Macintosh colors, which enables you to see how users of other operating systems will see your image. Color differences between platforms can occur because different users, computers, and operating systems use different graphics cards and having different color calibrations, as well as different models of monitors. These differences occur because of the contrast and value of the graphic or image. You can diminish these differences by properly balancing these attributes of the picture prior to saving. By verifying that the images look good on all platforms, you can reduce the chances that images will look poor because of different hardware and color settings.

In Focus

When changing optimization options, the Preview pane shows the updates automatically. Although you might not see obvious changes in the image itself, you will see changes in the size of the file and how fast it will download.

Optimizing a Selected File Format

You have several types of file formats to choose from, and for web photos and uploading web images you'll choose between GIF, JPEG and JPEG2000, or PNG when using Photoshop Elements. But once you've made a selection, how can you optimize it further, other than simply comparing the download rates? In this section, you'll learn a few tricks and tips for use with each type of file.

GIF

Be with you in a GIF! GIF images contain a maximum of 256 colors, and are best used for text, logos that are made up of a specific number of colors that have sharp or well-defined corners and edges, and illustrations with lots of white space. GIF supports transparency too, which enables the website's background to show through. Web items such as buttons and frames are best saved as GIF files. Any image used in an animation must be saved as a GIF file as well.

Consider the following settings when optimizing GIFs:

- Place a check in the Interlaced check box to show a low-resolution image while the full image is downloading.

- To make the picture's 256 colors more suitable to the human eye, choose Perceptual.

- ◆ To make the picture's 256 colors truer, choose Selective.

- ◆ If the colors in the image are similar, say all reds and oranges, choose Adaptive. This creates the 256 colors from the most common colors in the image.

- ◆ To use standard web colors, choose web.

Remember, GIFs are best used for images with limited colors, such as logos, illustrations, and web buttons. For photos, use JPEG, detailed next.

JPEG

JPEG stands for Joint Photographic Experts Group and is an option when saving and optimizing files in Photoshop Elements. It is a popular format on the web, and images saved in this format have specific characteristics.

JPEG images are generally used with images that contain more than 256 colors, such as photographs. JPEG photographs can contain a maximum of 16 million colors and are 24-bit color images. However, you will never use that many colors in a web image; that's where optimization and compression comes in. The JPEG compression technology is superb; a photo with millions of colors can be compressed so that the download time is short and sweet.

Consider the following settings when optimizing JPEGs:

- ◆ Choose a quality number from 1 to 100 that meets a compromise between the look you want from the image and the time it takes to download. Choosing 1–29 gives you low quality, 30–59 gives medium quality, and 59–100 offers high quality. Lower numbers offer faster download times, smaller file sizes, and lower image quality. Higher numbers raise download times, raise file size, but increase image quality.

- ◆ To make downloading seem to occur faster, place a check in the Progressing check box. This enables the image to display at a low resolution until the entire picture is up. The downside, of course, is that the image becomes larger.

- ◆ To keep the color profile of the original image after the file is optimized, check ICC. ICC is Image Color Correction.

Figure 23.3 shows a JPEG image optimized for the web. It is a picture of a screen-printing machine used for printing T-shirts and hats, and is located on my website. If you compare the original picture at 439 seconds at 28K, the second one at 9 seconds at 56K, and this one at 6 seconds for 56K, you can see just how important spending time optimizing your web photos can be. (When you first start optimizing, the default setting is 28K, however, 28K is a pretty old technology, so always see what 56K will provide, too.)

Figure 23.3

Use the Save For Web dialog box to increase download times and optimize images.

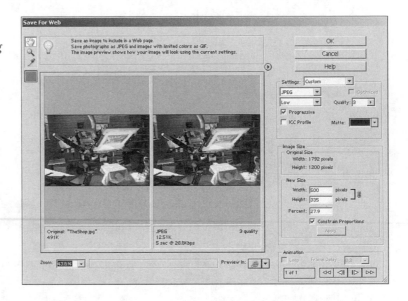

PNG

PNG stands for Portable Network Graphics and is an option when saving and optimizing files in Photoshop Elements. It combines the best of JPEG and GIF, and offers more colors and offers lossless compression. However, not all browsers support it, so you should be careful when deciding to use it. PNG comes in two flavors, PNG-8 and PNG-24. PNG-8 images contain a maximum of 256 colors, and are best used for text, logos, and illustrations with lots of white space. You can save web items such as buttons as PNG files, too. Because PNG-8 supports 256 colors, it is also referred to as an 8-bit format. Most times, PNG-8 compression creates files that are 10 to 30 percent smaller than GIFs, which might be a good reason to use it.

The other type of PNG is PNG-24. This file type supports 24-bit color just as JPEG does, but it goes a step further. It also supports transparency, background matting, and creates images that have sharper lines and better color than JPEGs. So, if you have a photo and want to configure transparency, you'll need to choose PNG-24 over JPEG. PNG-24 creates a much larger file, though, and, like PNG-8, is not supported by all browsers. Even though it's gaining popularity, for now, consider staying away from this format, at least until it becomes more widely accepted.

Transparent Images

When something is transparent, it means you can see through it. Clear plastic wrap is transparent; it lets you see through the cover to the food inside a container. Photoshop enables you to create transparent GIFs similar to this. These are images you can see through, and where the image is transparent, it lets the viewer see through it to the background of the web page.

If you want to use transparency tools and make images transparent, you'll have to use GIF files, not JPEGs. You can use PNG-24, too, although we do not suggest this due to the file size it creates.

To use the transparency tools, open a file that contains transparent areas or layers. Save the file using the Save For Web dialog box, and place a check in the Transparency check box.

Animated GIFs

Have you seen those cute little bouncing balls and other images on websites? Those are animated GIFs, and they're simply a collection of frames saved and played in a loop. If you've seen them, then you know that they are animated images that are flat, and that they aren't photos.

Animated GIFs don't do so well if they're made of photos because GIF images only display 256 colors, because the frames have to rotate or loop, and because photo files are much larger than other types of artwork. In addition, it takes photos much longer to download, and this could cause the animation to appear slow or jumpy. So, creating an animated GIF should be done from a small piece of art you've created, or a shape such as a ball or ellipse.

So how do you go about creating an animated GIF? Just follow these steps for a complete walkthrough from start to finish:

1. Create a single layer and place a ball or other small figure to animate on the layer.

2. Create a new layer from the original layer, and add the image again, this time in a different position.

In Focus

The Save For Web dialog box offers animation controls for playing back your creation. They work by enabling you to select the first or last frame, or any previous or next frame. You can see these controls in any of the previous screenshots; they are located in the bottom-right corner.

3. Repeat Step 2 until you have several layers with the same figure on it, where each layer has the figure in a different place on the screen. See Figure 23.4.

Figure 23.4

Place an image repeatedly and on separate layers to create an animated GIF.

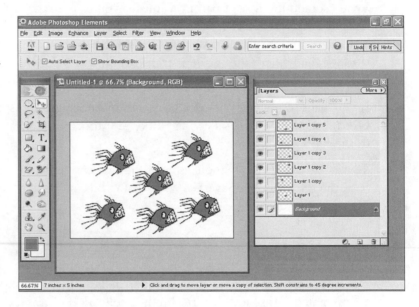

4. Click File → Save for Web.

5. Select GIF for the file type and place a check in the Animate box just below it. See Figure 23.5. (When you place a check in the animate checkbox, the images in the preview boxes will disappear.)

Figure 23.5

Use the Save For Web dialog box to create an animated image.

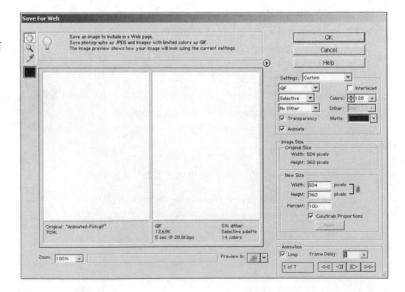

6. Place a check in the Loop box as shown in Figure 23.5. Set the delay to the desired time.

7. Click OK. When the Save Optimized As window appears, type in a name for the file and choose a folder. Click Save.

8. To preview the animated GIF, open the File → Save as Web dialog box again.

9. Make sure the file is open and repeat Steps 4 through 6.

10. Click the Preview In box to preview the animation in your Web browser.

Swatch Out! _____

We've surfed out of websites because of annoying little (and sometimes big) animated GIFs. While the instructions in this chapter say to check the Loop check box, that was really just for your previewing pleasure. If you are going to create an animated GIF for a website, you might want to rethink the whole "loop" thing. Configure it to run once, and then let it go away quietly. This way, the animated GIF you think is so cute won't annoy your website visitors, but you can still share your creativity!

One last note before leaving this subject: Photoshop Elements isn't a web-animation program, and doesn't really offer much for the serious animation designer (like automatically creating transition frames to connect two of your frames, resulting in a smoother animation). If you are serious about animation, consider purchasing a program designed for that purpose like Adobe GoLive, Adobe Live Motion, or Macromedia Flash. However, if what you need is a simple animation with a limited number of frames, then this tool allows you to easily create it.

Web Photo Galleries

So you've gone on a few vacations, had kids, gotten a dog, and purchased a new car. You've acquired lots of photos, and you want to show them to people across the globe. You've already tried making prints and mailing them through snail-mail, and you've spent plenty of energy cluttering up the e-mail in-boxes of your friends and family, too. We're not even going near the holiday letters you send. None of those turned out so well, did they? Well, we can solve that problem.

In Focus _____

Many other uses for galleries exist. You can quickly put together a portfolio for a client, get your small business on the web quickly, or set up a website to keep friends and family up to date concerning a family member's hospital stay or new birth— or show pictures of that new house you're building.

Gather around! Does Photoshop Elements ever have a deal for you! A Web Photo Gallery! Free for the taking and included in your Photoshop Elements software!

Using the Web Photo Gallery tools, you can organize all of your images in one place, have Photoshop Elements automatically size and optimize the images for the web, use preconfigured web pages, and more.

Getting Organized

Even if you're not so good at organizing stuff, you're going to have to at least create a couple of folders for your images before you can create a Web Photo Gallery. Photoshop Elements has to know where to look for your files and where to store the information it needs to send them to your website.

So, before we can get started creating a web gallery, let's create a couple of folders:

1. Create a new folder called Source on your hard drive. You can create this folder at the root level, in another folder, or it can stand on its own.

2. Create a second folder called Destination.

3. Locate the images you want to add to the photo gallery, and place them in this folder. You can do this on a PC by dragging the file from the old location to the new one. If you choose to drag the images over, left-click and drag to move them, right-click and drag to be given a choice to either move or copy, and on a Mac, just click and drag to move.

Now you're ready to start creating your gallery!

Creating the Gallery

One of this book's authors is thinking about naming a website "No comments from the Peanut Gallery!"—because he's got some pictures that are quite boring. Even though he thought the trip to Oklahoma was interesting, he doubts that many of his friends and family will agree!

In Focus

Choose the right look for your project. For work-related projects consider the Table, Office, or Simple styles. For wedding photos, try Spotlight or Vertical Frame.

No matter what pictures you want to feature (hey, you might even be a professional photographer), to create your own gallery, perform the following steps (note that not all options are available for all styles; if an option isn't available, just skip to the next step):

1. From the File menu, choose Create Web Photo Gallery.

2. The Web Photo Gallery dialog box appears. Browse through the Styles drop-down list and choose a style that suites your needs. You can see a preview of the style as you choose them from the preview window on the right.

3. Type in your e-mail address.

4. Click the Browse button to locate the Source folder you created earlier.

5. Click the Destination button to locate the Destination folder you also created earlier.

6. Click the arrow next to Options and choose Banner.

7. With Banner chosen, type in a name for your gallery in the Site Name field. Type in any other information if you desire.

8. Change the font and font size if you want. The larger the font size, the larger the banner.

9. Now you'll need to decide if you want large images or thumbnails. Choose the appropriate one for you from the Options drop-down list.

10. Depending on whether you chose large images or thumbnails, fill in the required information. Notice in both that you can choose how to configure their border size, their names, and font and font size for each.

11. Choose Custom Colors to apply a set of colors to the website.

12. Click OK when finished. The Web Gallery opens automatically in your Web browser. (You can close the browser without closing Photoshop Elements.)

If you want to edit the gallery after viewing it, which you might well want to do, simply repeat these steps. When you have the gallery the way you want it, you'll need to use an uploading program to actually upload it to a website. Photoshop Elements doesn't have that capability. You can upload your images to ftp sites, to a personal website, to a personal network's website, or even to your company's intranet website. Right now, only you can view it—or anyone who physically sits in front of your computer.

In this chapter, you learned how to create images for the web, including creating a Web Photo Gallery. You learned about creating transparent images and previewing images. Web images should be optimized so that they can be opened quickly, and an appropriate file type needs to be chosen.

In this chapter you also learned about three file types—JPEG, PNG, and GIF—and when and how to use them. GIFs are better for line art, logos, and illustrations, whereas JPEGs are better for photos. PNG is not widely accepted yet, but will be soon, and has advantages over the other two.

The Least You Need to Know

◆ Save files for the web using the File → Save For Web option.

◆ Save files as GIF if they are line art, logos, text, or have fewer than 256 colors.

◆ Save files as JPEG if they are photos.

◆ When optimizing images for the web, weigh the importance of download time, image resolution, and size.

◆ Create Web Photo Galleries for family or vacation photos, business photos and portfolios, and to maintain an updated website for emergencies or disasters.

Appendix A

Online Resources

When it comes to finding the latest and greatest information about Adobe Photoshop Elements 2.0, the best place to turn is the Internet. This appendix lists website and other resources you're sure to find useful. Keep in mind that, because the web changes constantly, some of the sites might have moved by the time you read this. You may have to use a search engine such as Google (www.google.com) to find exactly what you're looking for. You might also try shortening the URL—deleting everything after the *.com* or *.edu* part of the address, for instance.

Adobe Photoshop Elements: General Information

The following sites serve as good starting points for users who want to find out more about their favorite image editing program.

Adobe Photoshop Elements website
www.adobe.com/products/photoshopel/main.html
This is the place to turn if you're looking for updates to Photoshop Elements as well as additional recipes or other software you can add to the program.

Photoshop Elements Support Knowledgebase
pshopelementssupport.adobe.com
This site provides a searchable database of articles about Photoshop Elements. The articles highlighted on the front page of this site include tips and fixes for installation problems, particularly those confronting Mac OS X users.

About.com's Photoshop Elements Resources Page
graphicssoft.about.com/cs/photoshopelements
This site, which provides recommendations from a personal "guide," contains links to user groups, tutorials, add-on software, and other goodies that will help you use Photoshop Elements more effectively.

The Design and Publishing Center's Photoshop Elements Page
graphicssoft.about.com/cs/photoshopelements
At the time we were writing this, this site reviewed Photoshop Elements 1.0. By the time you read this, it will probably cover 2.0. The tutorials on color correction are particularly good.

Stock Photos and Images

Everyone needs some images from time to time to help them create posters and other publications. If you're looking for low-cost or even free artwork, you can turn to these sites.

Barry's Clip Art Server
www.barrysclipart.com
This website focuses on drawings you can add to your images to create invitations and other goodies. Artwork is arranged by holiday or occasion. You'll also find type fonts you can download and use to add text to your images. Artwork is free provided you use it for nonprofit purposes and give credit to the Barry's Clip Art website.

Dynamic Graphics
www.dgusa.com
Dynamic Graphics, another well-known name in the field of graphic design, offers a variety of clip art images on its website, as well as online magazines that cover digital design around the world.

Getty Images—PhotoDisk
creative.gettyimages.com/photodisc
The images on this site aren't free, but they're high-quality, and PhotoDisc is one of the best-known resources in the field of stock photography.

User Forums

It's hard learning in a vacuum. Sometimes, the key to solving a problem or getting something done more quickly and efficiently is to ask someone for help. The Internet is the perfect place to ask other Photoshop Elements users for advice. The following are some sites where you can find them.

Adobe Systems' User Groups
www.adobe.com/support/forums/main.html
Adobe presents a user group on Photoshop Elements itself, where you can ask questions of your fellow Photoshop Elements users, get tips, and do troubleshooting. In addition, you'll find links to user groups that discuss various topics related to graphic design and image editing, such as animation, typography, and color management.

Yahoo! Groups Forum on Photoshop Elements
groups.yahoo.com/group/photoshop_elements
This group is easy to join and easy to participate in. When last we looked, users were ready and eager to discuss the new features of Photoshop Elements 2.0. One particularly nice feature is a searchable archive of recent message postings.

Graphic Design and Image Editing

The web contains many sites devoted to topics in design such as color, retouching, scanning, and much more. Here are just a few sites to get you started.

Magic in RGB
www.pagelab.com
The graphic design company Before & After publishes an ongoing series of articles on topics in graphic design. Click the link on the site's home page labeled Magic in RGB to watch a series of animations showing how RGB color works.

DesktopPublishing.com
www.desktoppublishing.com/open.html
This site contains a wealth of information on graphic design, including clip art, books and magazines, tips and templates, and web design.

Lynda.com
www.lynda.com
This prolific author and graphic design guru offers a training CD-ROM on Adobe Photoshop Elements. She also offers articles on web color plus a downloadable file that helps Mac users adjust their monitor Gamma levels.

There's a lot more online than just these starter resources. If you don't find what you need from the preceding sites, keep searching—everything you need is out there.

Glossary

adjustment layer   A layer that contains colors that change the colors of any underlying layers.

aliasing   Jagged edges around raster or bitmap images. Compare to *anti-aliasing* (see also).

anti-aliasing   The capability of some image editing programs (such as Photoshop Elements) to smooth out the jagged edges of raster images by softening the edges.

artifact   A portion of an image that did not appear in the original and that usually results from *lossy compression* (see also).

batch processing   The act of performing a series of commands only once, and then configuring your computer to perform them automatically to multiple files.

bit   An individual unit of digital information.

bitmap image   An image made up of pixels, each of which has one or more bits of digital information assigned to it; also called a *raster image* (see also).

blend mode   A way of making the pixels in one layer interact differently with the layers beneath it.

burn Giving part of an image more contrast and making it darker.

Clone Stamp A tool in the toolbox that enables you to copy a part of an image to somewhere else in the image.

CMYK A color model commonly used in the offset print industry that reproduces color by mixing different quantities of cyan, magenta, yellow, and black (K). Compare to *RGB* (see also).

color cast An affect that occurs when the balance of colors in an image tips toward one color predominantly.

color depth A term used to describe the quality of an image in terms of the bits of information assigned to each pixel in that image. The GIF format uses 8-bit color, for example, and it can have a maximum of 256 colors.

color model A theory for reproducing color in an image (also called *color mode*).

compression The act of reducing the file size of an image.

contact sheet A way of viewing a set of thumbnail-sized images of an entire roll of film or a set of digital images contained within a folder or on a hard disk.

cropping The practice of identifying parts of an image you want to preserve and parts you want to cut out.

digital photography The process of capturing photographic images so they can be viewed and edited by computer equipment.

dodge Exposing part of an image to less light or otherwise make it turn out lighter than the rest of the image.

ellipse A shape that has two center (focal) points. The outer points on the ellipse that make up the line around the outside are determined by the sum of the distances to these two focal points, and the distance is a constant.

feathering A process in which the edges of an image or other object grow gradually more transparent.

File Browser A file navigation tool that Photoshop Elements provides for locating and viewing images.

file format A formula used to save the information in a file so a computer can process it and an application such as Photoshop Elements can display it.

fill layer A layer that lets you fill underlying layers with color.

filter A tool that lets you apply special effects such as distortion or texturizing that change an image's characteristics.

flatten   Change a group of layers into a single background layer.

gradient   A blending of two or more colors in a gradual way.

Graphics Interchange Format (GIF)   A raster file format that compresses digital images and uses a color model with a maximum of only 256 colors; ideal for presenting web graphics.

grayscale   An image that consists of multiple shades of gray.

Joint Photographic Experts Group (JPEG)   A raster image file format that works well with photographs and other images that display subtle changes in color.

hidden tools   Related tools that are found underneath a tool on the Photoshop Elements toolbar.

History   A palette that enables you to review recent actions you've performed with Photoshop Elements and change them individually or as a group.

image window   A window within the main Photoshop Elements window that displays an individual image, has a title bar, and can be resized.

indexed mode   A way of presenting color using a limited number of colors, each of which is assigned a number and a position in a color table.

inverse   The opposite shade of a color.

lasso   A tool that lets you draw a freeform selection.

layer   A subdivision of an image that sits amid other layers of the image like a transparent overlay or clear sheet of plastic; you can move a layer's contents independently of the other layers.

Layer Styles   A palette that enables you to add shadows, bevels, and other effects to a layer.

linking   A way of associating two layers so you can temporarily edit them as one.

Liquid Crystal Display (LCD)   The miniature screen that lets you preview images in a digital camera or other device.

lossless compression   A type of file compression that does not result in loss of information.

lossy compression   A type of image compression that results in some image information being discarded.

Magic Wand   A tool that selects all pixels in the vicinity of the pixel on which you click that are similar in color to that pixel.

Magnetic Lasso   A tool that enables you to draw a selection marquee around an irregularly shaped object by detecting the contrast in color within the image.

marquee   A rectangular or elliptical dashed line that is drawn around part of an image that is being selected.

opacity   A quality of an image that determines to what degree a drawn line, background, or other object reveals the layer underneath it. At 100 percent, nothing shows through from the layer underneath. At 10 percent, the entire background shows and the object is almost transparent.

optimize   The process of preparing an image so that is of a manageable file size while retaining as much image quality as possible.

options bar   A toolbar that appears by default beneath the shortcuts bar and that contains options that change depending on the currently selected tool.

output resolution   An expression of the capability of a printer or other output device to produce detail.

palette   A window that you can access from Photoshop Elements, that you can resize, and that contains its own buttons and popup menus so you can perform specific functions.

Palette Well   A container at the right edge of the shortcuts bar that contains palettes you can drag out into the working area.

path   The fundamental element that makes up a vector graphic; a mathematical description of a shape.

Photoshop Data (.psd)   The native Photoshop Elements image format.

pixel   A small rectangle that is the most fundamental element of a *raster image* (see also).

plug-in   A piece of software that works within another application and that adds functionality to that application.

polygons   Shapes with line segments that make up its sides, and that have at least three sides by definition.

Portable Document Format (PDF)   A file format created by Adobe that compresses documents so they can be easily transported across networks and then viewed by the Acrobat Reader software.

Random Access Memory (RAM)   A type of memory that your computer uses to run programs, remember temporary data, and calculate and apply changes to an image.

raster image   Computer image made up of pixels, also called a *bitmap image* (see also).

Reset Palette Locations   A Window menu command that enables you to put all palettes, toolbars, and default settings for the program back in place.

resize   Change the size of an image while changing the number of pixels to maintain image quality as much as possible.

resolution   A way of expressing the amount of information contained within a digital image, usually in terms of pixels per inch (ppi) or dots per inch (dpi).

retouching   The process of changing the appearance of selected areas within a photograph.

RGB   A color model that duplicates color by mixing different levels of red, green, and blue. Compare to *CMYK* (see also).

saturation   A term used to describe the intensity of colors.

scale   Changing the size of an object.

scan resolution   An expression of the amount of image information (pixels) stored in a file that is controlled by the settings in your scanning software.

Selection brush   A tool that lets you draw your own selection area using a brush.

shortcuts bar   A toolbar that appears by default just beneath the Photoshop Elements menu bar and contains buttons for opening, saving, and performing other functions.

toolbox   A set of tools for selecting, drawing, retouching, and viewing images in Photoshop Elements.

transform   The process of changing the appearance of an object—to change the shape of the object to make it fit better on the page, to distort it, or to give it perspective.

transparency   The capability of some image formats (GIF, JPEG2000, and PNG) to designate one color as transparent; when you identify the color as transparent, you can use it as the background of the image.

TWAIN   A standard set of instructions that enables your computer to connect with graphics hardware, including many scanners and digital cameras.

Type Mask   Two tools that create a "selection" that you can drag, change, or otherwise manipulate from the active layer.

vector graphics   Images made up of paths and shapes and that are defined by mathematical formulas.

web-safe color palette   A set of 216 RGB colors that are displayed with reasonable consistency across different web browsers and computer platforms.

Windows Image Acquisition (WIA)   An application programming interface (API) that enables Windows-based software applications such as Photoshop Elements to acquire digital images from hardware devices such as scanners and digital cameras.

Index

A Little Knowledge Goes a Long Way ...

Check Out These
Best-Selling
COMPLETE IDIOT'S GUIDES

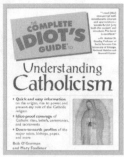

0-02-863639-2
$16.95

0-02-862743-1
$16.95

0-02-862728-8
$16.95

0-02-864339-9
$18.95

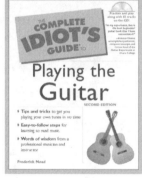

0-02-864244-9
$21.95 w/CD-ROM

0-02-862415-7
$18.95

0-02-864316-X
$24.95 w/CD-ROM

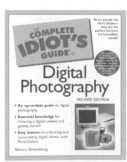

0-02-864235-X
$24.95 w/CD-ROM

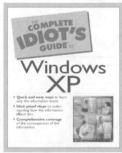

0-02-864232-5
$19.95

ALP